AQUINAS' *SUMMA THEOLOGIAE*

T&T Clark Reader's Guides are clear, concise and accessible introductions to key texts in theology. Each book explores the themes, context, criticism and influence of key works, providing a practical introduction to close reading, guiding students towards a thorough understanding of the text. They provide an essential, up-to-date resource, ideal for undergraduate students.

Forthcoming titles in the series:

Balthasar's Trilogy (Stephen Wigley)
Barth's Commentary on Romans (Donald Wood)
Kierkegaard's Philosophical Fragments (Tim Rose)
Bonhoeffer's Ethics (Philip Ziegler)
Schleiermacher's Speeches on Religion (Kevin Hector)

AQUINAS' *SUMMA THEOLOGIAE*

A Reader's Guide

STEPHEN J. LOUGHLIN

t&t clark

Published by T&T Clark International
A Continuum Imprint
The Tower Building 80 Maiden Lane
11 York Road Suite 704
London SE1 7NX New York NY 10038

www.continuumbooks.com

British Library Cataloguing-in-Publication Data
A catalogue record for this book is available from the British Library.

ISBN: HB: 978-0-567-51141-6
PB: 978-0-567-55094-1

Typeset by Newgen Imaging Systems Pvt Ltd, Chennai, India
Printed and bound in Great Britain by the MPG Books Group

This book is dedicated to Gerry Campbell, Floyd Centore, and Donald De Marco by whose charity and dedication I was taught all things Thomistic.

CONTENTS

PREFACE

This book endeavors to provide an undergraduate student with an introduction to Thomas Aquinas' *Summa Theologiae,* a work that has had a profound impact upon the whole of Catholic theology and holds an important place within the discipline of philosophy. This is not an easy task, given the length of the *Summa,* the depth and complexity of its material, the mode and language of its presentation, the wealth of sources upon which it draws, and the expectations of its author upon its reader (namely that he be familiar with these sources, be comfortable with the language and method used, be capable of sustained reading at a high level of difficulty, be able to expand what is often presented in an abbreviated way, and other such matters). These difficulties have often prevented the most eager of students from engaging this work profitably, a great shame given its importance to the Western Intellectual tradition. This situation has given rise to many and diverse books (such as this one), which have endeavored to mitigate these difficulties and encourage the reader to experience, at the very least, the spirit that animates this work with the hope that with this in place, further study will be undertaken to appropriate increasingly over time the treasures that it contains. Joining with these well-intentioned souls, I put this guide forward as my contribution to the *Summa*'s dissemination, and in gratitude for all that it has taught me over the years.

This guide is not intended in any way to replace a direct encounter with the text of the *Summa Theologiae* itself. It has often been said, and this from a very early time, that the most cogent presenter and defender of Thomas's thought is Thomas himself. I hold this firmly to be true and encourage the reader to grapple with the text no matter what difficulties it may present. For in doing this, one begins to acquire much more than just the material with which the particular treatises are concerned. One begins to develop the very intellectual dispositions that are required to penetrate to the very heart of this work, and to enjoy fully what it offers. To encourage these acquisitions, I have organized my considerations around the various treatises that make up the three parts of the *Summa*. Given my own (and others') experience in teaching this work, I have spent a good deal of time concentrating upon the *Summa*'s first part, as well as the first part of its second part. The material covered by these two parts usually occupies the lion's share of any class devoted to this work, given, first, that it lays much of the foundation for what is contained in the remainder of the *Summa*, and second, that its material is so complex that it begs for proper exposition. This should not prejudice one from not attending seriously to the second part of the *Summa*'s second part, or to its third. For these latter parts constitute, for all intents and purposes, the completion of all the materials that have preceded them, and in light of which much that was implicit in these prior sections are then revealed in their proper light. It is fortunate for the undergraduates that the material with which the third and the latter of the second parts deal is of a more accessible nature, and thus allow this guide to treat only of their major principles and arguments thereby situating the student to attend to a selective reading of these materials as determined not only by the professor who introduces them, but also by one's own interest in the topics of which they treat. I have attended in the first chapter of this reader's guide to the historical matters pertinent to one's first encounter with the *Summa*, as well as to some discussion concerning its structure, basic themes, unifying principles, the basic problems that one encounters in reading this work, and advice on how to minimize their initial impact. Having dealt in the second chapter with the work itself, as described above, I finish with a very brief consideration of the history of the *Summa*'s reception and the influence that it has had upon the Western Intellectual tradition. A bibliography is provided, as well as information as to where to look for more detailed works upon the *Summa* itself, and the man who wrote it.

I would like to thank DeSales University and especially its Philosophy and Theology Department for their support in the composition of this guide. I am greatly indebted as well to the several people who read portions of this work and offered their comments, particularly Gregory Kerr, Rachel Coleman, and Michelle McCarthy. Lastly, to my wife, Carol, I express my eternal gratitude for all that she has done.

CHAPTER 1

CONTEXT

A great deal has been written about Thomas's life, character, the times in which he lived, and the many and diverse influences that molded his thought and work. In this brief chapter, I will try to select judiciously among these materials to foster your initial encounter with his *Summa Theologiae*.

BIOGRAPHY[1]

Thomas Aquinas was born into an aristocratic family in 1224 or 1225 at the family castle at Roccasecca, Italy, a town midway between Rome and Naples. Being the youngest of the male children, the custom of the day was that Thomas take up a role within the Catholic church. So, at the age of five, he was brought to the Abbey of Monte Cassino where he studied for the next nine years, receiving his initial elementary education and spiritual formation in the Benedictine tradition. In 1239, upon the advice of the abbot, Thomas enrolled in a university at Naples, where he studied the arts and philosophy for the next five years. His time there had a profound impact upon his thought and character, specifically as he encountered both the richness of the Greek and Arabic intellectual culture (which had been denied to the West until shortly before his birth, especially the works of Aristotle), and the Dominicans, a religious order newly formed some ten years or so before his birth, which, together with the Franciscans, marked a return to the modeling of the religious life upon an imitation of the life of Jesus, one characterized by fervent prayer, itinerant preaching, assiduous study, and a serious commitment to the evangelical vows of poverty, chastity, and obedience. Thomas was attracted by the charism of the Dominicans, which strove to combine the contemplative with

---

[1] In this section and the next, I draw heavily upon Torrell (1993; 1996), Tugwell (1988), Weisheipl (1974; 1983), and O'Meara (1997).

1

the active life, that is to say, the monastic posture of meditation upon the Word with that evangelization which defines the mission of the Church to the world, particularly through teaching and preaching. He joined this Order in April of 1244 at the age of 19 or 20. His family, and particularly his mother, Theodora, were greatly displeased with his choice since it had been hoped that Thomas would become the abbot of Monte Casino, a position that would secure the family's future, again, an expectation of the day particular to the children of the noble classes. The Dominicans, being well aware of this and having suffered the wrath of another noble family who likewise did not agree with their son's choice, had Thomas leave Naples immediately. Theodora, however, had two of her sons pursue and intercept Thomas. It was the middle of May, 1244. He was brought back to the family castle at Roccasecca where he was detained until the summer of 1245, when his family, having tried unsuccessfully to convince him to abandon his choice of Order, allowed him to rejoin the Dominicans. He was sent to Paris where, in 1248 at the age of about 24, he completed the education that he had started at Naples. It was during this time in Paris when Thomas met and began to study under Albert the Great, one of the great theologians of his day who was pivotal in explaining Aristotle to the people of his time. Thomas continued his education under Albert, as well as being his assistant, following him to Cologne in 1248 where Albert had been asked by the Dominicans to establish a school of studies. During this time, Thomas was deeply immersed in the thought and work of his teacher, most particularly in his lectures concerning Aristotle's *Nicomachean Ethics,* an important source upon which Aquinas drew in his composition of the second part of the *Summa Theologiae.* So well did Thomas proceed in his studies that Albert entrusted him with some minor teaching duties, which have come down to us in the form of commentaries on the Old Testament books of Jeremiah, Lamentations, and Isaiah.

Having completed his formation with Albert in 1252, Thomas, upon the recommendation of his teacher, was sent to the University of Paris to take up the next part of the training required of one who was to become a master (or professor) in theology. He was 27, two years younger than the university allowed normally for one to take up the duties of lecturing/

commenting upon the *Sentences* of Peter Lombard (a work that expertly compiled the opinions of a wide number of Patristic writers covering the major areas and interests of theology), a process comparable to the modern day Ph.D. dissertation. Over the course of four years, Thomas lectured upon this work, as well as completing two much smaller although quite important works (*On Being and Essence*, and *On the Principles of Nature*), and in the spring of 1256, amid some controversy (mainly due to anti-mendicant animosity among some of the masters of the university), he was awarded a license to take up the regular duties of a master in the biblical sciences (or theology) at the University of Paris, a position that he occupied from 1256 until 1259. As a master, he had three primary responsibilities, namely, to comment deeply and meaningfully upon the Holy Scriptures (the primary task of a master, for the Bible was the primary text of the time; all scholarly work was oriented in some way to the Bible's elaboration), to hold private and public disputations (a formal and rigorous treatment of problems that arose from a mature consideration of the Holy Scriptures), and to apply the fruits gathered from the prior two activities to the pastoral duty of preaching. These activities produced corresponding works—biblical commentaries, collections of disputations, and sermons—of which many survive. His reputation as a teacher was excellent, particularly as his lectures were "terse, clear, and engagingly intelligible,"[2] as an early biographer states.

At the end of the school year in 1259, Thomas left his position at the University of Paris, having come to the end of his tenure, a normal practice among the Dominicans, one that allowed for the training of much needed masters within their order. He returned to Italy in the fall and continued his work on the first of his two *Summae,* the *Summa Contra Gentiles,* which he had begun toward the end of his time in Paris. In 1261, at the age of 36, Thomas was assigned as conventual lector to the Dominican priory at Orvieto. In this position, he was responsible for the formation of friars who had not been able to receive the kind of schooling that Thomas had in Naples (1239–1244),

---

[2] O'Meara (1997) quoting Peter Cavo, an early biographer of Aquinas, p. 19.

but who, nonetheless, had to be prepared to take up the duties of preaching and hearing confession. He spent four years in this capacity (1261–1265), during which he finished the *Summa Contra Gentiles,* composed many other important works (particularly his exposition on Job), took advantage of the monastic libraries in the region (which exposed him heavily to the theologians of the Greek tradition, something that had a great impact upon his thought), and gained valuable experience and insight into the conditions that called for the composition of a work of theology like that of his *Summa Theologiae,* specifically that many of the friars of his Order required a theological formation for the proper discharge of their duties, which was not provided for sufficiently by the texts or manuals of the day. In 1265, at the age of 40, Thomas was directed by his Order to address this problem, something that gave rise to a school of studies in Rome and the idea for the composition of his *Summa Theologiae.* This work occupied the rest of his life, and was left unfinished at the time of his death some nine short years later. In the three years when he was in Rome, Thomas probably finished the first of the three parts of the *Summa,* in addition to several other works. In 1268, Thomas found himself back in Paris to take up once again the master's chair of theology reserved for the Dominican Order. His return to Paris was occasioned by three problems that demanded his talents, namely, a renewed attack upon the mendicant orders, strong opposition from the more conservative theologians of his time to the use of Aristotle in the discipline of theology, and finally the popularity of certain theses of the Arabic philosopher Averroes that were dangerous to the Christian faith, particularly that there was only one intellect for the whole of mankind and not individual intellects for each person. Thomas wrote extensively concerning these problems, in addition to attending to his regular teaching duties. What many find amazing is that in addition to these tasks, Thomas composed several extensive commentaries on the major works of Aristotle (something that he had begun in Rome), important commentaries on Holy Scripture (specifically the Gospel of John), series of disputations, and the composition of the entirety of the second part of the *Summa,* as well as the first 20–25 questions of the third part, a massive amount of work in the space of four years (1268–1272) requiring several secretaries, a great deal of research on his part and others', time to read, and precious little time for food and sleep. Scholars estimate that Thomas had to have composed more than 12 pages of modern text each day to account for this literary output, an incredible amount even with the aid of several people and the habit of having worked in this fashion over the last 25 years of his life. In the spring of 1272, Thomas left Paris for Naples in response to his Order's desire to establish a school of theology. There, he lectured on the Letters of St. Paul, the book of Psalms, and continued his work upon the third part of the *Summa* and the commentaries on Aristotle that he had begun in Paris. Then, on December 6, 1273, while celebrating mass, Thomas "was suddenly struck by something that profoundly affected and changed him."[3] From this point forward, he composed nothing. When pressed for an explanation, he responded, "I cannot do any more. Everything I have written seems to me as straw in comparison with what I have seen."[4] While it is difficult to be precise concerning what had happened to him during mass, it is probable, especially in light of his rapidly failing health from that point forward, that the last five years of his life had taken a physical and psychological toll upon him. This, combined with the mystical experience that tradition holds he had had during mass, hastened his end. While on a journey to a council convened in Lyon by the Pope in the early months of 1274, he fell ill at the castle of his niece. He was brought to the Cistercian abbey of Fossanova where, after a time, he passed away on March 7, 1274. He was about 50 years old.

CHARACTER

Before we survey his works and method, something should be said about Thomas's character. For as you begin to read the *Summa,* you will quickly discover that both its method and dedication to the matters that it investigates make access to its author's character rather difficult.

From the brief biography just provided, one can readily discern that Thomas's whole life bespoke of a dedication to God

---

[3] Weisheipl (1974; 1983), p. 321 quoting Bartholomew of Capaua quoting Reginald.
[4] Torrell (1993; 1996), p. 289.

and the things of the Catholic faith. Reading, contemplating, teaching, and preaching the Word of God occupied and defined his life, seeking both for himself and others the ways by which God could be made most manifest in mind and heart, in thought and action. He was a Dominican priest, deeply committed to his Order and the responsibilities of forming his fellow Dominicans so that they too could discharge their duties beautifully. One should note carefully his decision to become a Dominican, particularly as this stood contrary to the wishes and aspirations of his family, and as it committed Thomas to a life lived in imitation of Christ, abandoning the comforts and positions that could easily have been his. He was a man of great prayer, particularly as he incorporated this into his work as a scholar and teacher. He was a true intellectual, having great confidence in the abilities of human reason, when properly trained and engaged, but always very aware of its limitations. He greatly enjoyed the interior life of the mind and was well known for his absent mindedness, something that became quite pronounced as he aged to the point where he would at times be unaware of the passage of events, of others in his presence, the experience of pain, and so on. Nevertheless, he did not spurn the advances of others. He was known to be approachable, kind, and generous with his time, particularly when called upon to resolve philosophical or theological questions, or to take up administrative duties on behalf of his Order. He was humble in his abilities, and did not abuse these powers, even in the heat of disputation. Ever the teacher, he was patient and would find the clearest and most succinct way to make his point. His written expression is very simple and direct, lacking all the rhetorical flair of an Augustine. He strove for the most direct and clearest order in his presentation of his materials so that the truth of the matter might best be presented. He was a lover of wisdom, and would seek it wherever it could be found. In this, he exhibited an exhilarating approach to his sources as he grappled with the theological concerns of his day, utilizing whatever he could obtain. The Holy Scriptures had pride of place, being the revealed Word of God itself, and that to which he dedicated his whole energy in trying to understand. He did this not only through prayer, but also through an appeal to the patristic writers (both Latin and Greek), and to Aristotle, the neo-Platonists, the Stoics, and the great Arab and Jewish thinkers and commentators. Clearly, he was a man of great stamina and dedication not only with respect to the voluminous output of his written work, but even in the miles that he travelled in the discharge of his duties, some 9,000 it is estimated.

WORKS[5]

Thomas composed a wide variety of works to address the varied responsibilities that he undertook and the requests that were made of him by family, friends, members of his Order and of the wider Church. In addition to the disputations on philosophical and theological problems that were a part of his duty as a professor of theology (the most famous among these being *De veritate, De potentia, De anima,* and *De malo*), and the commentaries he composed upon many of the books of Holy Scripture (particularly Isaiah, Job, Psalms, Matthew, John, and the letters of Paul), several of the works of Aristotle (some finished—*De anima, Physics, Posterior Analytics, Nicomachean Ethics,* and *Metaphysics*—others left incomplete at the time of his death) and other writers from both the theological and philosophical traditions (on Boethius's *De trinitate* and *De hebdomadibus,* Dionysius's *De divinis nominibus,* and *Liber de causis* by an Arab philosopher), Thomas wrote several treatises that continue to receive serious attention today (especially *De ente et essentia, De principiis naturae, Compendium Theologiae, De regno,* and *De substantiis separatis*). He was called upon for expert opinions on various matters, and left us some important works of a polemical nature, responding to the troubles that faced both his Order and the mendicants in general (*Contra impugnantes Dei cultum et religionem, De perfectione spiritualis vitae,* and *Contra doctrinam retrahentium a religione*) and to particular intellectual/theological problems of his day (*De unitate intellectus contra Averroistas* and *De aeternitate mundi*). Several sermons (on the Ten Commandments, the Lord's Prayer, the Apostle's Creed, and others) and prayers have survived (particularly the well-known hymn *Adoro te devote*), as well as some letters. It is, however, for his three great theological syntheses that Thomas

---

[5] For this material, I follow G. Emery's "Brief Catalogue of the Works of Saint Thomas Aquinas" as found in Torrell (1993; 1996), pp. 330–361.

is particularly remembered, namely, his commentary upon the four books of Peter Lombard's *Sentences,* and the two summas, the *Summa Contra Gentiles* and the work with which we are concerned in this book, the *Summa Theologiae.*

SUMMA THEOLOGIAE

Before we consider the text of the *Summa* itself, it is necessary that we engage in some propaedeutic considerations. We must consider the nature and purpose of this work, its unifying principle (macrostructure), its method (microstructure), and then consider the demands it makes upon its readers, as well as offering some general advice on how to read this medieval text of theology.

The Nature and Purpose of the *Summa Theologiae*[6]

It was mentioned previously that Thomas's experience at Orvieto had led him to conceive and write the *Summa Theologiae.* To expand upon this, it should be fairly clear that friars like Thomas, Albert the Great, and Bonaventure (the great Franciscan theologian, a contemporary of Thomas and one-time colleague during his first regency in Paris) were the exception and not the rule among the mendicants of the day; the majority of friars did not (or could not) take advantage of the kind of education these three men had received. Nevertheless, as Dominicans, they had to be prepared adequately to take up the duties that were central to their Order, those of preaching and hearing confession. Their education, then, had to cover the pastoral elements of theology, those that would make them proficient in these two areas with the ultimate purpose of caring effectively for the people that they served. To this end, there were a number of texts or manuals generated to meet this demand, texts that Thomas would have known well, especially as he was about to take up the duty of Lector at Orvieto. His experience at Orvieto led Thomas, it is argued, to consider these manuals as less than satisfactory insofar as they were so concerned with the pastoral and the moral that they did not provide for a wider coverage of the other parts of theology, especially as they could service or support the

[6] Much of what is presented here draws upon Torrell (1993; 1996) and Boyle (1982).

pastoral. To fill this "gap" in the practical theological training that the Dominican friars had traditionally received required attention to what we would today call sacramental and dogmatic or systematic theology with the purpose of putting this practical moral theology into "a full theological context."[7] The effect of this decision on Thomas's part was the idea for and the initial composition of the *Summa Theologiae,* a work that endeavors to present Christian morality as something grounded in the entirety of theology, and not as something that can safely ignore fundamental theology on the one hand, and Christology, sacramental theology, and eschatology on the other.

It is in light of these considerations that Thomas's *prologue* to the *Summa Theologiae* should be read:

> Since the teacher of Catholic truth has not only to build up those who are advanced but also to shape those who are beginning, according to St. Paul, *Even as unto babes in Christ I have fed you with milk and not meat* (I Cor. 3.1), the purpose we have set before us in this work is to convey the things which belong to the Christian religion in a style serviceable for the training of beginners. We have considered how newcomers to this teaching are greatly hindered by various writings on the subject, partly because of the swarm of pointless questions, articles, and arguments, partly because essential information is given according to the requirements of textual commentary or the occasions of academic debate, not to a sound educational method, partly because repetitiousness has bred boredom and muddle in their thinking. Eager, therefore, to avoid these and other like drawbacks, and trusting in God's help, we shall try to pursue the things held by Christian theology, and to be concise and clear, so far as the matter allows.[8]

The "beginners" that Thomas had in mind were very likely "young and run-of-the-mill Dominicans"[9] and not those in the

---

[7] Boyle (1982), p. 16.

[8] St. Thomas Aquinas. *Summa Theologiae: Volume 1 Christian Theology (Ia. 1) Latin text, English translation, Introduction, Notes, Appendices and Glossary* by Thomas Gilby O.P. (Cambridge: Blackfriars, 1964), p. 2.

[9] Boyle (1982), p. 17.

learned circles of a *studium generale* of Paris. Nonetheless, the difficulty of the work seems to argue the opposite point, that it is far more suited to the latter group. Torrell argues, however, that Thomas's concern was not so much materially driven, but was centered rather upon its arrangement into a direct, cohesive, and intelligible body of doctrine.[10] This synthesis, then, would allow them to take up their duties of preaching and hearing confession most effectively, and this without sacrificing a greater part of the body of Christian theology. To this, one might add Boyle's argument that Thomas may also have had a wider audience in mind, that is, not just his students at Rome, but all beginners of theology, at least within the Dominican Order from the general friar up to and including those who would become professors of theology.[11]

The Unifying Principle (Macrostructure) of the *Summa Theologiae*

Given the great size of this work and the amount of material with which it deals, it is vital that one understand its structure as well as the overall principles that give it its unity.

The division of this work is given by Thomas in the second question of the *Summa*:

> So, because, as we have shown, the fundamental aim of holy teaching is to make God known, not only as he is in himself, but as the beginning and the end of all things and of reasoning creatures especially, we now intend to set forth this divine teaching by treating, first, of God, secondly, of the journey to God of reasoning creatures, thirdly, of Christ, who, as man, is our road to God.[12]

This division is implicit in the solution to the problems Thomas faced both at Orvieto and Rome as discussed above, namely of embedding the friar's moral training in theology within the larger theological context. He does this by "prefacing" the

---

[10] Torrell (1993; 1996), p. 145.
[11] Boyle (1982), pp. 17–20.
[12] *Summa Theologiae Volume 2: Existence and Nature of God (Ia. 2–11)* translated by Timothy McDermott O.P. (Cambridge: Blackfriars, 1964), p. 3.

moral part of this work (the second of the three parts mentioned above in Thomas's preface, traditionally referred to by its Latin name, the *secunda pars*) by a fundamental theology (the first part or *prima pars*) and then by "rounding it off" with a Christological, sacramental, and eschatological theology (the third part or *tertia pars*).[13] The details of this structure can be discerned by looking to the material that Thomas covers in these three parts, something readily discerned in the prologues he offers to each of these parts. However, Thomas does not state explicitly a larger architectonic principle governing the whole of the work, something that many scholars have labored to supply. We will look at the most popular of these, that one offered by Fr. Chenu, and then consider Fr. Torrell's slight alteration of it, as well as another approach recently suggested by Rudi te Velde.

The introduction to Question 2 gives us the broad division into which Thomas divides the *prima pars*. He states that he wishes to treat first of those things that pertain to the divine essence (Questions 2 through 26); secondly, of those matters that concern the Trinity, that is, of the persons, and their distinctions, relations, and activities (Questions 27 through 43); and thirdly, of all matters that are related to the procession of creatures from His creative activity (Question 44 through to the end of the *prima pars,* Question 119). In considering the divine essence, Thomas questions first whether it can be shown that God exists. After establishing the conditions under which this is possible, Thomas then considers the manner of God's existence in the hope that we might be able to say something about His essence. Questions 3 through 11 are concerned with those essential descriptions that denote something positive in God, but which, from our perspective, denote at best what God is not. These negative or apophatic descriptions are followed, in Question 12, by an examination of the manner in which God can be present in human knowing, that is in distinction from the apophatic approach. With this determined, Question 13 details the nature of our naming of God. In the remaining questions of this initial section (14 through 26), Thomas concerns himself

---

[13] See Boyle (1982), p. 16. When the parts are cited, it is customary to replace the Latin with Roman numerals (I, I–II, II–II, and III, respectively).

with those operations, or activities, that follow upon the very essence or substance of God Himself. Questions 14 through 24 are directed to the nature of those activities that are immanent to God, that is to say, those that do not find their realization in anything external to God, but rather are realized within Him (such as matters that pertain to His intellect and will). He then considers in Question 25 God's power, that principle of the divine operation that proceeds toward an effect external to the unity of the divine essence itself. In light of all this, Thomas considers lastly the very state of God Himself, namely His beatitude.

Questions 27 through 43 complete Thomas's consideration of God, and constitute the second part of the *prima pars*. In these questions, he approaches God not in the unity of His divine essence, but rather according to the Trinity of the Persons that God is. He discusses their procession or origin (27) and the relations that these processions imply (28) before considering the Persons themselves, first in general terms, as "person" can be said of God (29 through 32), and then each Person individually (the Father in 33, the Son in 34 and 35, and the Holy Spirit in 36 through 38). He completes his consideration of the Persons of the Trinity by considering them in reference to the essence of God (39), His properties (40), the relations that exists among them (41), their equality and likeness (42), and lastly their respective missions (43). Thus, we have the first two parts of the *prima pars*, those which consider God as He is one and as Trinity.

Thomas then takes up the procession of creatures as they result from the creative act of God Himself. This will occupy Thomas's attention through to the end of the *prima pars*, and is divided by him into three broad sections. The first deals with general matters associated with the production or creation of creatures (44 through 46), while the second deals extensively with the distinctions that are to be made between them (47 through 102). The third then considers the preservation and governance of all that has been created (103 through 119). The second of the three, comprised of three treatises, distinguishes according to the kinds of creatures that had been created. The treatise on angels (50 through 64) deals with those creatures who are purely spiritual, while the treatise on the six days of creation (65 through 74) deals with those that are wholly material. The treatise on the human person (75 through 102) deals with those who are both spiritual and material. All of the three treatises are tempered in their scope by the context in which they appear, namely, first, as they derive from the creative activity of God Who is their beginning and their end, secondly, as they address the concerns particular to the theologian, and finally as they figure importantly in the second and third parts of the *Summa,* especially in light of the overarching principles that unify the entirety of the work. In this latter regard, the treatise on the human person is of particular importance, both as it constitutes the height of God's creative activity, and as it establishes the basic psychological doctrines central to the concerns that occupy the *secunda pars.* The third and final division of the *prima pars* completes Thomas's examination of the creative activity of God as it considers the whole of the created order as it is governed and preserved by God, and the varied ways by which He effects this in Himself (105), and through the roles played by the angels (106 through 114), material things (115), and the human person (117 through 119).

The concern in the *secunda pars* shifts to the pinnacle of God's creative act, namely the human person himself, and considers how the human person effects whatever he can effect in his journey to God. This part of the *Summa* deals with moral theology which, from a modern perspective, may seem somewhat peculiar insofar as it treats not just of what many consider to be typical moral matters, but also includes discussions concerning happiness, human psychology, and the varied activities and ways of living that characterize certain people within the Christian community. The reason for these "additions" lies in a conception of morality, which includes such matters as essential to its very project. Thomas's approach to morality is not one dominated by the solving of "hard cases," or centered upon the doing of the law, the defining and keeping of one's obligations, or acting according to one's conscience. Instead, it is one which seeks to answer what constitutes the happiness of man and how can it be attained.[14] In this, Thomas stands within

[14] Consider chapter 9 of Pinckaers (1993; 1995), especially p. 223 for Thomas's approach, and p. 229ff for its distinction from a modern approach.

what is characteristic of the ancient approach to morality, but in such a way that it is taken over and transformed in light of God's revelation and its investigation and articulation by the discipline of theology. The Prologue to the *secunda pars* is to be read, then, in this light:

> Since, as Damascene states (*De Fide Orthod.* ii. 12), man is said to be made to God's image, in so far as the image implies *an intelligent being endowed with free-will and self-movement*: now that we have treated of the exemplar, *i.e.*, God, and of those things which came forth from the power of God in accordance with His will; it remains for us to treat of His image, *i.e.*, man, inasmuch as he too is the principle of his actions, as having free-will and control of his actions.[15]

The human person, among all the things of creation, is found to be created to the image and likeness of God, which here implies, among other things, that he is not determined wholly by the forces that govern the material world; the human person knows not only the "what" and the "why" of things, that is, the essences and purposes of reality, but is able to determine himself or herself in accordance with this knowledge. Man, however, is not an end unto himself. Nor is his end something that consists simply in his self-determination, that is to say, in some absolute realization of his will as free in the act of choice. Man's freedom is relative, that is to say, he is free *for* something, and it is this something in which his destiny and his happiness are to be found. In discovering that for which he was made, the human person will have the chance to mold the entirety of his person so that in mind, heart, and action he might journey toward that wherein he might attain his perfection and happiness. Consequently, the *secunda pars* is divided into two sections. The first deals with an articulation of this destiny or end, that for which man is created, in light of which he finds his fullness, completion, and happiness. This is the treatise on happiness that begins the *secunda pars*, and extends for only five questions. The remainder of

---

[15] This translation is from the edition prepared by the Fathers of the English Dominican Province, published by Benziger Brothers (1947). The remaining translations will use this edition unless stated otherwise.

the *secunda pars* (298 questions) is concerned with the means whereby the human person might attain his end and happiness, namely, union with God Himself. This consideration of the means is itself divided into two parts. The *prima secundae* (literally "the first part of the second part") concerns itself with the general principles of morality, those that are directly relevant to the activities in which people must engage in order to attain to their happiness. What follows, then, might be considered a theory of human action, beginning with those activities that are particular to man, namely, activities that are voluntary, and all that surrounds or influences the volitional nature of such activities (Questions 6 through 21). Having dealt with the intellectual appetitive impetus to human action, he then considers the sensitive appetitive impetus common to both man and the other animals which lack reason and will. What follows is a detailed examination of the passions, or what we might call the emotions (Questions 22 through 48). The remainder of the *prima secundae* concerns itself with the principles that can be brought to bear upon the human person's appetition, those principles that are all important to the effecting of his happiness. They divide into principles that are intrinsic to the person and those that are extrinsic. Having dealt with the nature of the powers of the human person in the treatise on human nature in the *prima pars*, he considers here how these powers can be brought to bear upon man's activity for the sake of his happiness, and particularly the formation that these powers, but especially the appetitive, can receive. This formation is effected through the virtues and the vices. Thus, he begins with a general consideration of these insofar as they are generically defined as habits (Questions 49 through 54), and then moves on to a more specific consideration of these as they can be either good (virtuous) or bad (vicious). Questions 55 through 70 consider the nature of virtue and its division into intellectual, moral, and theological (55 through 67), and then those matters connected with them, namely, the gifts of the Holy Spirit (68), the Beatitudes (69), and the fruits of the Holy Spirit (70). Questions 71 through 89 consider vice and sin, those ways by which the human person "misses" or "strays from" the end and happiness for which he is made. The *prima secundae* ends with an examination of those principles external to the human person that are directly relevant to the attainment of his happiness, namely, through law (90 through 108) and grace (109 through 114).

The *secunda secundae* (literally "the second part of the second part") is the longest of the parts of the *Summa*, composed of 189 questions. The majority of this part is dedicated to a detailed description of the theological and moral virtues (faith, hope, and love—Questions 1 through 46—and prudence, justice, fortitude, and temperance, what traditionally have been called the cardinal virtues—Questions 47 through 170), and the vices that are opposed to them. These are the virtues (and vices) that pertain to all people regardless of their vocation. The remaining questions of this part deal with those matters that pertain to specific people within the Christian faith. Thomas considers three things, namely, the gratuitous graces (of prophecy, rapture, the gift of tongues, the gift of the word of wisdom and knowledge, and miracles: Questions 171 through 178), the active as compared to the contemplative life (179 through 182), and lastly specific duties and states of life (what these are, what is the state of perfection, and then the perfections of the episcopacy and the religious life: Questions 183 through 189).[16]

The Prologue to the *tertia pars* shows the way Thomas intends to complete what was started in the *secunda pars*, namely, the means whereby the human person can effect his happiness:

> Foreasmuch as our Savior, the Lord Jesus Christ, in order to *save His people from their sins* (Matthew 1.21), as the angel announced, showed unto us in His own Person the way of truth, whereby we may attain to the bliss of eternal life by rising again, it is necessary, in order to complete the work of theology, that after considering the last end of human life, and the virtues and vices, there should follow the consideration of the Savior of all, and of the benefits bestowed by Him on the human race. Concerning this, we must consider, first, the Savior Himself, secondly, the sacraments by which we attain to our salvation, and third, the end of immortal life to which we attain by the resurrection. Concerning the first, a double consideration occurs, the first, about the mystery

---

[16] The Prologue to the *Secunda Secundae* will be treated in the next chapter when this part of the *Summa* is considered in greater detail.

of the Incarnation itself, whereby God was made man for our salvation; the second, about such things as were done and suffered by our Savior, that is, God incarnate.

The journey of man to God is brought to its completion, then, only insofar as the Word becomes Incarnate, suffers and dies on man's behalf, and rises again on the third day. It is he who offers himself as the second Adam, he who is the perfect model for man to imitate in his journey to God, he through whom all graces will flow, and by whom man can actually attain to his happiness. Thomas dedicates the first 59 questions of the *tertia pars* to Jesus Christ. Questions 1 through 26 deal with the Incarnation itself, while 27 through 59 are concerned with the particulars of Christ's life, the things that he did or suffered while united to human nature culminating in his resurrection, ascension into heaven, taking up his seat at the right hand of the Father, and his judiciary power. Question 60 begins Thomas's consideration of the sacraments. After treating of their nature, necessity, effects, causes, and number (60–65), he begins to examine each sacrament separately. He considers baptism (66–71), confirmation (72), and the Eucharist (73–83), but is interrupted in his writing by the events of December 6, 1273, related above. He leaves off at Question 90 in the midst of his treatment of penance.[17]

By considering Thomas's own expressed principles concerning the structure of this work, as found in the prologues to each part of the *Summa*, one can begin to appreciate its overarching structure, and this particularly in light of the situation to which he responded as lector at Orvieto and in Rome. The amount of material, nonetheless, seems to demand a more succinct way by which one could represent how this multiplicity is formed into the cohesive unity that constitutes this work. For it is the mark

---

[17] Thomas's disciples, if you will, tried to complete the *Summa Theologiae* by appealing to his *Commentary on the Sentences of Peter Lombard,* and carefully selecting material appropriate to the general indications that Thomas had given in the *tertia pars* concerning the overall plan of this part. Recalling that this commentary stands at the beginning of Thomas's career, some 20 or so years earlier, the *Supplement,* as it is called, should not be considered as definitive concerning his mature views of the remaining sacraments and the last things.

of Thomas's *Summa Theologiae* (and also of other *summae* that were composed in many different disciplines both before and after his work) that it is a systematic work, one which is neither wholly encyclopedic/exhaustive, nor summative, but one which endeavors to combine both of these, being somewhere between them, aiming at "an exact, complete, and especially organically structured presentation where nothing essential is missing."[18] Such an endeavor thus demands an overall plan, a macroprinciple, to assure the synthetic nature of the work and its intelligibility as a whole.

Fr. M.-D. Chenu, in a work entitled *Toward Understanding Saint Thomas*, has presented such a principle that has been very helpful to many people who read and study the *Summa*.[19] He proposes that the architecture of this work has at its heart a Christian appropriation of the neo-Platonic principle of *exitus—reditus*, that is, of emergence/emanation and return. This movement is understood in metaphysical, psychological, and historical terms. God is the Creator of all, and there is nothing or no one prior to Him. He determines all things in their descriptions or essences, is the ultimate cause of all order and intelligibility, is the one who governs all things, and is the reason that all of this perdures. Wisdom is found in beholding all things in light of the Creator's mind, in light of this highest and ultimate cause. The human person himself is best understood in this light, and is revealed for the dignity and nobility that he is, as he has been created to God's image and likeness. He strives not only to realize this wisdom in his understanding, to take on the mind of God, but also to order the whole of his life in light of it. By this, he not only realizes what is implicit in his

---

[18] Torrell (2005), p. 70. Fr. Chenu (1950; 1964): "the word *summa* designates a literary work undertaken with a threefold purpose: first, to expound, in concise and abridged manner, the whole of a given scientific field of knowledge (this is the original meaning of *summa*); second, to organize, beyond piecemeal analysis, the objects of this field of knowledge in a synthetic way; finally, to realize this aim so that the product be adapted for teaching students . . . encyclopedic, synthetic, and in line with good teaching requirements." p. 299.

[19] Chapter 11 of this work. One might also consider Torrell's exposition of Chenu's position, some critiques it faced, and his responses (1993; 1996, pp. 150–158), and O'Meara's exposition with diagrams (1997, pp. 56–64).

very nature as a human being, but discovers that his ultimate completion and perfection, his happiness, is found not in the things of this existence, as good as they are, but rather in the striving to be united with the origin of all these goods. Wisdom has become a person with whom the human person is invited to commune imperfectly here and now, but perfectly in the time to come, something that cannot be effected by human effort alone, but requires the gift of God Himself, specifically in the person and life of Jesus Christ, the sacraments that He established, in the graces and gifts poured out by the Holy Spirit, in the virtues that are received both natural and infused, and in the gift in the next life of that very union and communication with the font of all being and intelligibility. God is the Alpha and the Omega from whom all things arise and in whom all things find their ultimate perfection, peace, and happiness. This, Fr. Chenu argues, constitutes the primary ordering principle of the materials of the *Summa Theologiae*. The *prima pars* describes the emanation of the whole of creation from God, its Creator or efficient cause, whose activity culminates in the establishment of the human person, and who conserves everything so created through His governance. The *secunda pars* shifts its focus to the theme of return, specifically of the human person whose happiness, perfection, or end consist in God Himself. Being created to God's image and likeness, and thus capable of knowledge and self-determination, the human person is considered in light of those activities that are required of him in order to begin his return to God. It is, however, only in the *tertia pars* that the " 'Christian' conditions of this return"[20] are determined, namely as God is made man in Jesus Christ, and the salvation that he effects for man through the salvific act. In this, the entirety of this work and of theological discourse in general, are brought to their completion, specifically as the *tertia pars* represents that transition from an examination of those necessary metaphysical and psychological structures at work in creation and especially in man, to that historical, freely willed and loving intervention of God in the person and actions of Jesus Christ.[21]

[20] Chenu (1950; 1964), p. 305.
[21] Chenu (1950; 1964), p. 315.

Fr. Torrell offers a slight modification of Chenu's approach in light of the literature that surrounds this topic. He suggests a distinction that he says was familiar to the patristic tradition between "theology" and "economy," that is, between investigations of God in Himself, and those which concern the work of God in time. He argues that Thomas could be read as dividing the *Summa* into these two parts, the first covering the *Prima Pars* from Questions 2 through 43, and the second covering the remaining questions of the whole work. The principle of *exitus—reditus* would then apply only to the "economic" part of the *Summa*, with the *exitus* corresponding to Questions 44 through 119 of the *Prima Pars* (that is, from the biblical account of creation up to its governance), and the *reditus* to the Second and Third Parts. He states:

> These parts are perfectly unified under the sign of the "return" of the rational creature to God under the leadership of Christ. The incarnate Word takes the lead in this movement for he alone is able to bring it to completion. The whole project is brought (ought to have been brought) to completion at the end of the Third Part by the glorious return of Christ at the end of time and the beginning of new heavens and a new earth. Between the two creations is placed the entire history of salvation in its diverse stages. Thomas can thus integrate the historical and existential evolution of the work of God in a perfectly organic way within a harmonious structure that, of itself, helps us to understand his project.[22]

This modification of Chenu's approach accounts nicely for the problem of the simple attribution of the *reditus* to the *secunda pars* when clearly the *reditus* begins much earlier in the *prima pars*.[23] Noting other problems with the *exitus—reditus* scheme, Rudi te Velde suggests a modified way of describing the basic scheme of the *Summa*.

As powerful and as reasonable as the *exitus—reditus* scheme is, Velde argues that a careful reading of the prologues cited above would seem to indicate that Thomas's approach to the

---

[22] Torrell (1993; 1996), pp. 49–50.
[23] One of several problems that troubles Rudi te Velde (2006), pp. 13–14.

material of the *Summa* is less theocentrically structured than is supposed. The entirety of theology, as Thomas argues in the first question of the *Summa*, does indeed treat of God primarily, and of all other things only insofar as they are referable to God as their beginning or end,[24] and that the *prima pars* has God as its primary concern. However, God is not the primary agent in the *secunda pars*. "The principal acting subject of the *Secunda Pars* is, perhaps surprisingly, not God under the aspect of final causality, but man inasmuch as he is a rational, free agent."[25] The focus shifts from the work of God, as it has established, conserves and governs creation, to the work of man, who, having been created to the image and likeness of God, exercises the work of a being who is rational and free. In the *tertia pars*, the principle agent is Christ, and the focus shifts there from the created freedom that man is to Christ's work of salvation and the benefits that this confers upon all people. He argues, then, that the *Summa* does not appear to be ordered according to Chenu's *exitus—reditus* scheme, but rather according to the three agents of God, man, and Christ and the work that they accomplish. Thus, the *prima pars* concerns God and his "work of creative freedom," the *secunda pars* concerns man and his "work of the created freedom," and the *tertia pars* concerns "Christ and his work of salvation, that is, the work of restoring and reopening the fallen freedom of man towards God."[26] Under this description, all the things of theology continue to be treated as they concern either God Himself or His creatures as they are referred to Him as their beginning or end. But they become unified in the *Summa* not so much by the movement of the *exitus—reditus* scheme, but rather by "a linear movement of increasing concretization in which two shifts in perspective occur," both of which give rise to the second and third parts of the *Summa* and the subjects of which they treat.[27] The *prima pars* concerns God both with respect to his nature and all that flows from this, culminating in the establishment, conservation, and governance of the whole of

---

[24] ST. I. 1. 3. ad1.
[25] Velde (2006), p. 16.
[26] Ibid., p. 17.
[27] Ibid., p. 18.

creation. The human person, however, being a rational creature and thus free to determine his course within and with respect to God's creation and His consequent governance of it as he seeks his happiness, "transcends the perspective" of the *prima pars*, thus requiring a refocusing of the *Summa* both upon the being and activity of man as he realizes his image and likeness to God as created freedom in his search for happiness, and upon the kind of governance that God exercises with respect to man "whose freedom requires a new and different way of divine guidance which cannot be thematized from the perspective of creation.[28] This, then, forms the concern of the *secunda pars*. The *tertia pars* becomes necessary insofar as "man has turned away from God, from his graceful and saving presence, by committing sin, the result of which is the corruption of his freedom." The Incarnation, then, becomes

> the divine answer to the human condition of damaged freedom. As a result of the first sin of Adam, all mankind, on its way through time and history, stands in need of redemption and restoration of its freedom, and this can only be accomplished by the action of an agent who unites, in himself, the divine and the human. In the *Tertia Pars*, therefore, we see that God's presence assumes another form, namely, as incarnate in Christ. The Incarnation, I want to suggest, should be understood as the final and most 'intense' concretization of God's grace with respect to human freedom corrupted by sin.[29]

Its Method (or Microstructure)

One of the greater difficulties that anyone faces upon reading the *Summa* for the first time is the method that Thomas uses in the presentation of its material. It is quite unlike the scholarly writings of either the present day or even of the ancient world, and is something that arises out of the teaching and learning style of Thomas's day.

A greater part of teaching was accomplished in Thomas's time by a close reading of a text considered authoritative in the

[28] Velde (2006), p. 17.
[29] Ibid., pp. 17–18.

area being taught. Proceeding line by line, the teacher would either offer explanations sufficient to an initial understanding of the text in question without dwelling on any problems that it might contain or occasion (what was called a "cursive" reading) or expound upon the text more carefully, detailing and considering the issues that arose from it (an "ordinary" reading).[30] From these readings arose problems that could not be solved easily and would thus occasion much discussion and research far beyond that from which they began. This gave rise to a literary form called the *quaestio* or "question," which consisted generally of a consideration of an issue through a presentation of the positions both pro and con, a considered solution offered by the teacher, followed by an addressing of the positions pro and con in light of the determination that had been offered. The purpose of this was to achieve a deeper, more profound understanding of the text before one, and not the modern practice of questioning the authorities as something fuelled by skepticism and doubt. This procedure not only influenced the way by which a text was "read" (in the sense just spoken of previously), but also became the basis for its evolution into the *disputatio* of which there were two forms. The "private" dispute was occasioned by the master or professor who would introduce his students to a particular thesis who would then be required to put forth positions contrary to this thesis, to which the master's assistant would then respond. This allowed students not only to develop their skills in debate, but also to behold the issues or "knots" that "bind" the mind so that, in a full understanding of these puzzles, a way might be discovered to their "loosening" or solution.[31] It also served as excellent training for the master's assistant who was engaged upon his own study and training to become a master. This would be done in one session. In a second session (either later in the day or on the next), the master would summarize the objections, offer his own determination of the thesis, and then respond

---

[30] Chenu (1950; 1964), p. 84, Marenbon (1987), pp. 16–19, and Torrell (2005), pp. 64–65.
[31] This aporetic approach to understanding follows Aristotle's method of investigation. See Thomas's *Commentary on Aristotle* Metaphysics, Book III, Lectio 1 for more on this.

to each of the objections that had been raised against it in the prior session in light of his determination. The second kind of dispute was held publicly and would mirror the procedures of the "private" dispute. These were called "ordinary" disputes, and they were required of the masters on a regular basis throughout the school year. There was a particular form of the public disputation called the "quodlibetal" disputation that was quite popular among the audience, but not generally for the master. These were held infrequently (in Thomas's time at Paris only at Easter and Christmas), and were conducted much like the "ordinary" dispute except for the fact that the thesis and the objections to it were not determined by the master and his students, but rather could be offered by anyone in the audience concerning any issue of interest.[32]

The *Summa Theologiae* is a work that very likely was never taught to students. However, it bears directly the marks of the "ordinary" disputation. As Torrell states, "What was originally simply the reflection of a more or less animated oral discussion became a process of personal reflecting on and writing about."[33] We have seen that the *Summa* is composed of three parts, and have dealt briefly with the material found in these parts, as well as the unifying principle of the work as a whole. In a more proximate approach to this work, you will find that each part is made up of questions (which are collected together further in the form of treatises), and that the questions themselves are determined through a series of "articles." It is important to note that although the article will proceed very much after the manner of the "ordinary" disputation, nonetheless, the article always serves the purpose of detailing what needs to be investigated in order to treat adequately of the question within which the article is found, the question that is proposed for discussion. For example, when you consider the second question of the *prima pars*, that famous question dealing with the existence of God, Thomas put forth three matters that need to be addressed in the course of considering this question, namely whether the existence of God is something that is self-evident (or not, in which case it would lead to the

---

[32] Torrell (1993; 1996), pp. 59–63, and ibid (2005), pp. 65–66.
[33] Torrell (2005), p. 67.

next article, namely), whether God's existence is something that could be demonstrated, that is, approached in some way other than by faith alone, and (if this is found to be the case, this then leads to the next article, namely) whether there are ways by which this demonstration can be effected. These three matters are treated separately in three distinct articles, all of which share the same basic structure. Each article begins by considering what are called "objections," that is, arguments that are contrary to the position that Thomas will take in his determination. These arguments were drawn from the authoritative writings at Thomas's disposal of either a religious or a secular nature, or from the arguments made by the men of his day. The purpose here, as was said before, was to illuminate the difficulties that one had to face in the answering of the issue before one. For without a consideration of these difficulties, Thomas and others considered any solution to the difficulty to be arrived at accidentally. This affirms, then, the cogency, at least, of the objections, arguments that must be taken seriously in one's search for the answer to the issue at hand. Three or four objections are usually entertained, although the number could be much higher. After the objections are stated, there follows the declaration of a position that is an alternative to that proposed in the objections. This is called the *sed contra*, or "on the contrary" something that is not intended to be read as directly contradicting the objections, but rather as presenting the position in support of the issue at hand. For the course of the discussion, or debate if you will, has not yet positioned the master to offer a direct argument against these objections. This can occur only after the magisterial determination of the author has been presented. This is the next part of the article, and is called the *respondeo* or "response." Sometimes, it is referred to as the "body" or *corpus* of the article. As was the case in the disputation, it is only in light of the response that the initial objections can be answered. Sometimes, the "response to the objections" will simply indicate the error that underlies the position. It is quite common, though, for these responses to allow Thomas the opportunity to expound further upon his initial response, but this time in light of the particular issue upon which the objection dwells. Finally, it is sometimes the case that the response is so definitive and clear that Thomas will forego responding to the initial objections, deeming them to be obvious to the reader.[34]

Some Final Considerations and Advice

In spite of all that has been said here of a propaedeutic nature, the *Summa* still presents the reader with some unique problems. In addition to its size (it treats of "512 questions, 2,669 articles, and approximately 10,000 objections with their solutions"[35]), and the exacting method that is employed in its investigations (the disputational method just discussed, often referred to as the "scholastic method"), the *Summa* requires a good understanding of the sources upon which it draws in its composition.

The source from which all theology arises is the revelation that is contained in the Holy Scriptures. Thus, the *Summa*, as a work of theology, is compenetrated by the whole of Sacred Scriptures, which requires that the reader be well read in these if he or she is to appreciate the work as a whole. It is often pointed out that Thomas was a master of Sacred Scripture, that the central text of the theologian was the Bible, and that the greater part of his duties both as a master and as a Dominican revolved around teaching and preaching the macroprinciples discussed above. These, combined with Thomas's great devotion to Jesus Christ, should be kept in mind as one reads the *Summa* insofar as they constitute insights into the very tenor of the work, and of the man who wrote it. In his desire to know the things of God and to understand His revelation, Thomas depended greatly upon the tradition of commentary upon the Bible and

---

[34] There are many ways to cite Thomas's text. Generally, the three parts of the *Summa* are referred to by Roman numerals (I, I–II, II–II, and III, respectively). It is typical to refer, next, to the question followed by the article, and these in Arabic numerals. So, the third article concerning whether God exists as found in the second question of the First Part of the *Summa* is indicated as ST. I. 2. 3. If one wishes to indicate something within the article itself, this is added after the article number in the following fashion: the first objection by *obj. 1* or *arg. 1*; the "on the contrary" by *sc*; the corpus or body of the article by *resp.* or by no reference other than the article number itself; and the response to the first objection by *ad 1*. You will note variations on this way of citing, but they all follow the same order (part—question—article—*obj. 1 / sc. / resp. / ad. 1*).

[35] Weisheipl (1974; 1983), p. 222.

the works of theology that were available to him. Most notable here, in the Latin tradition, were the works of Augustine who figures most prominently throughout the *Summa*. As is pointed out by Fr. Torrell, the whole of the *Summa* could be considered as an " 'uninterrupted dialogue' with Augustine,"[36] quoting the scholar L. Elders. Thomas also had the opportunity to immerse himself in the theology of the Greek tradition, particularly during his stay at Orvietto, a fact that deeply influenced his Christology and Trinitarian theology. Not content to restrict himself to this abundance of theological work, Thomas cast his net wide, looking to the works of the ancient Greek philosophers (and to their Arab and Jewish commentators) for anything that would aid him in the understanding and exposition of the matters with which the *Summa* was concerned. Although he made generous use of the neo-Platonic and Stoic materials that were available to him, Aristotle figures most prominently in this regard, so much so that one can be greatly hampered in appreciating the *Summa* if one does not have at least a general understanding of the teachings of Aristotle, particularly his logic, epistemology, psychology, ethics, physics, and metaphysics. This is immediately noticed in both the logic employed throughout the *Summa* (the scholastic method just mentioned) and the "technical" language it often employs in its determinations. It is not unusual to find a glossary of these technical terms in anthologies of the *Summa*.[37] While these are helpful, it is more to the point to engage directly the works of Aristotle, or at the very least to avail oneself of a good summary of his work.[38] Thomas's use of Aristotle (and of philosophy in general) in treating of matters of revelation and of the faith is most complex and has been the subject of great controversy

[36] Torrell (2005), p. 74.
[37] For example, *A Summa of the* Summa edited by Peter Kreeft (San Francisco: Ignatius Press, 1990), pp. 23–30 and *A Summary of Philosophy* translated and edited by Richard Regan (Indianapolis: Hackett, 2003), pp. 209–216.
[38] For example, *The Cambridge Companion to Aristotle,* edited by Jonathan Barnes (Cambridge: Cambridge University Press, 1995), *Aristotle: A Very Short Introduction* by Jonathan Barnes (Oxford: Oxford University Press, 2001), and W. D. Ross, *Aristotle,* 5th edition (Cleveland: Meridian, 1953).

both within and outside of Christian circles. Be that as it may, within the context of the *Summa*, one best approaches its non-theological material, vocabulary, and formal structures initially as the Christian appropriation of a wisdom that is put at the service of the very things of which theology treats, those things for which the ancient philosophers strove but were unable to attain. Thus, Thomas's use of philosophical materials and methods in the *Summa* should be viewed in light of the aid they offer in the ascent of the mind and soul to the things of theology and ultimately to man's beatitude, God Himself.[39] Of all the difficulties that the neophyte experiences in reading Thomas's *Summa Theologiae*, this to my mind is the most difficult to overcome.[40]

In the next chapter, the text of the *Summa* will be our concern. Given the quantity, let alone the quality, of the materials with which it deals, it would be prudent to organize our reading in light of the treatises that make up the work. This approach accommodates both the nature of this introductory text, as well as the macroprinciples that are at the heart of the *Summa*. If one can address the varied treatises in light of these principles, as well as the many other concerns noted in this chapter, one will receive not only a decent first exposure to this work, one which may encourage continued reading and reflection, but also avoid what seem to be perennial errors in its understanding and interpretation.[41]

---

[39] Among the many works written on these issues, consider Jordan (1992), and Velde's "Understanding the *Scientia* of Faith: Reason and Faith in Aquinas's *Summa Theologiae*" in Kerr (2003), pp. 55–74.

[40] For a more extensive survey of the sources, consider Torrell (2005), pp. 72–85.

[41] Some of which can be gleaned in Mark D. Jordan's "The *Summa*'s Reform of Moral Teaching—and Its Failures" in Kerr (2003), pp. 41–54.

CHAPTER 2

READING THE *SUMMA THEOLOGIAE*

This chapter will divide according to the three parts of the *Summa* and will consider the varied treatises that comprise each part. A discussion of each treatise will be offered, some longer, others shorter, with attention dedicated to the more pertinent questions of the treatise under consideration.

PRIMA PARS

As stated in the last chapter, the *Prima Pars* can be divided into two parts, the first dealing with the theology of God, that is to say, an examination of God's inner being and life, and the second with His economy, that is to say, His work in time, the *exitus* or emergence of all things from His creating power. In considering the former, Thomas composes two treatises, the first dealing with the *Divine Essence* (Questions 2 through 26) and the second with the *Trinity* (Questions 27 through 43), both of which are preceded by a short, yet very important *Treatise on Sacred Doctrine*. The remaining questions dealing with God's transitive activity (44 through 119), span five treatises, namely, the *Treatise on Creation, the Angels, the Work of the Six Days, Man,* and *the Divine Government.*

Treatise on Sacred Doctrine (Question 1)[1]

In this very short treatise, Thomas considers sacred doctrine or teaching by looking to, first, its necessity (Article 1), secondly, its definition (Articles 2 through 7), and finally its particular method (Articles 8 through 10).[2]

The issue of necessity is introduced by the objections to Question 1 that ask why one would require any other doctrine or

---

[1] One might wish to consult Velde (2006), pp. 18–35, his article in Kerr (2003), pp. 55–74, and the appendices of Blackfriars's *Summa*, Volume 1 for more detail on what is presented here.

[2] See Weisheipl (1974; 1983), p. 223.

teaching than those that have already been developed by human reason and pursued by the arts and the sciences. For it seems, they say, that the intellectual traditions of the day have already addressed the entirety of reality, even God himself, as is accomplished through the study of metaphysics in philosophy. There may indeed, they say, be a teaching that is beyond the reach of reason. This, however, cannot be the concern of the human person who must restrict himself, by reason of the limitations of his reason, to those things that fall within his natural grasp. It would seem, therefore, that a sacred doctrine or teaching is superfluous or, at the very least, unattainable. The *sed contra*, on the other hand, states that the necessity of sacred doctrine is assured by its very source, namely, God himself, particularly as He reveals this teaching, which otherwise would be unattainable by natural means, to the betterment of the human person. Before proceeding to Thomas's solution, one should note how well the objections and the *sed contra* present the field of engagement, the issues to be addressed and the dilemma that needs to be resolved if the question is to be answered properly. Thomas presumes that the reader will be able to understand this field, and be able to expand upon these arguments appropriately so that the knot, so to speak, of the issue might be clearly revealed, allowing one to see one's way to a definitive answer. Clarity concerning Thomas's response always begins with how he perceives the problem before him, something that the objections readily supply. It is well worth the effort in one's reading, then, to attend carefully to these matters.

Thomas addresses the issue of redundancy by looking to the very root from which the arts, sciences, and especially philosophy arise, namely that they manifest collectively the human person's characteristic manner of striving to understand, articulate, and acquire that in which his completion, perfection, and happiness consist. As will be seen in the first five questions of the *secunda pars*, all created things, all products of human making, doing and learning contribute to the realization of man's happiness, but do not, either singularly or collectively, stand as that in which man finds his ultimate completion and happiness. And yet, man, in his very essence, is oriented naturally in all that he does to his happiness and cannot but strive for this end. Thus, in light of this necessity, it is reasonable to suppose that there is some doctrine or teaching that addresses this very situation, offering guidance with respect to the attainment of this ultimate of pursuits, as well as the means by which it might be realized by both the learned and unlearned. This teaching, Thomas argues, is exactly that which is revealed by God for the sake of the salvation of the human race. It supplies precisely what is lacking in man's intellectual and cultural traditions, namely, the very object of human happiness, that for which humans were made, for which all strive, but which only a very few could even begin to approach, namely the philosophers who glean something of the divine through their engagement in metaphysics, a study sometimes referred to as natural theology. But, this pursuit is itself imperfect, requiring a great dedication of time and effort on their part as well as the suffering of the misfortunes that attend such an endeavor (the inevitable errors of speculative philosophical thought, the difficulty in finding teachers adequate to the task, the leisure and the economics required to conduct such a life of study, peace in their country, and so on). But this doctrine or teaching is something required by *all* people for their happiness, and is not something to be restricted to those who happen to be learned and fortunate. Thus, it is reasonable to argue for a doctrine such as this, one that communicates effectively to all human beings that for which they strive, that in which their happiness consists, something gleaned by the arts and sciences, but only realized by them in an imperfect and propaedeutic way. The fullness of man's happiness and perfection can only be revealed in light of the communication of the divine himself both with respect to those things that the human intelligence could never comprehend on its own, and even with respect to those things that man could discover on his own but does not do so assuredly.[3]

It is in light of this determination that Thomas can then address properly the initial objections, answering them and even indicating in what way they were accurate. He affirms that which is beyond the natural reach of human reason is not something for which one can grasp. However, it is a different matter when such things have been brought into one's grasp,

---

[3] Consider also the treatment of this same question in chapters 3 through 8 of Book I of the *Summa Contra Gentiles*.

something accomplished through revelation and the acceptance of such by an act of faith. The fact itself that there is a part of philosophy that treats of divine matters does not of itself hinder another discipline (theology) from treating of the same things. Thus, just as the philosopher, the psychologist, the psychiatrist, and the biologist can be concerned with human happiness, albeit from differing perspectives suitable to and definitive of their respective disciplines, so too can the theologian occupy himself with matters concerning God in ways proper to his discipline. The matter of redundancy, then, is not so obvious. At the very least, that this doctrine should exist is reasonable in light of the natural and historical insufficiency of the natural human striving for happiness.

Articles 2 through 7 consider the nature of sacred doctrine. Thomas describes this doctrine as a *scientia*. The literal translation of this term as "science" does little to indicate what Thomas means here, and thus requires some explanation. He is referring to the ancient use of the word, specifically as found in Aristotle's works, where it stands for any knowledge that one acquires through discovering the causes of an effect. Different *scientiae* are distinguished according to the manner by which the thing under investigation is approached. Thus, we can speak of varied *scientiae* of the human person as we approach him biologically, psychological, politically, metaphysically, and so on, developing, over time, the organized bodies of knowledge that we now call by the aforesaid names. The question is posed: Is sacred doctrine of this nature? Thomas says that it is. He appeals to one of the foundations of any organized body of knowledge, namely that it arises either from principles that are not proven by it but rather are discovered in relation to the thing under consideration, or from principles that are borrowed, so to speak, from another organized body of knowledge that is more universal, or of greater extent, than the one that does the borrowing. Consider Thomas's examples. The former could describe Euclidean geometry, a *scientia* that is established upon axioms or postulates that define the elements upon which the whole of the study is founded, axioms that are discovered, are self-evident and thus do not derive from a more universal *scientia*. The latter could describe the structural or theoretical dependence of music upon mathematics. Clearly, there are mathematical structures foundational to the whole of music, something that the musician is not required to explain, prove, or demonstrate from within the *scientia* of music itself so that he might engage in his discipline. He presumes, so to speak, the existence and operation of these principles, and engages accordingly in his art. It remains to a more universal *scientia,* mathematics, to investigate these principles that music as a *scientia* has borrowed and upon which it depends for its nature, operation and integrity. It is in this second way that sacred doctrine deserves to be called a *scientia.* The *scientia* of greater extent upon which it is based, from which it takes its foundational principles and consequently its logical coherence, is the knowledge that God has of Himself, something which He communicates through revelation in the Holy Scriptures, which requires an act of faith on the part of man to be possessed and to become the very foundation from which theology arises.

The unity of this *scientia* is found in the formal principle or primary perspective under which this revelation is considered. Thus, just as physics treats of a wide diversity of things as they are material and thus subject to the principles that govern the change, so too does sacred doctrine treat of a wide variety of things under the perspective that they are divinely revealed. And as the reply to the first objection states, this revelation, which gives rise to sacred doctrine, is concerned primarily with God, and secondarily with creatures insofar as they are referred to God as their beginning and end. Consequently, this *scientia* is both practical and speculative, the former insofar as it concerns the doing of the Word, and not just the hearing of it, and the latter as it concerns God Himself and all creation in reference to Him, with the primacy lying with the speculative for the sake of this doctrine's unity, and that the doing of the Word is possible only in the hearing and the understanding of it.[4] Article 5 argues that sacred doctrine is most noble and

---

[4] ST. I. 1. 4. The practical and theoretical aspects of this knowledge and the principle that the former depends upon the latter is mirrored in the organization of the *Summa* itself as the *prima pars* details the theoretical aspects of God's revelation, which is necessary to its practical realization in the both the *secunda* and *tertia pars.* This also reflects well Thomas's addressing of the problem of a moral theology done in distinction from the other parts of theology, as discussed in the first chapter of this work.

certain among all other *scientiae* due to its source (the mind of God Himself), its subject matter (the highest of all causes, those entertained by God Himself that constitute the very basis of all creation), and the benefit that it confers upon all people (that it supplies both the answer to what is man's ultimate end and happiness, and the means whereby it can be attained). Thus, certitude is not something to be judged, in Thomas's view, primarily from the perspective of man's understanding, something that can err quite easily and cannot on its own aspire to that *scientia* that allows him the chance to become happy. All other *scientiae*, particularly philosophy, can be used for the sake of the investigation and clearer communication of this sacred doctrine or teaching, particularly as all other *scientiae* can treat of and present divinely revealed matters in terms that are more familiar to the human intellect. It comes, then, as no surprise that this *scientia* is properly defined as wisdom, that highest of knowledge that allows the mind to behold all things from the perspective of their highest causes, thus beholding all reality in light of its ultimate foundation. Through this knowledge, one is able to order most effectively and beautifully all the things of one's making and doing. Such a person is considered to be truly wise, that is, one who is best able to judge rightly of all things and to order them well. One sees all things not only from the perspective of the revelation given by God, but can be said to take on the mind of God in all that one thinks, does, makes, and feels. God, then, forms the very object of this *scientia*, both in Himself, and as all things come forth from Him (*exitus*) and as they find their fulfillment and perfection in their relation to Him (*reditus*). It is this mind, this *scientia,* this wisdom that man is called to take up if he is to be happy.

Articles 8 through 10 describe what are particular to the method of this *scientia*, that is to say, what is characteristic and appropriate to its manner of investigation. Given that sacred doctrine is a *scientia*, its procedures must have something of the argumentative about them. With respect to its foundational principles, this *scientia* does not argue about such things. Instead, these principles constitute the articles of the faith and are accepted as such, which then allows one to argue from them to other positions in a logically coherent manner. The articles of the faith are contained within the canonical books of Holy Scripture and are accepted by reason of the authority of these writings. However, all other knowledge within this sacred doctrine, which includes the contributions made by the Church Fathers, the arts, and the sciences, but especially philosophy, are subject to the same criteria for soundness as any other argument is.

Given the argumentative nature of this *scientia*, its reasonability and logical coherence, Article 9 asks whether there is an appropriate use of metaphor and symbol within it, especially given that both of these are used abundantly throughout Holy Scriptures. Thomas argues that there is, insofar as these literary devices accommodate the way by which people come to know, namely through sensible things and images, thus making the knowledge contained in sacred doctrine available to all. His reply to the second and third objections supplies, as is often the case, refinements to his initial answer in light of the concerns that each objection presents. Although a metaphor does indeed hide the truth, something the objection considered inappropriate to a *scientia* that concerns the highest wisdom, three "safeguards" are built into Scripture to prevent an unnecessary clouding of the truth, namely that the mind is never allowed to rest merely in the image or metaphor, but is always invited to ascend to the truth that it reveals; second, that whatever is taught metaphorically in one place of Scripture is discussed more openly elsewhere; and third, that the hiding of truth is a useful thing whereby the mind of the believer is exercised, and the truths that the Scriptures contain are hidden from unbelievers and thus not exposed to their ridicule. The reply to the third objection proceeds in a similar fashion.

Finally, given the argumentative nature of this *scientia*, it is asked whether it is appropriate that the Scriptures that communicate this *scientia* employ the several senses in which words can typically be used. The concern of the first objection is important, namely that one of the conditions necessary for a *scientia* to proceed soundly is that the meaning of the words employed in its arguments retain the same meaning throughout the argument. Reasonable, logically coherent argumentation avoids not only symbols and metaphors, but also the equivocal usage of its terms. Univocal use of language is one of the conditions for the validity of an argument, something that every theologian of Thomas's day would have known from his training in logic.

This concern allows Thomas to develop a characteristic that is particular and unique to this *scientia*. On the one hand, this doctrine is like all others, namely that the words employed are used to signify the things with which they deal. However, on the other hand, the very things that are signified by these words are themselves occasions for further significations. The former constitutes the historical or literal sense of Scripture, while the latter refers to its spiritual sense, a sense that is based on the literal, presupposing it insofar as it gives rise to the occasion where this sense can be realized. Thomas describes three forms of the spiritual sense: the allegorical, the tropological or moral, and the anagogical. The allegorical sense allows one to see how the things of the Old Law signify those of the New. The tropological or moral sense offers the things that Christ did, or those things that signify Christ, as examples of what Christians themselves ought to do. Finally, the anagogical sense allows one to see how the matters of which the Scriptures treat signify the eternal glory to which all are called. Given this special mode of signification, one which is based upon and arises from the things of the literal sense and not just a further playing out of the words that are used in the literal sense to signify such things, it must be the case that the spiritual sense is not intended by the human author of Scripture, but can be effected only by the author of the whole of the Scriptures, namely God Himself.[5] Consequently, equivocation of argument is avoided insofar as the words themselves are not in play, but rather the things that they signify, significations that are directly intended by God, and the meaning of which is guided by the literal sense as well as by the action of the Holy Spirit.

Sacred doctrine, then, is a knowledge that concerns God and all things as they are related to Him. It is a knowledge that concerns both the world itself and its source, a knowledge that considers these from the perspective or mind of God Himself, a perspective that is necessary to the salvation of man, and a perspective that can be acquired only by an act of faith consequent

---

[5] Thomas holds that the literal/historical sense is also authored by God. For an initial consideration of the contributions made by the human authors of Scripture, consider appendices 12 and 13 of Volume 1 of the Blackfriars' edition of the *Summa Theologiae*.

upon God's communication of this through the revelation that is contained in Holy Scriptures. This knowledge is necessary to all Christians and carries with it the three concerns that form the three parts of the *Summa*, namely, a knowledge of God from whom all creation issues, and for which the human person thirsts as He in Whom he will find his completion and happiness; the moral means whereby the human person can begin to effect his happiness; and finally, the Christological and sacramental means whereby human happiness is really attained. The theologian makes these matters the focus of his study, and in the present case, allows these matters to structure the very work of the *Summa* itself. The entirety of his mind is turned to this revelation so that it might behold the articles of faith upon which the study of theology itself stands, and thus acquire the foundation from which all that theology does arises as a *scientia*. Sacred doctrine calls the theologian forth both personally and professionally to render the divine matters understandable and actionable, seeking not only the literal and historical sense of the Scriptures (something that would probably include the historical-critical approach to Scripture study today), but primarily its spiritual sense. Sacred doctrine and theology themselves can have the character of a *scientia* only insofar as they are based upon and derived from the *scientia* enjoyed by God both of Himself and of the whole of creation in relation to Him. This makes possible their reasonable and logically coherent character, and justifies the order and method used by Thomas in the theological treatment of it, something which strives not only to do justice to the inherently intelligible character of this revelation, but also to satisfy the pastoral duty a theologian has in relating its teachings to his students, or in Thomas's case, to the Dominican friars under his tutelage at Orvieto and Rome.

Treatise on the Divine Essence (Questions 2–26)

Introduction

Thomas divides his consideration of God into two treatises. The first of these, extending from Questions 2 through 26, is devoted to God's essence, while the second, Questions 27 through 43, considers the Trinity that God is. This division and the order in which the are treated "serves only a pedagogical function," according to Torrell, and should not be interpreted as the development of a specifically philosophical approach to God followed by a theological expansion of the former in light of what has been revealed in Holy Scriptures concerning the Trinity.[6] Nevertheless, the seemingly heavy use of philosophy in a theological context does require some comment.

Although Thomas was deeply read in philosophy and made liberal use of it throughout the *Summa*, he did not consider himself (or anyone who called himself a Christian) to be a philosopher as the ancient Greeks understood this.[7] The Christian understanding of reality that revelation affords perfects the ancient wisdom, correcting what is erroneous in it as it is viewed with the eyes of faith. The Christian, then, does not yearn to become a philosopher, does not forsake the perfect for the imperfect, but appreciates, instead, the learning, truth and wisdom that can be found in the philosophical literature, and appropriates it for the sake of the higher learning of sacred doctrine. This appropriation, however, "cannot simply be reduced to a use of philosophy internally to faith, aiming at an analytical and argumentative clarification of its doctrinal statements."[8] Instead, it must be respected for what it is, namely as that *scientia* that regards the highest causes, and thus wisdom itself, according to the natural access that the human person has to these. In this natural acquisition of and approach to the highest things, the human person manifests a knowledge that is indeed true and good, but one that is reflective of his natural access to such things, and thus in keeping with the nature of his mode of approach and the understanding that this affords. In this, philosophy (and every other art and science) becomes a way by which the human person, in light of the nature of his knowing, can bring what his intellectual traditions can provide to his encounter with theology, so that he might progress in his understanding of that *scientia,* which deals with the supra-rational gifted to him by God. In this, "philosophy serves as a powerful pedagogue in the ascent towards beatitude."[9]

---

[6] Torrell (2005), p. 21.
[7] This point is well brought out in Jordan (1992), pp. 30ff.
[8] Velde (2006), p. 28.
[9] Jordan (1992), p. 38.

Question 2: The proofs of God's existence
The treatise on God begins with a question concerning whether He exists. There is much discussion among scholars as to the reason why Aquinas begins in this fashion. On the face of it, one could see this question as something that arises naturally out of the prior treatise. If one is concerned here with sacred doctrine as a *scientia* of God Himself and all things in relation to Him, then it follows that one must establish the existence of God, the very subject matter of this doctrine, as the precondition for detailing any other knowledge about Him. This, however, does not seem to fit well with the greater theological principles that order this material, let alone Thomas's intent in the composition of the *Summa*. In light of all that has been said, both here and in the prior chapter, it would seem more appropriate to approach these proofs in the spirit offered by Velde, namely that

> Although there are several objections to the assumption that God exists, which should be taken seriously, we Christians firmly hold, by the authority of Scripture itself, that God is existent. Now, granted that this is true, as we believe it is, let us then try with the help of arguments found in the philosophical tradition to show how the human mind may be led to an understanding of this truth.[10]

The approach to these proofs in Article 3 is made carefully through the considerations of the prior two articles. Article 1 establishes that the knowledge that God exists is something that is not self-evident to the human person. The reason for this is twofold, first that one can logically entertain the proposition that He does not exist, something to which even Sacred Scriptures attest (knowledge that is self-evident does not allow one to entertain its contradiction. Thus, if it is evident that someone is dead, you cannot logically entertain the proposition that this person is not dead; it is either one or the other, and cannot be both); secondly, that self-evidence requires that the ideas involved be understood. Thus, our understanding of the proposition that "the whole is greater than any one of its

---

[10] Velde (2006), p. 39. See also (2003), pp. 70–72.

parts" is self-evident only insofar as we understand the ideas of "whole" and "part," and the nature of the relation that is established between them in the context of this judgment. In this knowledge, we see that "part" is included in the essential description of "whole" and that the judgment is evident in its truth without any need for demonstration. However, if we were unable to comprehend the ideas of "whole" and "part" in this way, such a judgment, although continuing to be self-evident in itself, would not be self-evident to us. Now, in the judgment that God exists, the ideas of "God" and "exist" are not understood by the human person in this fashion to allow for the self-evidence of this judgment to be revealed, a knowledge that is enjoyed only by God Himself. And even if there were an understanding of the idea of "God" within the mind of the human person, this itself would not necessarily lead to the establishment of the real existence of the thing, that is to say, its existence outside of or nondependent upon the mind.

In light of this, Article 2 asks whether it is possible for the existence of God to be proved. Again, the authority of Scriptures (Romans 1.20) and the arguments offered by philosophy state that this judgment can be made if it is connected directly to some experience that people have of the things of this world. These things, being well known or even self-evident in some cases, might provide the opportunity for a demonstration, specifically when they are considered as effects requiring an examination of their causes so that these effects might be made intelligible both with respect to their essential descriptions and existential conditions. In this approach to the things of man's experience, an approach characteristic of all the arts and sciences, one discovers what a thing is, how and why it exists, and hopefully the ultimate or first cause that accounts for these things in the first place.

Article 3 offers five ways by which one can aspire to this first cause. These are the well-known proofs for God's existence that have received a great amount of attention in the secondary literature and in the history of philosophy. I will restrict my discussion of these proofs to their basic elements, enough to permit an understanding of their structure and the opportunity to investigate their details further, as well as the debate that swirls around their soundness. The strategy that Thomas employs in each of the arguments is to find some aspect of man's everyday experience that, when examined carefully, necessitates the existence of a first cause that, if denied, leads to the denial of the experience with which the proof itself began, something that would be very difficult to do in light of the foundational nature, or even the self-evidence, of this experience. The first proof deals with the experience that we have of change in the world. It uses the example of the change that wood undergoes as it becomes hot to illustrate the principles that apply here and to all manner of change. Thomas states that the heating of wood is not something effected *by* the wood itself. Rather it requires an agent, namely fire, to act upon it so that it might be brought from the condition that it is in (namely, not currently hot but with the potential to become so) to the state of actually being hot. To deny this requirement of all change and to argue that a thing can effect change on its own without an agent, results, Thomas states, in a contradiction, namely that this could occur only if at one and the same time, the subject of change, in this case the wood, possessed both the absence of heat and the presence of heat, that it be both potentially and actually hot at the same time and in the same respect, an impossibility; its potentiality can be realized only through the activity of something other than itself upon it. Now, if one considers the cause that effects this change, and discovers that it itself is subject to change, then the same argument just stated would apply to it as well. The question then arises: Does this complexity of cause and effect extend infinitely, or is there a first cause in this complexity of cause and effect by reason of which all change becomes a reality? Thomas answers that the former is impossible. For if it were the case that there is no first cause, then the very effect with which this proof began, namely the experience of change itself, would not actually occur. For the multiplication of cause and effect relations would never result in that first activation necessary to explain change, that situation where something could be the cause of its own change; all change would be potential. To save, then, the experience of actual change in the world, one must posit a first cause which itself is the cause of all change, and is itself not changed by anything prior to it, being fully realized in all that it is, and thus having nothing of the potential about it. This fully actual, fully realized cause is what "everyone understands to be God." Thomas considers this proof to be the most evident way to establish God's existence, and this based seemingly on the fact that of the five experiences with which these proofs begin, change is the most obvious and certain of them all, being directly experienced at the sense level, and thus not requiring a certain degree of learning and argument for it probative force, as the other four seem to require in order for them to function as they do in these demonstrations.[11]

The second proof concentrates upon the experience that whatever acts as an agent or efficient cause, acts in this capacity only insofar as it has been made capable of doing so. Thus, the fact that I am something capable of effecting the establishment of another as an agency of change is something that I myself do not effect. If this were not the case, if one could be the cause of one's own status as an agent of change, then this would require that the agent exist as an agent before it made itself into an agent, a contradiction, especially if the agency in question results in the establishment of the existence itself of the agent in question (that I, being the cause of my existence and thus of all agency consequent upon this, had to exist before I existed). At this point, the proof follows the same line of reasoning as the first. There is observed, as before, a complexity of relations of cause and effect, but this time the emphasis is upon the agency of the cause rather than the change that the effect undergoes in this relation. Again, Thomas denies that this complexity of relation at the level of agency is infinite. For the multiplication of the series of cause and effect in this regard does nothing to establish the actual agency that one experiences in the world, since nothing could have initiated on its own that first realization of its agency without contracting the contradiction just noted. Thus, there must be a first agent or a first efficient cause to the whole of agency and to the whole of the complexity of their inter-relations in the world, an agency that is fully active in this capacity, not requiring anything to establish this condition but is this absolutely.

---

[11] Nonetheless, this first proof admits of far greater detail and complexity than is presented here, as is witnessed by the extended treatment of it in Book I, Chapter 13 of the *Summa Contra Gentiles.*

The third proof considers the contingency of the things of our experience, which is to say that their existence is not necessary but is something that arises in their generation and passes away in their eventual destruction. If one assumes that all things are of this nature, then given an infinite amount of time in which all variables have been realized, one would have to conclude that there would be no existing things right now. For at some point in an infinite amount of time, all permutations would have been realized, including that one where all things would have passed out of existence, leaving nothing. Since the being of something cannot arise out of the pure negation of nothingness, the fact that there is something now contradicts the original assumption, and that there must be a being whose existence is necessary. Now the necessity of this being is caused either by another, or not at all. If by another, then the same question applies to that which has caused this necessity. Thomas then argues, as he did before, that one cannot posit an infinity in these causal relations since this would eliminate the actual existence of the contingent beings with which the proof began (let alone the necessary ones to which he has argued). There must, therefore, be a first being whose necessity is not a consequence of another, whose necessity is its own, from which all other beings, both contingent and necessary, have their being.

The fourth proof addresses the observation that things exhibit varying degrees of perfection in the ways in which they exist. The good, for example, describes a perfection attributable to a wide diversity of things, but not in exactly the same way, some being better than others. Thus, it is that we describe food, clothing, one's car, spouse, parents, government, virtue, and other such things as good, not equivocally or univocally, but analogously. However, for this kind of naming, and thus for this comparison or determination of the greater and lesser to be realized, there must exist a maximum or a standard against which the measure of such things is made possible. Consequently, in light of our example, there must be something most good, which is goodness itself and in participation with all other things can be denominated as good in varied ways. Now as we apply the term "good" to the things of our experience, we are making note of a perfection of the very being of the things in question. If this is the case, then as we compare the varied things that we have denoted as good in the manner just spoken of, we are in fact comparing degrees or gradations of being, which then leads to the conclusion that there must also be a maximum in being in order for these comparisons or determinations to be effected. The same can also be said with respect to all other perfections of being, like truth, nobility, and beauty. Since what is maximal in being is the cause of all that is found within any instance of being, such as the varying degrees of goodness, truth, nobility, and the like, it must be the case that there is a being which is not only the cause of the being of all things, but also of every and any perfection that they enjoy, perfections that are properly found in and characteristic of this very being.

The fifth proof deals with the observation that the world and all its parts do not act haphazardly but rather in an ordered and regular way, both with respect to their individual natures and in the relation of these natures to the whole itself. In Thomas's language, all things work toward an end both individually (for the perfection of their own natures) and collectively (for the sake of the good of the whole itself), whether consciously or unconsciously, by intention or instinct. That both intelligent and nonintelligent things do this indicates that it is not by chance that such occurs but rather that this arises through the governance of the universe, and that consequently, there is a governor, one who is responsible for this order in its establishment, maintenance and culmination.

Before we consider Thomas's discussion concerning the essence of God, it is good to recognize a problem that many have upon studying the proofs for the first time, namely that the conclusions for each proof do not seem to correspond closely with the God of Holy Scriptures and revelation, but rather to some impersonal deity common to religious beliefs outside of and/or prior to Christianity. While this may appear to be the case, one should remember that the intent of these proofs is not to determine the essence of God, but rather to establish the ways available to human reasoning by which the existence of God can be shown. To then make this critique ahead of Thomas's examination of the essence of God and of the Trinity itself, that is to say, to critique his vision of God on the basis of this one question without its proper integration not only into the treatise to which it belongs, but also to the following treatise and to the *prima pars* itself, bespeaks a lack of understanding of how Thomas develops his subject matter. As was stated earlier, these proofs do not intend to establish a natural philosophical theology propaedeutic to theology proper. They intend to show, among other things, that the doctrines of the Catholic faith have an intelligibility and reasonability proper to them, something that can be shown by appealing to those disciplines, particularly philosophy, which strive for these same realities by means of the natural tools at their disposal, tools developed by and suited to the nature of human reason and the ways by which it comes into possession of its knowledge. The conclusions, then, of these philosophic proofs are something that the *scientia* of theology can expand upon within the context of its more universal discipline and the source it enjoys in the revelation found in Holy Scripture. It is only in light of this more universal context that the philosophical material of the *Summa* begins to reveal its true sense and contribution to the work of theology.[12]

Question 3–11: What God is as He is in Himself
Having demonstrated the ways in which it is possible to show that God exists, Thomas now considers the manner of His existence so that he might be able to say something about His essence, a difficult matter dealt with in Questions 3 through 11. As we will see in the *Treatise on Man,* Thomas argues that a person's knowledge, as was noted earlier, depends entirely upon his sensible experience of the things of this world from which he abstracts all that he knows at the intellectual level, particularly the essences of things. The difficulty in articulating these accurately is quite clear from the histories of the disciplines that make up our intellectual traditions. An even greater difficulty arises, however, when one begins to consider the foundational principles and causes of reality, causes that are not directly met with in one's experience, but are known only in relation to the sensible things of one's world. Man's knowledge, then, of the higher things, and

---

[12] Consider a more detailed description offered by Velde in Chapter 2 of (2006).

particularly of God Himself, is acquired discursively and indirectly, something that demands the best that the mind and his intellectual traditions can offer in their pursuit. This, together with the Holy Scriptures' affirmation of this difficulty, requires great care in one's approach to the divine.

Clearly, then, the knowledge of God's essence is something that is not attained by the human mind in a direct fashion; God is not met as we meet other beings in the world. Nor, as was seen in Question 2, do we have an intuitive, self-evident knowledge of Him. God's essence, moreover, is not something that can be encompassed by the human mind in the manner in which other things, both directly and indirectly encountered, become available to its consideration and investigation. For only God beholds His own essence. It would seem, then, that the most appropriate way to speak of the divine essence would be to deny of it anything that is clearly inappropriate. This apophatic way of describing the divine essence reflects the lack of access that human beings have to such an object, and respects the profundity of the Creator's essence. However, Thomas does not consider the whole of man's knowledge of the divine essence to be negatively approached. When one considers that the knower himself and the world of which he is a part, is a product of God's creative activity, an effect of which God is the ultimate cause, there is in this fact a possible positive approach to the knowing and the naming of God, at least a knowing and a naming that is not inappropriate to what He is. The strategy that Thomas employs is to look to the arguments that have established His existence, and derive from these, the manner in which He, as cause of the very things with which the proofs themselves began, can be described in light of them. And so, to quote Thomas directly, since all created things

are His effects and depend on their cause, we can be led from them so far as to know of God whether he exists, and to know of Him what must necessarily belong to Him, as the first cause of all things, exceeding all things caused by Him. Hence we know that His relationship with creatures so far as to be the cause of them all; also that creatures differ from Him, inasmuch as He is not in any way part of what is caused by Him; and that creatures are not removed from

Him by reason of any defect on His part, but because He superexceeds them all.[13]

Thomas describes here the approaches of causality, remotion, and eminence, with the first and the third being the means by which we can articulate something positive about God's essence. Thomas begins, then, by considering God's essence from these three perspectives in Questions 3 through 11, resulting in a knowledge that is negative for the most part, but which also includes the ways of causality and eminence.[14] This allows for an examination of the subjective appropriation of whatever knowledge the human person can have of God, (Question 12), and then how this knowledge can be named appropriately (Question 13).

Question 3 takes up the question of God's simplicity. Everything that man meets in his experience is of a composite nature; absolutely simple things, not having any parts to or divisions within their being, are simply not encountered. In each of the articles of this question, Thomas appeals to the different areas of philosophy to see whether any aspect of composition or division might be attributed to God. In each of these areas, he finds that this is not the case. Whether we examine the physical, metaphysical, logical, or psychological sciences, we find that the principles with which they deal, the concerns that they have and the terminology that is specific to each, are all of them denied of God, and are affirmed, as a consequence, as appropriate to the condition of created things. Thus, God must be wholly simple, which is to say that He lacks any and all compositional aspects in His essence. Even when it comes to those most basic distinctions between the essence of a thing, its individuality (a person is not identical to his humanity, but rather is an instantiation of it), and existence (one's humanity is not equivalent to nor does it necessitate one's existence), Thomas will deny these of God (God is His essence, and God's essence and existence are the same). All of this follows from the manner in which the first cause has been described in the five

---

[13] ST. I. 12. 12. The line of exposition here is heavily indebted to Velde's discussion in Chapter 3 (2006), pp. 72–77.

[14] Also see ST. I. 13. 1 for these three ways.

proofs of Question 2. Thus, for example, God cannot in any way be material since this would introduce potency into His being, something denied of God in the first proof (He is purely actual, having nothing of the potential about Him). Again, God's essence and existence must be identical, for if they were not then God's existence would derive from another (something denied by the conclusion of the third proof).

Perfection, for Thomas, indicates the extent to which nothing is lacking in a thing's actuality, that it has attained, so to speak, to the height of what is possible to it. Question 4 argues that perfection is said properly of God insofar as He is purely actual and thus has nothing of the potential or the unrealized about Him. Moreover, as the Creator of all things, He has in a most perfect way all that is perfect in creation, but this in a more eminent way in keeping with the mode of His existence. Thus, for example, while He does not have the perfection of a body, he could be said to have the perfection of the integrity of a body, or any other number of perfections that could be associated with the body, but more eminently and appropriately. This applies most especially to the being, the actualities and perfections that all creatures enjoy, all of which are possible only insofar as they derive from this most perfect of beings. The question then arises: To what extent is the human person's perfection like that of God's? Clearly, the likeness is not of the same kind (human beings are not gods), nor is it some lesser likeness of the same kind (people are not less powerful or less intelligent gods). It is in the line of causality that people are like God, not as He begets another like Himself (human beings are not little gods or god-children), but rather as the Maker instills something of Himself in people, which minimally includes the capacity to reason and to choose freely, something that will be taken up by Question 93 of the *Prima Pars*, and with which the prologue to the *Prima Secundae* begins.

The consideration of God's goodness is covered by Questions 5 and 6, with the former dedicated to the idea of the good in general, which then, in the latter, is discussed in relation to God. The use of the word "good" indicates, for Thomas, those things that people find desirable, something that arises when people have judged something to be perfective of their person or simply is perfect in itself. A musician, then, might judge a particular instrument to be good insofar as it is well and beautifully constructed, being a fine example of the luthier's art. He might then desire it for itself, or as the means whereby it will allow him to engage more fully and beautifully in the performance that is such an important aspect of his art, and thus be considered as one who plays well, worthy of the title of a good musician, or perhaps a virtuoso, if he is among the best. The good, then, is associated with the desirable, with one's being, perfection and activity. But it is something that is ultimately associated with purpose. For the good, as Aristotle noted, has the aspect of an end, is that for the sake of which one does whatever it is one does. The desire of the musician for the good of performing well orders his life and his activity so that he might aspire to achieve whatever he must so that he might engage fully in being what a musician is, and thus fulfill his potential in this particular fashion. When one considers a person to be good, we would say not only that his being human is good (which is to be perfect in a way), but that he also, by reason of the good of his humanity, can engage in a whole host of activities to realize the potential that is found in being human. Becoming a musician allows one to perfect oneself in a particular way, to aspire to the goodness particular to this art. But with respect to one's being human, and not just a musician, the good here is found in the degree to which one acts in accordance with the fullness of one's humanity, seeking the purpose or good for which one exists and to do this over the course of one's entire life. In this, the human person realizes the goodness and perfection that is implicit in his humanity, all that lies potentially in the good of his being. In this is found the happiness of the human person, that in which he finds his highest actuality, perfection, and good, something that will occupy Thomas's attention in the *secunda pars*.

In light of these brief comments on the notion of the good and with an eye to the prior questions, one can see that God is not only good, but that He is the greatest of all goods, the source of all goodness and that His essence is identical with His goodness. For what a thing is or has is possessed in a more eminent way by the agent that has caused it. Thus, as there exists perfection, actuality, and goodness in created things, so too will these exist in their first cause in a most eminent fashion. Since there is a likeness between cause and effect, a likeness spoken of in Question 4, the human person discovers a desire to be united to that to which he has been made, that in which he finds his true intelligibility, completion, and peace. The desirability of the first cause is fuelled not only by the fact that God is goodness Himself (He is fully actual, wholly simple and perfect, and undivided in His essence: He is His goodness), but that the desire that the human person has for the good itself is satisfied not by the external, bodily, or spiritual goods of his person, but only by the very source of these things, namely, the perfect absolute good that God is (something that will be discussed further in the treatise on happiness at the beginning of the *prima secundae*).

Question 7 considers the infinity of God. Unlike all other things that He has made, God is not finite, and this by reason of the fact that He is fully realized in all that He is, thus finding within His being nothing that limits or restricts His essence and His existence. The question of God's omnipresence (Question 8) follows closely upon His infinity, as the latter implies the former. Each thing, as we have seen, is a contingent being, and, as such depends upon God at every moment for its existence. This necessitates, then, that God be present in all things and everywhere so that He might hold every being and the whole of creation in existence. He does this not as some agent extrinsic to the things that it holds in existence, but by being present intimately to all things.

Question 9 draws out what is implicit in the preceding, namely that God is immutable. It was shown earlier that God is pure act, having nothing of potentiality about Him. The consequence of this is that whatever God is, exists wholly, completely and, from the human person's perspective, at all times. He does not change since change requires the presence of potentiality, something totally lacking to God Himself. In every change, there is the realization of some new actuality. But since God is infinite and perfectly actual, containing in Himself the perfections of all being, there is no new actuality for Him to gain. Thus, change would be pointless for Him. Nor could God lose any aspect of His being. For He is uncaused, and thus exists necessarily and not contingently. God cannot cease to be in any respect. Now, if God is immutable, then He is eternal (Question

10), which Thomas defines, following Boethius, as the "simultaneously complete and perfect possession of life without beginning or end." The latter part is self-explanatory—eternity has no beginning or end. The former refers to the way in which an eternal being is measured, so to speak, as something which has no succession in its being, is simultaneously whole in all that it does and is. From man's perspective, as beings in time, God is at any moment what He always was and what He always will be. From God's perspective, He is His own eternity; He was, is, and will always be the simultaneously complete and perfect possession of life without beginning or end. Other beings are said to be eternal only insofar as they receive their immutability from Him. In this sense, such things share in God's eternity, but, nevertheless had a beginning, something missing from God entirely.

Question 11 argues the unity that God is, which is to say, that there is not only an integrity to His being, but also nothing within Him that divides Him, an important point in light of the many and varied descriptions that have been just presented concerning His essence. Thus, He is supremely one, as opposed to the human person's experience of what is one in relation to composite and contingent beings that, although enjoying an integrity and unity of being, cannot be described as supremely one in the way in which God is.

Questions 12 and 13: How God is in human knowledge, and how He is named accordingly
Having considered these descriptions of God's essence, Thomas turns to their subjective appropriation by the mind of man, which, then, not only allows him to consider how God might be named appropriately consequent upon man's knowledge of him, but also the precise reference of this knowing, that is to say, in what manner it designates the divine essence given the manner and the limitations of human knowing.

There must, first, be a knowledge of God enjoyed by the human person, one which is not encompassed wholly by the negative approach. For if man's knowledge were restricted to the *via negativa* in his understanding of the divine essence, then not only would such a knowledge frustrate the fulfillment of his nature, but also the very promises made by Scriptures, namely that the faithful will behold God as He is. The question for Thomas, then, is not whether man can behold the essence of God, but rather how this will be effected.

The vision of God's essence will not be something effected through the senses, nor through a created likeness of Him encountered in the things of this world. This knowledge can only be acquired if it is gifted to man by God, but in such a way that it respects the psychological processes that characterize his knowing. It will be strengthened by what Thomas calls "the light of glory," making possible the beholding of God where otherwise it would not come about. This sight will be accomplished through the eye, so to speak, of the intellect, as it has been strengthened in this manner. We encounter here an important principle that permeates the entirety of Thomas's thought, namely that grace does not destroy nature, but rather perfects it, that grace is not opposed to the natural, but is the means whereby its fullness might be realized and this without violence to its constitution. This principle is further exemplified by the fact that although all who receive the gift of God's essence receive the same gift, nonetheless the understanding and appreciation of this gift depend upon the disposition of those who receive it; those will behold the essence of God better who have prepared themselves to receive Him, who have led a life devoted to virtue and holiness. In the vision of God's essence, one's mind does not entirely encompass what is gifted. Such an encompassment is reserved only to God who, being infinite, is alone capable of encompassing His own infinity. Man's vision will always be incomplete, and yet will be of such a nature so as to satisfy his desire to know Him and be united with Him, a vision that, given its infinity, will satisfy throughout eternity. While this vision is normally reserved for those who have passed on to the next life, Thomas states that it can be gifted to one here and now in the experience of rapture: God's gift is given as and when He so desires. This, however, is quite rare. For the most part, the human person anticipates this heavenly vision in this present life as he aspires to achieve a glimpse of God's essence through the ways discussed earlier. This brings us, then, to the consideration of how the knowledge that man currently has of God can be designated.

First, the human person's naming of something is consequent upon its presence in his knowing, and that the name he assigns reflects importantly this subjective appropriation. Since man, then, does not in this life acquire a knowledge of the divine essence, he cannot name God in this fashion, but only according to the three ways of causality, remotion, and eminence. This leads Thomas to determine carefully the references of the names used up to this point. Negative names (such as "immutable" or "immaterial") and names signifying God's relation to creatures (such as "Creator" or "Lord") do not signify God properly, but describe respectively the distance of creatures from Him, and the relation that creatures have to Him. Positive names (such as "good" and "wise") are intended by Holy Scripture to signify God, but still fall short of representing Him. Thomas explains:

> When we say, "God is good," the meaning is not, "God is the cause of goodness," or "God is not evil;" but the meaning is, "Whatever good we attribute to creatures, pre-exists in God," and in a higher way. Hence it does not follow that God is good, because He causes goodness; but rather, on the contrary, He causes goodness in things because He is good.[15]

The consequence of this is that these positive names do indeed signify what God is. However, man's appropriation of this reality so named occurs in light of the manner in which the perfections that are God are encountered in the things of this world. Thus, words like "wise" and "good" have their genesis and are understood in relation to the things of this world, and thus fall well short of being applied to God their Creator in this fashion. However, in light of the causal relation that creatures enjoy with respect to God, and that all perfections found in this world have their origin in God Himself, one might ask whether there is some way by which man's experience and understanding of these positive names might really indicate something about God Himself. Clearly, positive words are not used synonymously; the intention is to indicate His eminence, not to draw some vague similarity between Him and the

---

[15] ST. I. 13. 2.

things that people call "good" or "wise." Nor is it the case that these positive words name God in the same way that people use them (univocally) or in a wholly different fashion (equivocally or metaphorically). The intent rather is to name God in such a way that at one and the same time the difference and the sameness just indicated are implied, something accomplished through an analogous use of words. This occurs where a word, such as "good," "healthy," or "father," is used to signify many diverse things by reason of a reference to some one thing which each enjoys in differing proportions and which must be included in their definitions. Thus, "father" has been used to signify one's male parent, a teacher, a priest, and God Himself, clearly different things but each joined by what is essential to the notion of father, namely, one who introduces another to some aspect of life (biologically/socially, intellectually, spiritually, and absolutely, respectively). The primacy of the sameness is found in God who is properly called "Father." But from the perspective of man's knowing and consequent naming, he can only begin to approach what "Father" means by taking his cue from the realizations of "father" in the things of his experience. Thus, the reality of "father," and of "good," "wise," and other such positive terms, are things that will only be comprehended properly in the vision of the divine essence, until which time man anticipates analogously in an imperfect fashion by means of his reflection upon the effects of God's creative act. Of all the names that are given to God, the most proper of them is the one that He Himself reveals to Moses at Exodus 3.13, "I Am Who Am." For, as Thomas explains, a name is given as it signifies a thing's essence. But this name signifies being itself, a formulation that implies that God's being is His very essence, something discussed earlier as the most appropriate way of describing God's essence. Moreover, the name itself does not limit God in any way; He is His own existence. It is a name, then, which best respects what one can know about the divine essence, and what God is as He is in Himself, that is to say, from the perspective of both the subjective knowing of Him and the objective reality that He is. One, however, must always remember that the analogous naming of God, although designating something proper to Him, is nonetheless something that defies one's full understanding as it is found in Him, if only in light of the fact of His simplicity wherein all these positive names attributed properly to God are not realized in Him in a plural way, or in distinction from His very being. God is His goodness, His wisdom, and His beauty, whereas human beings are never considered to be their goodness, wisdom, or beauty, just as they are never considered to be their humanity. God is these in His very being, while the human person is these in the manner of being a creature. Thus, one can make affirmative propositions concerning God, both of a negative and a positive nature, the latter giving rise to a diversity of knowings of something that in itself is absolutely simple, something that reflects ultimately the inadequacy of the human mind in its approach to the most intelligible of beings, an inadequacy that manifests plurality as the only approach it can take in the beholding of such a being through His effects.

Questions 14–24: Those activities immanent to God (His intellect, life, and will)
Since the activities of a thing flow directly from what that thing is, Thomas passes from the description of God's essence to a consideration of those activities that are proper to Him. Activity is of two kinds: intransitive and transitive. The former refers to that activity that is immanent to the agent, having its genesis and termination within it, while the latter refers to activity that begins within the agent but finds its termination outside of it. God's intransitive or immanent activity occupies Thomas's attention for the majority of the remaining questions of this treatise. His transitive activity is treated briefly with respect to its principle, namely his power (at the end of this treatise in Question 25), and is taken up more directly in the context of the Trinity and in the remainder of the *prima pars*, especially in the treatise concerning creation.

The difficulties that surrounded the description of God's essence continue with the descriptions of His intellect (Questions 14 through 17), life (18), will (19 through 21), and the interactions that exist between His intellect and will in His providence and predestination (Questions 22 through 23). His intelligence and consequent knowledge are negatively and analogically described. We know that God's intelligence and knowledge are themselves perfect. However, unlike our experience of rationality, God is not limited in His. Rather, it extends most perfectly over the whole of creation and is His very nature. He thus knows all things both universally and particularly, the former as a whole and according to the natures that compose this whole, and the latter through His very presence to all things, something that establishes and keeps them in their being and directs them to completion in Him. He comprehends himself fully, there being nothing hidden to His gaze or unrealized in His being. This understanding is not something that is discursive, as it is for the human person. Instead, it is accomplished all together and always; God does not "awaken" to Himself, but is, rather, His very understanding (a consequence of the simplicity and the fullness of His actuality). As the first efficient cause, God's knowledge is the cause of every thing's existence and essence, containing within Himself the exemplars of all things, which constitute the basis for all truth and of the order and intelligibility of the whole of creation and it individual parts. His knowledge encompasses not only all that actually was and is, but also future contingents both on His part and on that of man; His vision is not successive but eternal. It extends also to the evil that exists in the world, and this to a far greater degree than man himself would know it, given the comprehensive nature of His knowing, and the perfect manner in which He knows that all things do not embody or aspire to the good that is theirs. In light of all this, God is truth itself, the greatest wisdom to which one could aspire, a wisdom in light of which one understands all things in the best possible way.

God's life is most perfect and full. In man's experience, "life" is said of that which has an intrinsic capacity to determine itself in its movement or activity. Thus, a stone is not said to have life insofar as its movement or change is effected by forces external to it, while a plant, on the other hand, is considered to have life as its activities are importantly effected from within, that is to say, by it itself. However, plant life is also influenced directly by things external to it, things that it requires for the activities that characterize its living, namely, nutrition, growth, and reproduction. As one considers animals and then human beings, one notes a greater capacity for self-activation and a wider variety of activities. Thus, the animal not only enjoys the ability to go from place to place, but also enjoys the whole of the sensual life, which includes the capacity to know its surroundings through its sensitive cognitive powers: the animal is the first among life forms to know. In this, the animal is said to exhibit and enjoy life more perfectly than the plant, particularly as it engages in sensation. However, it does this in a less perfect way than man insofar as the animal is determined in its reactions to what it knows, being bereft of reason: the animal knows where it is going but not why. The human person, then, is said to enjoy life most fully insofar as he engages not only in sense but also in intellectual cognition (he knows both the essences and the reasons for things). He is not determined wholly by his knowledge but is free to pursue those things that are good or appear to be so. Nonetheless, this freedom is something made possible insofar as he is activated by both the true and the good, by the principles that are foundational to his thinking, and his desire to be happy. God, however, is said to be life perfectly insofar as there is nothing that He requires to activate His knowing: He is truth and wisdom itself. There is nothing that He requires to activate His will: He is perfect goodness, fully activated in His being, requiring nothing to make Him better. Thus, since His understanding, His truth, His goodness, and His love are His very essence, something that is eternal, simple, perfect, and complete, God's life is not only the perfection of man's life, his very happiness, it is also God's very happiness.

Will manifests the height of a rational nature's appetition and constitutes that inclination which decidedly pursues, in love, that which is considered to be good as such and thus as perfective of the one who lacks this good. When possessed, the will rests in this good, a rest that is manifested in the experience of delight and joy. This inclining of the rational being to that which is good and perfective of it also manifests in lesser ways in the sensitive appetition of animals and in the natural appetition that characterize all things. The operative notion in all forms of appetition is that the thing is naturally inclined to that in which its perfection lies. With the rational nature, there is clearly a great deal more at work than just the instinct that characterizes the animal nature; the human person makes definite judgments concerning the nature of what perfects him, and the manner in which he pursues them. The point to be made is that where there is intellect, so too is there will; as there is a comprehension of what is good, so too is there a directedness toward this so that what is known as good might be attained in fact. Not only, then, does God have a will, but it is directed primarily to the perfect good that He is, for there is nothing lacking to God, and nothing that can make Him any better than He is. However, lest one think that this restricts God's activity only to Himself, Thomas notes a third aspect to the nature of appetition, namely that in addition to one's desire for a good not possessed, and then the repose and joy that one experiences in its possession, there is also a natural effusion of this good to others insofar as this is possible. In this is found the root of the explanation of God's creative act, as the establishment of things other than Himself insofar as the good that He is over-flows, so to speak, in the establishment of the whole of creation (more will be said about this in the next few treatises).

What strikes modern readers oddly is the seeming limitations that are imposed upon the will of God. Contrary to the suppo-sition that God's will is absolute in all ways, even with respect to its own nature and that of which He makes or commands, He is said by Thomas to will necessarily the good that He is, much as the human person necessarily wills his own happiness, this being a natural manifestation of his will over which he does not exercise choice. Just as the human person wills all that he wills under the description of good, so too is it that God wills in like manner the good that He is. He wills all other things freely, and these, not for the satisfaction of something unrealized in Him (for He is realized perfectly in His being, requiring noth-ing external to Him to be who He is), but rather as they are a manifestation of the willing of His own good, so that all is cre-ated as a consequence of the good that God is, and is ordered to His own goodness as to their ultimate end and perfection. Thus, God wills Himself as an end, but all other things He wills as to that end. And to prevent a link between the necessity with which God wills Himself and the consequent willing of things other than Himself, one should note that although God neces-sarily wills His own good, He can do this without willing any of the things of creation, or the whole of it, into being. God's will is fulfilled in an absolute sense in the establishment of that which He wills. This is seemingly tempered, so to speak, in His establishment of creatures who exercise choice in the adhering to the things that God has commanded. Thus, His will may be frustrated by such creatures as they commit sin. However, in the larger scope of things, the sinner does not escape the order established by the will of God that is effected in the judgment and punishment of the sinner. Thus, what He wills conditionally need not happen, but the conditional exists ultimately in the context of His absolute will that is always satisfied. His will does not change as it intends the good that He is eternally and completely, having nothing ever left unrealized in His willing. He in no way wills evil. However, He permits the evil committed by other intelligent agents, as well as natural defects and punishments to occur, insofar as He intends not these evils themselves but the goods to which these evils are attached. "Thus in willing justice he wills punishment; and in willing the preservation of the natural order, he wills some things to be naturally corrupted."[16]

Lastly, Thomas considers three aspects of God's will implied by the foregoing, namely, His love, justice, and mercy. His love is understood initially in the way by which man experiences the will's first and most fundamental manifestation, namely in the binding of it to some good whether it be possessed or not. From this arises, in the human sphere, the desire for the good when it is not possessed, and joy when it is. While desire, then, could only be said of God metaphorically (for in its proper sense it would indicate a lack of being and goodness on God's part, something already seen to be impossible), both love and joy can properly be said of Him insofar as the good which He is, loves and possesses, is that which is most perfect, is most intimate to Him, and is not divided in any way from Him. This love extends to all things insofar as whatever good they possess is something that is willed to them by God as the cause of their existence, description, conservation, and happiness. However, there is not a democracy, so to speak, in this extension of God's love to all things, something that can be discerned in the degrees of good spoken of in the fourth proof (some things are better than others insofar as God has extended His goodness and thus His love more to the former than the latter). His justice is

---

[16] ST. I. 19. 9.

demonstrated in the order that He effects in the creation of the universe, and establishing the good for each thing, and thus determining those things that are due to each, and the responsibilities that each thing has in relation to all others. His mercy is displayed not so much in the goodness that He effects in created things, nor in the order that He establishes among them in His justice, nor in the liberality of His creative act, but rather in the fact that what He gives serves to ameliorate the hardships and defects to which the human person is heir, even those which he has brought upon himself and for which he deserves the punishment demanded by His justice. However, justice presupposes mercy insofar as in His creative act and in His conservation of all things, God gives to creatures a goodness that excels anything proportioned to their desert.

Drawing all of these matters together, one can perceive the providence of God at work wherein the entirety of creation is brought into existence, is established in its order, is preserved in this and directed to its consummation in God according to the understanding that He has in mind of all of this, together with His intention that these things be so. Thus, Thomas states that all things occur in accordance with God's understanding and intention, that the being, the descriptions, the powers, and the activities of each and every thing are realized only insofar as they are manifestations of the providence that God exercises over the whole of the created order. In this providence, nothing is or occurs outside of the causality that God effects. Even chance events are possible only insofar as God has willed a forum, so to speak, within which they can occur. The free activities of the human person for good or ill also fall within the plan of creation that God has effected and directs to its fulfillment in Him. Here, we encounter his views concerning the existence of evil, namely that evil is not something created or intended by God, but is nonetheless permitted insofar as God, providing for the good of the whole of creation, will "permit certain defects in particular effects that the perfect good of the universe may not be hindered, for if all evil were prevented, much good would be absent from the universe. A lion would cease to live, if there were no slaying of animals; and there would be no patience of martyrs if there were no tyrannical persecution." The force of this view, namely that God permits evil so that through His omnipotence, goodness, and providence, He might produce good out of it (or at least preserve goods greater than the evils perpetrated), is tempered somewhat in light of God's providence, namely that although such do occur, and that they are permitted for the sake of a greater good, nonetheless all things effected by the will of man cannot escape the providence of God, and especially the judgment to come. One must also remember the nature of the knowledge with which we are dealing. The governance or providence that God exercises, particularly in light of the existence of evil, is not something that can adequately be approached in terms univocal to our own experience of it. This is a mistake that is often made by those who argue against God's existence in light of the contradiction they say exists between God's omnipotence and absolute goodness, and the real existence of evil in the world. As David Bentley Hart points out,

> The entire case is premised upon an inane anthropomorphism—abstracted from any living system of belief—that reduces God to a finite ethical agent, a limited psychological personality, whose purposes are measurable upon the same scale as ours, and whose ultimate ends for his creatures do not transcend the cosmos as we perceive it. This is not to say that it is an argument without considerable emotional and even moral force; but of logical force there is none. Unless one can see the beginning and end of all things, unless one possesses a divine, eternal vantage upon all of time, unless one knows the precise nature of the relation between divine and created freedom, unless one can fathom *infinite* wisdom, one can draw no conclusions from finite experience regarding the coincidence in God of omnipotence and perfect goodness. One may still hate God for worldly suffering, if one chooses, or deny him, but one cannot in this way "disprove" him.[17]

In these considerations, one should recognize that there is a space, so to speak, effected within the created order that allows

---

[17] Hart (2005), pp. 13–14. One may also wish to reflect upon ST. I–II. 19. 10.

for the causal activity of man wherein his volition is authentic and his responsibility is real. The things that man effects are in fact things that he effects, and are not to be seen as occasions for God to exercise His causality as if He were the direct and immediate efficient cause of every efficient causality that is effected in the created order; things properly take on their role as secondary causes consequent upon the primary efficient and final causality effected by God in His providence. Nevertheless, the freedom of man is not absolute, but is assured only insofar as it is established in its nature, activity and directionality by God's providence. In the relative nature of the will, then, and its consequent freedom, are found once again a principle central to the *secunda pars*, namely that man must determine his standing before God, whether he will be directed in all that he is and does to the source of his being, or not and thus choose himself over God, a situation that can exist only in light of the result of God's creative activity and governance of the world and the nature that He establishes man to be. Finally, God's predestination is manifested in His providence with respect to the human person, specifically that all people be directed to God as to their ultimate end and happiness, something that they, however, cannot effect themselves, but must receive as a gift freely given by God in the next life. Predestination is this intentional ordering of all people to eternal life, an integral aspect of the providence of God, and something central to the treatise on happiness which grounds the considerations of the *secunda pars*.

This treatise concerning God's essence ends with a consideration of His power (25) and His beatitude (26). Having dealt with the latter previously, we end with some brief comments concerning the former. His power describes that principle that gives rise to what we would describe as God's transitive activity, that is to say, the activity that establishes all that is distinct from Him, namely creation itself. Since God has nothing of potentiality about Him, His power is fully active and of the highest degree. He can do anything, not in a purely absolute and arbitrary sense, but rather only with respect to that which is possible. This seems to impose a limitation upon God's power, but in fact is something that is a consequence of His nature as a being whose very essence is equivalent to His existence, who is His own being and perfection, and from whom all being and perfection flow in His creative activity. Thus, everything that is possible in the realm of being is something that falls under His power. This excludes everything that stands in contradiction to the realm of being, namely, non-being absolutely considered.

> Therefore, that which implies being and non-being at the same time is repugnant to the idea of an absolutely possible thing within the scope of the divine omnipotence. For such cannot come under the divine omnipotence, not because of any defect in the power of God, but because it has not the nature of a feasible or possible thing.[18]

Consequently, God cannot deliberately do what is evil, cannot make past events not to have occurred, cannot make a square to have more than four sides, and anything else that involves a logical impossibility. Thus, God could have created in a way other than He did, which affirms the difficulty of determining things concerning His essence from His effects, and the wisdom of proceeding with such care in our negative and analogical understanding of Him. However, with respect to the things that have been created, God cannot have made the essences of things any better than He did; God does not fail in the realizing of His providence, given the perfection and infinitude of His power. And yet, when it comes to those things over and above a thing's essence, such could have been made better (the knees of man being a good example, along with his wisdom or moral virtue). He can also make something else better than anything He has made.

Treatise on the Trinity (Questions 27–43)[19]

Of all the knowledge that the human person has concerning God, that of the Trinity holds pride of place as it defines Christianity in distinction from the other forms of monotheism. It is a doctrine that does not derive from a reflection upon the effects of creation, but is gifted to man by God's revelation,

---

[18] ST. I. 25. 3.
[19] In this section, I concentrate on Questions 27–30 and 32, with passing reference made to Questions 33–38.

specifically through the statements Christ makes in the New Testament. Be that as it may, this treatise bears witness to Thomas's conviction that although this doctrine has its genesis in the revelation effected by God, nevertheless philosophical reasoning and the teachings particular to philosophy can be applied effectively in the "unpacking," so to speak, of the inner life and activity of God.

The difficulties that the reader faces in studying this treatise are familiar. First, the ideas central to explaining the doctrine of the Trinity seem to conflict with the ways by which we understand these ideas in the first place, specifically that the relations that are implied by the procession of the persons of the Trinity seem to be contrary to the divine simplicity. For in our experience, the way by which a relation is established typically is to affirm first the substantial reality of at least two things that then can be related to one another. Relation, then, seems to be secondary to the substantial reality of the things related, making relation something added to the being of those things related, and, consequently, accidental to them, something that is quite opposed to God's essence. It is thus quite difficult to approach this most definitive of doctrines when the very basis of our understanding of the ideas necessary to its explanation seems to contradict the very essence of the doctrine itself, namely that although there is a real relation of three persons, Father, Son, and Holy Spirit, in God, and a real distinction between them as persons, that nevertheless, the divine simplicity must be maintained, that these three do not constitute three gods but rather are one God. The difficulty, then, is to retain a firm hold on the nature of our understanding of God's essence, as developed in the prior treatise, together with this exploration of the Trinity. It would be a serious mistake to consider this treatise as somehow secondary or supplementary to the prior treatise on God's essence, as if Thomas's views concerning God were essentially non-Trinitarian, and that he is captivated with the deity of classical theism. Recalling what was discussed earlier, namely Thomas's dedication to the Holy Scriptures and thus to all that they contain concerning God's very being, one, at the very least, must see this treatise as a continuation of the discussion of God's life, and maybe go so far as to see this treatise as the climax of those investigations that constitute the initial section of the *prima pars* and foundational to all that follows. As one grapples with the difficulty of this material, one should keep in mind the role that paradox plays not only in the theological and philosophical realms, but also in all the arts and sciences, that just because the nature of a doctrine carries with it seemingly unresolvable paradoxes, it cannot thus be pushed aside as unimportant or unintelligible. For there are times when the matter at hand can be dealt with in no other way, particularly when we come face-to-face with the limitations of human knowing. Thus, just as the advances in modern physics lead us to posit realities that patently contradict our experience of the world but which nevertheless allow us to explain it in a far better way, so too is it even more the case with matters that concern the inner life of God.

In Question 29, Thomas accepts Boethius's definition of *person* as "an intellectual substance of a rational nature." His understanding of this, however, is qualified in two important ways, first, as it is developed within the context of three larger considerations, namely that of the *procession* of the persons (Question 27), the *relations* that are enjoyed between them (Question 28), and how one distinguishes their use with respect to God from their more familiar application to man.

The notion of *procession* is drawn not from philosophy but is taken from the Holy Scriptures, specifically from Christ's declaration at John 8.42 that "From God I proceeded." Relying heavily upon the writings of the Church Fathers, both Greek and Latin, and varied Church councils, Thomas appeals to a division made earlier between the intransitive and transitive activity of God, as well as to an analogy utilized by Augustine in his own treatise concerning the Trinity to explain this notion. Every activity, he explains, implies a procession, a coming forth that finds its completion either in something external to that whence the activity arises (transitive activity, the subject of the remainder of the treatises of the *prima pars*) or within the very agent itself (intransitive or immanent activity). With respect to the latter, Thomas concentrates upon the activities of thinking and willing. Now it is basic to Thomas's views concerning human psychology that such activities are attributed not primarily to some organ or system within man, but rather to the person whose nature is characterized by such organs or systems; it is not the intellect that thinks or the will that wills, but rather the human person who thinks and wills by means of these powers. In short, the immanent activities of the human person are what the human person himself performs, activities that constitute a procession from his very person. In giving birth to a thought, something proceeds from the human person, something that in one way can be distinguished from him. This is the *concept*, the internal re-presentation of the thing itself whereby the human person knows it. Although it can be distinguished in this fashion from the knower, nonetheless, this distinction also implies an intimate union between the knower and the thing itself. For in Thomas's understanding of human knowing, the concept is the means by which the thing to be known (external to the knower) is made present exactly as it is to the knower, that is to say, the means by which the knower becomes the thing itself, not really, but cognitionally. The thoughts of the human person, then, are not to be seen as radically distinct from him. They are indeed generated within him and can thus be distinguished from him, from that which generates them. Nonetheless, his thoughts are related most intimately to him, to that whence they arise, an intimacy that becomes more intense as he progresses in his understanding. This is not as mysterious as it first seems. It is a basic presumption of scientific thought that our minds are capable of taking on the intelligible structure of the things external to our cognition, that we, through careful investigation and reasoning, can comprehend and represent the things of the universe, that in knowing we can discover its intrinsic order and in our knowing, take this order on, becoming, as it were, the thing itself in our knowing of it. For both science and Thomas, this is something that must occur if we are to be assured of the objectivity of our knowing, that what we know at the end of a careful investigation is objectively reflective of the reality external to us. To deny this would be to deny the reasonability of any investigation, scientific or not, and to despair of ever offering an objective account of the things that we come to know.

The immanent activity of knowing, then, is that whereby we become, cognitionally, the thing itself, and as the mind of the human person turns toward the things of the universe through the arts and the sciences, he not only effects an understanding of that of which he is a part, but also grasps the opportunity of knowing himself in relation to and distinction from that which he has come to know; the more profoundly he knows his universe, and turns this knowledge in investigation toward himself, the better and more accurately does he represent himself to himself in his understanding. This knowing of all things including that of ourselves constitutes the perfecting not only of our intellectual powers but also of our very persons. For Thomas, happiness itself is essentially a cognitive activity whereby we are united to the very source of all intelligibility, namely God Himself. Leaving this, for the moment, to the later discussion of the treatise concerning human happiness in the *secunda pars*, one should note that the perfection of this activity in the human person does not generate another person; the concept, or as Thomas calls it in this setting the *verbum cordis*, the "word of the heart," is the means by which we realize our potential to be united to, and thus to know, all things that are knowable, and it is the very basis of language itself, where the concept, or the word of the heart, is signified by the *verbum vocis*, the "word of the voice," the spoken word.

In God, however, things are different. His immanent activity of understanding is perfect, lacking in no way at all; He is omniscient. Likewise, there is nothing discursive about His understanding; He comprehends all things together in a single thought in His eternal now. His understanding is His essence, His very being; He is wholly simple. He understands himself perfectly, and understands all things in Himself. Consequently, his immanent activity of understanding, while indicated in some fashion by the human experience of it, nonetheless manifests in a procession far different from that which is enjoyed by man. The first procession, then, that emanates from God is an intellectual one. But instead of a *verbum cordis* or concept being generated, there is instead generated the Word in God, "and the Word Himself proceeding is called the Son,"[20] someone who is of the same nature of God insofar as the act of understanding in God is the same as His existence. Thus, the Word first conceived is not accidental to the being of God, nor the result of Him working efficiently, as if the Son where some substantial

---

[20] ST. I. 27. 2.

being created in distinction from God (as will be the case with the things of creation). Instead, the Son proceeds "as subsisting in the same nature, and so is properly called begotten"[21] and is thus not some modality of God's essence, but is rather a person. As we understand ourselves, we represent ourselves to ourselves through the concept that is formed in self-reflection and self-understanding. Thus, while we are distinct from this concept, we are, nonetheless, possessed of this concept, are united to it intimately, and enjoy an identity with it; the thing itself (in this case one's person) is identical, cognitively speaking, to the one who knows it. However, with the human person, this concept never rises to the status of equivalence to his being. In God, however, His thought is His being, and what is brought forth in his act of understanding Himself is the Son.

The other immanent activity that can be attributed to God is that of His willing. In the human person, the will constitutes our intellectual appetite. Unlike our animal appetites, the will is something over which we exercise an almost absolute control. In its constitution as a power, the will is naturally determined to goodness absolutely considered. Thus, whatever the human person wills, he wills under the description of good; one cannot will something evil insofar as it is evil, but only with respect to some goodness that attaches to it. But since perfect goodness is not found in any created thing, the will is not bound necessarily to any created thing, and, consequently, the human person enjoys the capacity of self-determination with respect to the goods of his experience, both those which he judges as good for him and those that are good in themselves. The will's activity, then, follows upon his cognitive and intellectual activities; knowing gives rise to desiring. Now, just as there is a procession involved in intellectual activity, so too is there with volitional activity. The intellectual procession of the concept is the first movement of the mind as it seeks truth, its proper object, that which will perfect it as a power. Truth, for Aquinas, denotes what is called an adequation between the thing itself and its presence in the knower, a conformity of one's understanding to the thing external to oneself. The generation of the *verbum cordis* is the beginning not only of knowing, but also of the

[21] Ibid., ad2.

appropriate investigations whereby one's understanding is more greatly conformed to the being and intelligibility of the thing itself. With regard to volitional activity, there is a like process, one which Thomas regards as less well articulated by the language available to him. Nonetheless, there is the presence of the thing in the knower that is seen, however, not with respect to its truth but rather with respect to its goodness. This presence gives rise to the procession particular to volition, namely that of love, that initial impulsion of the lover to the beloved as the beloved is united cognitively to the lover. This procession, then, is characterized not only by the initial repose that the lover enjoys in his beloved as the two are cognitively united, but primarily by this impulsion or movement toward the beloved so that the beloved might actually or really be attained. Thus, as one plumbs the essence of justice and comes to understand its intrinsic worth and goodness, one's volition becomes united to justice in an act of love, an act which includes and is perfected by the impulse to realize justice in all of one's activities with other people. In short, unlike the activity of the mind which is realized in the cognitive presence of the thing itself and perfected in truth and wisdom, the activity of volition is realized in the inclination of the will to the thing willed, in the impulsion that arises toward the beloved, and lastly in the joy that arises in the real possession of the beloved.

Applying our experience of the immanence of willing to God's, the procession of His love can be said to follow upon the knowledge of Himself in the person of the Son, who, as so understood, is loved by the Father. But given that the Word subsists in the same nature of God, and that the Son knows as the Father knows, so too does the Son love the Father. It is this mutual love of the Son and the Father that gives rise to the person of the Holy Spirit. This third person is manifested not in the generational terms appropriated to the procession of the Son, but rather in accord with the essential notions of impulsion and movement, as one would expect given the Scriptural witness together with the human experience of volition as previously described. This procession of the mutual love of Father and Son is described as *spiration*, a notion that preserves and expresses the movement or impulse of love familiar to human experience, but now an impulse that results in the third person of the Trinity (for what proceeds from God's immanent activity is equivalent to His being). Again, unlike the human experience of love, this mutual love of Father and Son is perfect insofar as it is directed to that which is most perfectly good, and as it rejoices in the actual possession of this most perfect good, a love and delight that manifests as a person, the person of the Holy Spirit. This love is devoid of all need, of all want; God suffers from no privation to His being, but is fully actual and fully active in all that he knows and loves (remember we speak of the immanent life of God Himself, a life from which all else will follow, specifically the creation of the world). This love, then, has the very nature of gift, that gratuitous donation of all that the Father is to the Son, and all that the Son is to the Father, a love realized in the procession of the Holy Spirit.

Since there are the two processions of the Son and the Holy Spirit from the Father, questions naturally arise concerning the relations these three enjoy. The difficulty, as noted earlier, in talking about these relations is that in our experience a relation commonly implies two substantially different things, which then makes the relation possible. For example, before the relation of husband and wife can be realized, there must be a man and a woman wherein the relation can then be realized as one is referred to the other in Holy Matrimony. This, however, is unhelpful in trying to explain the relations that arise in the processions of the three persons in God, how there can be these relations within God without violating His simplicity. The psychological analogy helps to ameliorate this difficulty. However, unless one can offer some account of relationality that is not secondary or accidental as it seems to be in man, then there will be little to no clarity concerning the use of the word *person* to denote Father, Son, and Holy Spirit, let alone how there could be three persons but only one God.

Thomas begins by explaining that relation is not like a thing's weight or color that exists only insofar as it qualifies the thing itself. Instead, relation is something external to a thing, something that qualifies the thing in the reference that it has to another thing. Thus, I am a *citizen* of a certain country, not because of anything that I find in my nature, but rather because of the specific circumstances of my life that refer me to the country of which I am said to be a citizen. In this reference,

I can then say that my citizenship qualifies my person, or, to use Thomas's language, denotes an accidental modification or realization of my being. This reference, then, is "assistant" to my being, something that is "not intrinsically affixed," but rather signifies "a respect which affects the thing related and tends from that thing to something else."[22] Sometimes, this reference is between two things by reason of the natures they possess insofar as these natures have a natural reference to one another. Thus, man and woman share a mutual inclination to each other, the relation of which gives rise to many things required for the realization of their persons, specifically, friendship, marriage, family, culture, and so on. At other times, the reference between two things is purely logical, one that exists only insofar as reason compares one thing to another. Thus, the ideas of "man" and "animal" are related insofar as the latter is the generic description of the former, and the former being a species of the latter. In these two examples, we have the difference between a real and a logical relation.

When we apply these notions to the Trinity, the first thing to be noted is that these relations are real, and not merely logical. This avoids the view that the doctrine of the Trinity is a metaphor that allows the human person to somehow imagine the life of God better, but which in itself does not reflect anything real about Him. Keeping in mind the processions that characterize the immanent activity of God, giving rise to Son and Holy Spirit, and the Father from whence they proceed, Thomas states that the reality of the relations thus implied by both processions is assured by the relative opposition that exists between the terms in these relations. Thus, in the relation of mother to daughter, there is a real distinction between the two insofar as the former gives birth to the latter, giving rise to the opposition of generator and generated, something properly called a relative opposition insofar as the very terms themselves, although opposed, contain in their essential descriptions a mutual reference to one another. Thus, the mother is only so insofar as she has given birth to her daughter, and the daughter is only so insofar as she has come forth from her mother. In the procession of the Son from the Father, there is, then, a real relation and thus a real distinction between the two,

---

[22] ST. I. 28. 2.

insofar as the Son is so called by reason of having been generated by the Father, and the Father is so called by reason of being the origin or the principle of the Son whom he begets. The language of relation is less clear, although the relative opposition is just as real, in the procession of the Holy Spirit from the mutual love that both the Father and the Son enjoy, as described previously. In these real distinctions, we have an insight into what constitutes the very life of God, that in His perfection, unity and simplicity, there is, by revelation, afforded a seemingly contradictory understanding of this in the processions and consequent real relations and distinctions between Father, Son, and Holy Spirit. For these relations, resulting from the processions of both Word and Love from their Principle, arise "from a principle of the same nature" and that what proceeds and that from which the procession arises are in the same nature.[23] In contradistinction, then, from other rational beings, the processions and real relations that God enjoys are identified with His very essence, although such could never be arrived at rationally insofar as the essential descriptions of God do not imply this relational life at the very heart of the being of God, and thus constitutes another reason why the inner Trinitarian life of God had to be revealed by God Himself.[24] From these processions and consequent relations, we can discern four real relations within God, namely those of paternity, filiation, spiration, and procession, the first two of which are associated with the procession of the Word, while the latter two belong to the procession of Love. With respect to either procession, there are the relations of that which proceeds from the principle, and the relation of the principle to that which proceeds. Accordingly, in the procession of the Word, to which is associated the language of generation, there is *filiation* and *paternity* respectively, while in the procession of Love, there is *procession* and *spiration*. And yet, "although paternity, just as filiation, is really the same as the divine essence, nevertheless these two in their own proper idea and definitions import opposite respects. Hence they are distinguished from each other."[25] And, the same applies to the procession of the Holy Spirit.

[23] Ibid.
[24] Ibid.
[25] ST. I. 28. 3. ad.1.

This brings Thomas to the use of the word *person* (in Question 29). Accepting Boethius's definition of person as "an individual substance of a rational nature," Thomas states that this definition is fittingly applied to the Father, Son, and Holy Spirit, but not without some modifications to the generally understood thrust of this definition, namely as it applies to created rational beings. The definition of *person* designates what is most perfect in creation, namely a subsistent individual of a rational nature. Consequently, *person* is fittingly attributed to God insofar as He is the source of all perfections in creation, and this in much the same manner as the other perfections were analogously attributed to God in Question 13, in whom *person* exists in its most perfect and objective manner, something which is only gleaned imperfectly in our use of the term. Part of the use of the word *person* with respect to God indicates His dignity, a dignity that excels every other *person* and grounds this use of the word with respect to created rational beings.[26] Again, the notion of *individual* contained in Boethius's definition implies a material principle that although quite necessary in our experience of individuality, nonetheless cannot be applied to God, as explained earlier. Instead, this notion is used of God only insofar as it denotes the notion of the *incommunicability* of the person in question, his uniqueness, and the incapacity that such could be instantiated in any other person.[27] Again, the notion of *substance* in Boethius's definition is understood to denote in God the *self-subsistence* of whatever the word *person* is used to designate.[28] And finally, *rational nature* must be qualified by what has gone before in the treatise concerning God's essence, namely that although God is eminently rational, this immanent activity is not to be understood as one which discursively arrives at knowledge, but as something which is perfectly actual at every moment from all eternity.[29] He thus asks in Article 4 whether *person* designates the relations that result from the processions, or the very essence of God Himself. Noting the difficulties that other writers have faced in considering this question, Thomas

---

[26] ST. I. 29. 3. ad2.
[27] ST. I. 29. 3. ad4.
[28] Ibid.
[29] Ibid.

appeals to something that is implicit in the analogical use of the word *person*, namely that its application to man and God will include notions that, although appropriate to each, are not necessarily found in or appropriate to the other. Specifically, when said of a human being, the notion of *individuality* betokens something undivided in itself and distinct from others, as one is divided from them by the things particular to one's very substance—"this flesh, these bones, and this soul, which are the individuating principles of a man, and which, though not belonging to *person* in general, nevertheless do belong to the meaning of a particular human person." This point serves to disaffect the reader of importing into the use of the word *person* things that, while appropriate to his proximate experience of persons, nevertheless are not essential to the notion itself. The perfection of person is found in God and is approached only insofar as it has been revealed to reason that such is the case, using our experience and understanding of person in the created realm to begin to approach its perfection in God. Picking up on the notion of distinction, Thomas states that this, in God, is realized only insofar as the processions spoken of previously manifest in relative oppositions within Him. These relations are not accidental as is the case for created things. Instead, they are subsistent realities equivalent to the divine essence itself. "Therefore, as the Godhead is God (*deitas est deus*) so the divine paternity is God the Father (*paternitas divina est deus pater*) Who is a divine person. Therefore a divine person signifies a relation as subsisting." Thus, in the words of Fergus Kerr, the persons of the Trinity "are entirely constituted by their relationships, in the sense that the divine persons are nothing more (or less) than subsisting relationships."[30] Thus, the word *person* primarily signifies these relations that follow upon the processions noted previously. The person of the Father, when said of God, indicates the relation of paternity, God considered as that principle from which the Son is generated or begotten, and who, together with the Son, spirates the Holy Spirit. The person of the Son, when said of God, indicates the relation of filiation, God considered as Word proceeding from the Father in His immanent intellectual activity, the perfect Image of the Father proceeding as the Father

---

[30] Kerr (2002), p. 198.

understands Himself perfectly. Finally, the person of the Holy Spirit, when said of God, indicates the relation of spiration, the procession of love that is the Holy Spirit from both the Father and the Son, and this so that the procession of Love might be distinguished from the procession of the Word, and that the order of word and love noted above in the human experience might not be confused in the immanent activity of God in His intellection and willing (where the impetus which is love proceeds from the word as understood), avoiding the collapsing of Love into Word, and will into intellect.[31] Nonetheless, as stated before, these processions, relations, and persons denote the very essence of God, an essence whose simplicity and unity is manifested in these very processions and their consequent relations and persons, as revealed through the Holy Scriptures.

Conclusion to the treatises concerning God (Questions 2–43)
From this very brief rehearsal of the major aspects of Thomas's views concerning God, a few things should be clear. The God that is presented here is not that which might be derived by natural reason or a philosophy working diligently upon the things of this world, teasing out the characteristics of its first cause, which then can be supplemented by whatever revelation and theology have to offer. His account is more complex than this. There is a clear attention to God's revelation of Himself in the Holy Scriptures, and a careful attention to everything that the community of faith and the tradition of the Church offer in their interpretation. Thomas draws heavily upon the rich theological heritage to which he is heir in the formulation of his answers to these perennial concerns, taking particular advantage of the writings of the Greek and Latin fathers of the Church, as well as the determinations of the various councils dedicated to these very questions. Materially speaking, then, there is great continuity and congruity between Thomas's understanding of God and the traditions and sources on which he depends. Throughout both treatises, he shows himself to be very aware of

---

[31] See ST. I. 36. 2. See, however, the next article where Thomas allows that the Holy Spirit proceeds from the Father *through* the Son, something Brian Davies considers to be a conciliatory move on Aquinas' part to the Eastern Church (1992, pp. 204–206).

the difficulties one faces in God's revelation of Himself in terms appropriate to our human knowing. He is most especially aware of the conditions and the limitations that define the human cognitive experience under which this knowledge is acquired, and is careful to show just how far one can proceed in knowing and naming God accordingly. One of the most notable differences between his writings concerning God and that of the tradition upon which he draws is the degree to which he and the theological milieu of his day had been influenced by the thought and method of the ancient Greek philosophers, and the Arabic commentary tradition upon them. Far from compromising the theological and spiritual nature of these considerations, this appeal to the philosophical discipline both heightens Thomas's awareness of the difficulties involved in describing God's essence, and also allows for a new approach to this most pressing of concerns. What is the result? In contradistinction from the common charge leveled against Thomas, that his God is that of the Greek philosophers, wholly actual and therefore "a static entity, lacking potentiality, and therefore lifeless,"[32] Thomas's descriptions of God throughout these two treatises are primarily verbal rather than substantive, that God is best described in terms evoking activity, or "event" as Kerr states.[33] The proper name for God is that which He gives to Moses at Exodus 3.14, "He who is," a name that at least requires that the substantive be interpreted in categories evocative of what is essential to verbal language. Thus, for example, God's essence is simply identical to His existence; He is *ipsum esse per se subsistens,* that being whose very being (in the sense of existence) is self-subsistent, is simply identical with what He is, something that is especially manifest in Thomas's description of God's intellectual and volitional activity, the nature of His life, happiness and power, and finally the whole of the doctrine of the Trinity. In the processions and relations that define the persons of the Trinity, Thomas does not speak of a process that ends in the generation of three distinct substances that are related one to the other. Instead, we have three persons who are constituted by the very processions that establish these relations, the eternal generation of the Son, and

[32] Kerr (2002), p. 200.
[33] Kerr (2002), p. 190.

the mutual love of Father and Son that spirates the Holy Spirit. It is this description of the Trinity "as activities which eternally flow from the Godhead," of God as pure activity or pure actuality, as "a ceaseless emanation of active and personal forces," that Thomas deems as the most suitable way to regard God's subsistence.[34] In sum, then, we have a description, if you will, of God that is respectful of the fact that God is not an object to be comprehended in Himself, but is that to which all things in their being and their essence point, a description that is respectful of the manner in which this pointing arises (through the contingency of all that we are), and the degree to which that to which they point can be indicated by our language, a being who is believed to be, a belief that is itself reasonable, and whose inner life is approached analogously beginning with the perfections that we find in our world which must be and be perfectly and properly in the very being of that whence they derive originally, a being who has been described most reverently by indicating what is not appropriate to His being, seeing Him as source of all that is, the source and perfection of all being, intelligibility, wisdom, truth, goodness, and so on, a being who must reveal not only the dynamism of His life if it is to be known, but also His very Trinity, the persons of Father, Son and Holy Spirit, persons that ground our own notion of person and act as a potent opportunity to reflect upon how this might reveal something to us about the use of the word *person* in relation to our own natures.

Treatises on Creation (Questions 44–49), the Angels (Questions 50–64), the Work of the Six Days (Questions 65–74), and Man (Questions 75–102)

At this point of the *prima pars,* Thomas begins his examination of God's transitive activity, that activity which proceeds from God and finds its completion in the establishment of some thing, or more generally of some effect, external to Him. The first treatise, that on Creation, deals generally with this procession of all things from His power. The following three treatises deal with the varied distinctions that can be made between created

---

[34] O'Meara (1997), p. 95. One would do well to read Chapter 11 in Kerr (2002) for an excellent treatment of these two treatises on God.

things, specifically, as the Treatise concerning the Angels deals with those creatures which are purely spiritual, the Treatise on the Work of the Six Days deals with those that are purely material, and the third treatise reserved for that creature wherein the spiritual and the material meet, namely man or the human person, who is thus described accordingly as a microcosmos or horizon. The *prima pars* will then end with a consideration of the preservation and governance of creation so described.

Treatise on Creation (Questions 44–49)

The teachings of this treatise are quite direct and definite. Thomas begins with a return to the description of God encountered earlier as that being who is subsisting existence itself. His being and thus His existence is not only necessary, having nothing of the contingent about it, but is also His own: He is simple, undivided, a perfect unity—God alone is His existence. Whatever else, then, is found to exist, cannot be its own existence, cannot be necessary, or enjoy the simplicity or unity that is properly God's. All other things are said to exist only insofar as they enjoy a *participated* being, that is to say a "nonreciprocal relation of dependence,"[35] that is to say, an existence that arises in complete dependence upon God Himself who wills all things into existence, and by whose will all things are thus preserved, a relation which is nonreciprocal insofar as God, being existence himself, relies in no way upon those things He has created for His existence. Thus is established the distinction between the Creator and the created, as well as that most special and intimate of relations wherein all that man is comes to be and is preserved in its being. In distinction from the ancient Greek philosophers, God's creative act extends even to the material out of which all things were made. Creation, then, cannot be seen as God's working upon a pre-existent material that happened to be laying about. The point, then, that Thomas makes, one startling to the ancient world view (insofar as it considered the universe and all its materials to be noncreated and eternal), is that all things, the universe itself, and even the material out of which all is fashioned, is the result of God's creating activity. All that is ordered and formed, all that is determined both

[35] Burrell (2005) in Nieuwenhove and Wawrykow (2005), p. 87.

in themselves and in their relations among one another, derive from the very ideas that God has of them all. This is the divine wisdom that has determined the very order of the universe, and the intelligibility of all its parts. Finally, in addition to God being the first efficient cause of the being of all things including the very matter from which things are made, and the exemplar cause of the order, relatedness and thus the intelligibility of both things themselves and the universe as a whole, God is the final cause of all things, both insofar as all created things find their perfection in their Source, and as God Himself acts as a perfect agent, intending by His creative activity the communication of His goodness, wherein He is considered to be "the most perfectly liberal giver,"[36] acting not for the sake of His own profit but simply out of His own goodness.

Question 45 emphasizes how different the idea of creation is from that of making or change generally considered. First, creation is from no thing (*ex nihilo*); it presupposes no material from which it could be fashioned. In our experience of making, there is always a material presupposed; we do not effect something from nothing where the "nothing" is understood as pure negation, pure non-being. Creation, then, is an activity that is proper to God alone, and when used to describe human making is clearly used only in a metaphorical sense. One cannot call creation a change insofar as change, properly understood, implies something that existed prior to the change that one wishes to signify, something that has already been denied of creation. For the same reason, there can be no movement or process or a series of gradations involved in creation. The creative act lacks these notions familiar to our experience of both making and change, and denotes, instead, the instantaneous or the nonsuccessive. If we remember what was said earlier concerning the contingent nature of all things created, then creation is to be understood not only as the emanation of the being of all things from God, but also as including an essential reference to the maintenance of the being of all things. Thus, the doctrine of creation includes what Brian Davies calls a "doctrine of continuous preservation."[37]

[36] ST. I. 44. 1 corpus and ad1.
[37] Davies (1992), p. 35.

Special note should be taken of Articles 6 and 7 of Question 45 as they deal with the relation of the persons of the Trinity to the act of creation, and thus serve to connect this treatise with the preceding one. Thomas begins by stating that the activity of creation belongs properly to God Himself and not to any one of the persons specifically, since creation denotes the causing of the being of things, the principle of which belongs to God, as described previously. Nevertheless, he affirms that although creation is not proper to any one of the persons, it is an activity that is "common to the whole Trinity" insofar as the essence of God is common to all three. Moreover, greater precision concerning the causality exerted by the persons of the Trinity can be achieved by looking to their respective processions. Appealing to the example of the craftsman who in his work effects the making of something through "the word conceived in his mind, and through the love of his will," Thomas states that in this way, "God the Father made the creature through His Word, which is His Son; and through His Love, which is the Holy Spirit." In light of the processions themselves, since the Father is the principle from which both the Son and the Spirit proceed and that the Father, consequently, does not receive the power to create from another, he is called Creator. The Son, proceeding from the Father, and thus receiving His power to create through this generation, explains what John says at 1.3 namely that *Through him all things were made.* Finally, the Holy Spirit, receiving the same power from both the Father and the Son, is said to govern the whole of creation. To the Father then is appropriated Power, to the Son, as Word, Wisdom, and to the Holy Spirit, Goodness, "to which belong both government, which brings things to their proper end, and the giving of life."

Article 7 concerns the image of the Trinity in the effects of their creative activity. Again, based upon the processions within the Godhead, the image of the Trinity is found most especially in rational creatures, those possessed of intellect and will and which, in their respective activities, is found "the word conceived, and the love proceeding." But even in nonrational creatures, a trace of the Trinity is found insofar as "every creature subsists in its own being, " and thus receives its being from the Father, "has a form, whereby it is determined to a species," through the Son who proceeds as Word of the Father's intellect and establishes all things in light of this, "and has relation to something else" through the order that the Holy Spirit effects in creation as the love and the will of the Creator. In this, then, "the processions of the persons are the type of the productions of creatures inasmuch as they include the essential attributes of knowing and willing," as image in rational creatures and trace in nonrational ones. Thus, the whole of creation is modeled, so to speak, after the very processions found within the Trinity, something which, for the human person, establishes not only that He is made to the image of God, but also roots the possibility of the human person's *reditus* in that whence he arose, something that is played out in the *secunda pars*, and intensified as these invisible missions become visible in the incarnation of the Son and the indwelling of the Holy Spirit, the subject matter of the *tertia pars*.[38]

Establishment, conservation, and governance are all included in the description of creation. It cannot be viewed as something static, but rather as a dynamic ongoing activity of the Trinity. The being, the intelligibility, and the order of all creatures are a direct result of the characters of the processions within the Godhead, and, by extension, so too is the distinction and multiplicity of things in the world. Thomas states in Article 1 of Question 47 that this distinction and multiplicity has its roots in the communication of God's goodness in the act of creation, something that could not be represented adequately by just one thing, but required many and diverse creatures so that "what was wanting to one in (this) representation . . . might be supplied by another." In this way, the simplicity and uniformity of God's goodness is found in the diversity and multiplicity found in creation, which when taken together, "participates the divine goodness more perfectly and represents it better than any single creature whatever." In a like manner, the inequality that we notice in the things of creation is the result of the inadequacy of any one grade or level of goodness representing the goodness of God, a representation that is approached by the perfection of the universe in its diversity, multiplicity, and grades of goodness.

[38] For the development of this point, see Rikhof (2005), pp. 36–57 and Emery in (2005), pp. 58–76.

Thomas devotes the last two questions of this treatise (48 and 49) to the nature and causes of evil in creation. When one considers that God's creative activity proceeds from One who is perfectly good and thus incapable of doing evil, the very existence of evil presses one to explain its existence in both its natural and moral forms, that is to say, as evil is a part of creation itself and thus suffered naturally, and as it is undertaken and committed intentionally by a rational agent and thus is something suffered by both its recipient and its perpetrator, but of course in different ways, the former suffering the ill effects of the evil perpetrated, the latter suffering a deprivation to or imperfection of his very nature in the committing of such an act. Thomas begins his explanation by accepting Augustine's general discussion and definition of evil, namely as a privation of goodness, a deprivation in a thing of some perfection or actuality that it should have according to its nature. Thus, blindness would be considered an evil in a human person, who, according to his nature, should have that of which he is deprived. Evil, then, is not something that is created. Rather, it designates that deprivation, or relative nonexistence, that one suffers, a state that could only exist in relation to a positively really existing thing. One must be careful here. Its existence in things is not to be understood in the way that color, weight, or height exist in things. For, these manifest a certain positive qualification of one's being. Evil, on the other hand, denotes that very absence of something that ought to be there. Thus, evil exists only insofar as good exists, but it is possible for the good to exist without evil, as is the case with God. The two, then, are not co-principles, but rather the good or being is primary, and evil indicates some deprivation or failing or falling away from the good or from being itself. Now, the cause of this is something implicit in the very multiplicity, diversity, and inequality of the things of creation, specifically insofar as there are things created which can suffer the loss of some good proper to them, extending from some corruption of their being up to and including the loss of their existence. That such things are possible and do indeed happen are a consequence of the perfection of the universe. Material things, for example, are not naturally eternal but are subject to the principles which govern change, and this not only for the better, but also for the worse, and the latter either by accident (through some chance circumstance, like the breaking of one's arm consequent upon falling from a height) or by some defect in their constitution (as in, say, a genetic disposition to cancer or diabetes). The things of creation are not determined to such things.[39] Nor is the human person determined to abuse the reason and free choice that he possesses. All are created good, and as a consequence naturally seek out those things in which their perfection resides and naturally repel those things that are destructive of it. In the case of rational and volitional beings, everything that they will is willed under the description of the good, even those things that are destructive of their nature. Thus, suicide, for example, is not willed in itself and for the evil that it is, but is intended and sought out only insofar as it is judged to be good, namely as the means whereby pain is terminated, or one is delivered from an impossible or intolerable situation, and so on. Evil results, then, as it is something that is caused incidentally or indirectly as one primarily intends the good in one's activities, whether this be in the creative act of God or in the activities undertaken by the human person himself. In this way, Thomas argues at Question 49, Article 2 that God does not directly intend the evils of corruption and death but rather the good of the order of the universe, in which the failure of some things to achieve their good is a consequence of His intention of the good. Moreover, since God is fully realized in His being and thus suffers no defect, the defective disposition of things as well as the chance occurrences that characterize the lot of many of the things of creation cannot be attributed to God as their cause. The good order of creation and the nature of the things of which it is composed are what God intends in His creative activity, and not the consequences of it. And when we consider the evil that is intended and committed by created rational beings, it is, again, the case that God is not its cause, but rather that it arises from these very rational agents in question acting contrary to what is their true good and the good of others.

---

[39] that is, at least before the fall. Aquinas will say later that the natural things to which the flesh is heir would have been avoided by the special graces bestowed on them by God.

The difficult nature of Thomas's answers to the existence of evil and how it is to be reconciled with what we can know about God in relation to his creative activity was noted earlier when dealing with God's providence. It is fairly clear that God willed the creation of a world in which physical and sensitive beings are subject in their very natures to be both good and evil, that in the willing of the created realm, He directly intends its good, and in so doing permitted the evils of the natural order as something inevitable,[40] a position that follows reasonably from His omniscience. Likewise, it is also fairly clear that God permitted the situation to arise wherein freely acting rational agents could intend and undertake activities of an evil nature, and that He permitted this not as something inevitable (for the nature of the human person and of human freedom does not necessitate the intention and committing of evil, whereas in the natural order the accidents and defects are things that do follow from the ontological constitution of things in their being), but rather for the sake of a greater good, namely that the human person might maintain the integrity of his freedom (which includes the power, not the necessity, of acting immorally) and aspire to what God directly intends in His creative act, namely to seek the good and perfection of his nature through his rational and volitional activities, especially as this culminates in his desire for union with Him. The question, however, for modern thinkers has been how and why God, who is perfect goodness, is all-powerful and enjoys omniscience, freely created a universe in which is found so much natural and moral evil. Thomas himself was well aware of the reality of evil in the world. In the prologue to his commentary on the Book of Job, Thomas judges, according to Copleston, that "nothing is more difficult to reconcile with divine providence than the sufferings of the innocent."[41] And yet this does not become a reason for him to argue against the existence of God. This is not only because arguments of this type are unsound, something well presented by David Bentley Hart earlier in this chapter. And it is too simple to say that he does not have the concern of a philosopher or a modern thinker for

---

[40] at the very least inevitable to a world that fell from its originally intended condition subsequent to the sin of the first parents.

[41] Copleston (1955), p. 154.

whom this issue has so much force. Instead, one must remember the theological context out of which this work, and the treatment of its materials, arise.[42] The fact that evil exists is something to which all people would readily give their ascent. So, pervasive is evil that one cannot but describe it as a basic given of life in the world, something necessary to one's existence over which one can exert little or no control. The Christian addressing of this reality both accepts this given of his experience, but considers how it is manifested in the light of the Christian story, and, consequently, distinguished from it. Thus, the evil of this world is revealed to be an important consequence of the sin of man, something that reveals that this evil need not have been in both its moral and ontological forms.[43] This reveals not only that God is not the creator of evil, but also that His goodness takes priority over our initial experience of the seeming primacy and inevitability of evil itself. And when one considers the means of redemption made available by God through His Son's incarnation, suffering, death, and resurrection, there is cause for great hope. This, as Robert Sokolowski states,

> is part of the good news of Christianity. But when we understand the Christian "nonnecessity" of evil and suffering by holding it in contrast to the necessity that evil and suffering have for natural experience . . . (w)e are less tempted to ask questions like Why did God ever permit evil and suffering? . . . It is not that we now have answers to such questions, but we do appreciate more vividly that they are inappropriate

---

[42] What follows to the end of this paragraph parses Robert Sokolowskis' discussion of "The Theology of Disclosure" as found in chapter 8 of (1982; 1995), pp. 88–103.

[43] Many of the diseases of the body are considered to be a result of the disorder introduced into his nature and into creation by sin. As for accidents or chance events, while such were possible, given the human person's passible state, nonetheless, his reason and the grace of Divine Providence would have prevented such from happening—see ST. I. 97. 2. ad4. As for death, although the human person was different in nature from the angels who, by reason of their constitution, do not suffer death, nonetheless by reason of the grace of God, the human person would have remained incorruptible and immortal "so long as it remained itself subject to God" (ST. I. 97. 1).

questions. The important thing is that evil and suffering, which seem so dense and so dark, somehow did not have to be, that God is not subordinated to them, and that we can be saved from them. Questions about why God permits evil, or why he permitted a particular evil to befall us, begin to look like idle questions when we appreciate the impact of the truth that evil is not a last word.[44]

It is in this context that one can best understand his approach to this question, that his adoption of "a less anthropocentric attitude toward suffering and death"[45] than many in our own age would be willing to adopt is an indication that Thomas thought out of a context that differs markedly in some ways from that of the modern who is concerned with such questions, a difference that cannot be excused as simply a manifestation of the inadequacy on Thomas's part to consider what, from the modern's perspective, is an obvious and pressing concern.

Treatise on the Angels (Questions 50–64)

Having dealt with the general principles of God's creative act, Thomas turns to the specifics of this activity. He first considers those creatures that are purely spiritual, namely, the angels themselves. This somewhat lengthy consideration of what some have considered to be a minor matter has for its inspiration not only the clear interest that the Fathers before Thomas had in these beings, something inspired, no doubt, by the biblical witness to these creatures and the use to which God put them throughout Scripture (specifically, in the role they play, at the end of the *prima pars,* in the governance of creation and in the affairs of human beings), but also as they bear witness to the fecund nature of God's creative act. Recall that the multiplicity and diversity evident in creation, as well as the perfection found in its unity and intelligibility, follow upon the fact that any one created thing is unable to represent adequately God's goodness, but that it requires the entirety of creation in all of its multiplicity, diversity, order, intelligibility, and inequality to approach this. In the perfect order of creation, it is fitting, Thomas argues,

[44] Sokolowski (1982; 1995), pp. 94–95.
[45] Copleston (1955), p. 154.

that there be found not only intellectual creatures, but that there be among these some whose intellectual nature and consequent activity are not manifested in a corporeal way, as is the case with the human person. The challenge of Questions 50 through 53, then, is to describe the substance of these beings, followed closely by an examination of both their intellectual and volitional activity, first in themselves (Questions 54 through 58, and 59 through 60, respectively) and then in their first realization consequent upon their creation (61 through 64).

With respect to their substance, the angels, as already noted, are wholly incorporeal. While this may seem a somewhat obvious point to make, it does present Thomas with the opportunity of addressing how these purely spiritual beings differ from the purely spiritual being of God Himself. By the fact that they were created by God,[46] the essence of an angel is something that is distinct from its existence, something which, consequently, reveals that the angel is not pure act, as is the case with God. Rather, the existence of its essence or nature is contingent, standing as something which is potential to existence, potential to that participation of that being which is properly God's, something spoken of in the prior treatise.[47] Since, then, the "composition" of this created being is not at the level of matter and form, but rather with respect to its essence and existence, the way by which a species is typically multiplied (through its matter—thus one human person differs from another not in their humanity but rather as this is instantiated here and now in this particularly existing thing having its own matter which it does not share with any other human person) does not apply here. The result is that there are as many different species or kinds of angel as there are individual angels, of which there are a multitude far greater than all material things taken together. Thus, unlike the word "man," the words "angel" or "separate substance" do not directly indicate an essence shared by one and all alike but rather is the manner in which we can refer to this group of created intellectual beings as a whole in distinction from both the human person at the one extreme, and God

---

[46] ST. I. 61.
[47] Consider Etienne Gilson's consideration of this point in (1956; 1994), pp. 164–168.

at the other. Within this middle ground, so to speak, that the angels occupy, this multiplicity of species also manifests the inequality that characterizes the material creation with which we are more familiar. Here is found the basis for the doctrine of the hierarchy of the angels from the highest of the Seraphim to the lowest of the Angels properly so named, something that will be treated of in its proper place in the Treatise on the Divine Government at the completion of the *prima pars.*[48]

After having considered the angelic substance in relation to the bodies they sometimes assume (as recounted in the Scriptures: Question 51), the angels' relation to place (52) and how it can be said that they move (53) lacking a corporeal condition, Thomas considers the nature of their knowledge (54–59). Once again, given the immaterial nature of the angel and thus its likeness in this respect to God, Thomas is careful to note that the angel's knowing is not identical with its substance, existence, and essence.[49] On the other hand, he is also careful to distinguish the angel's knowing from that which the human person enjoys. The central difference between these two ways of knowing deals with the access each enjoys to both the intelligibility of things and their instantiation in particular material things. The human person's knowing is such that whatever he knows has it beginnings in his senses: the individual, particular material things of the world are encountered through his sensitive cognitive powers, and it is from these that his intellectual powers abstract the intelligibility that lies latent, so to speak, in them. While this will be discussed in greater detail in the next treatise, it is important to note that the intellectual activity of the human person is something that requires a fair bit of work. Two powers are required, one that works naturally to reveal, so to speak, the intelligible natures of things (something he calls the active intellect), and the other that is receptive of these intelligible natures and seeks to clarify what is implicit in them (the passive intellect). It is the latter that is familiar to us as performing those activities that we associate with being rational, namely, defining, judging, making distinctions, constructing arguments—in short, the discursive nature

[48] For a good summary of this, see Gilson (1956; 1994), pp. 168–173.
[49] ST. I. 54. 1–3.

that characterizes the human rational process. This is something that is proper to the human person as an enmattered soul whose intelligence is manifested under the corporeal conditions proper to his humanity. Given that the angel is wholly immaterial, the intellectual operations in which it engages are quite different from that experienced by human beings. First, there is no need to posit in them the two elements of the active and passive intellect necessary to human cognition.[50] Nor is it the case that they need to engage in the investigative processes so familiar and necessary to human knowing.[51] Their experience of intellectual cognition is not based in the senses, but is one which is innate to their being, one that arises insofar as God has gifted them, in varying ways, with the intelligible essences or ideas that are contained in His mind, and which serve as the exemplars of all created things, which themselves are instantiated in the particular material things of this world, these being the basis upon which all human knowing rests. The intellectual sight of the angels, then, goes immediately and in a nonsuccessive way to the very essence of those things for which we, being human, must strive discursively to attain, and even then we know only imperfectly for the most part. This knowledge is said to be "connatural" to their being, one appropriate to an intellectual substance separated from the conditions and limitations of matter, one which constitutes their experience of being and the knowledge that follows upon this.

Their volitional activity (Questions 59–60) is in many ways much like that of the human person's. Their will is naturally inclined to the good, is engaged in freely, and gives rise to their love of themselves, others, and God. The difference, however, is found when one considers how their voluntary activity manifested consequent to their creation together with the particular nature of their knowing, the subject matter of the remaining questions of this treatise (61 through 64).

Upon their creation, the angels, enjoying the kind of knowledge specific to them, were from the beginning possessed of what Thomas calls in the treatise on happiness a natural happiness, one that is within the natural grasp of the angel consequent

---

[50] ST. I. 54. 4.
[51] ST. I. 58. 1–5.

upon the contemplation of the highest things, something with which they have been naturally graced but for which man seeks discursively through the arts and sciences. However, there is something further to be attained here, given the fact that one's ultimate happiness or beatitude properly speaking cannot consist in any created thing, but is found solely in God Himself. This union with and subjective possession of God is beyond the power of any created being, and must be gifted to one if it is to be enjoyed. Thus, even though the angels possess a kind of knowledge for which the human person could only dream, it is nonetheless not equivalent to the beatitude that God Himself enjoys, and to which all rational beings are invited to participate through God's gracious gift of Himself to them.[52] There is, then, from their very origin, the requirement that the angels, like the human person, turn to God for their ultimate happiness, a turning that in its initial manifestation is a grace they received from their creation, making possible the orientation to that which is above and perfective of their natures.[53] As with man, so too with the angels is it the case that the gift of beatitude is a gift freely given by God for which the rational being can do nothing to necessitate its giving. Nonetheless, the human person is required by God to live a life of virtue so that he might be found ready to receive this gift, something of which we will talk in greater detail in the *secunda pars*. With the angels, however, the situation is somewhat different owing to the differences in their nature, specifically with respect to the mode of their knowing as this impacts directly the quality of their choice. Those angels who receive the gift of beatitude do so immediately following upon their first act of charity, determining in this one act all that is asked on God's part for the gift to be given. This is possible given the nondiscursive, nonsuccessive nature of the angel's knowing, something which does not allow for the vacillation of will, or the passing from one level of moral development to another, as is the case with the human person, but rather allows for the immediate orientation and ultimate determination of the angel to God in this act of charity which then allows for the immediate manifestation

[52] ST. I. 62. 1.
[53] ST. I. 62. 2–3.

of their beatitude.[54] This can be seen clearly in the case of those angels who do not receive the gift of beatitude, those evil angels who fell from grace in the committing of their original sin, that of pride. In this their first sin, they refused, consequent upon their creation, to be subject to God, a subjection that was appropriate to them in their created nature and due to Him as their Creator.[55] Instead, they desired to be as Him, not in the sense of enjoying an equality with Him, but rather in likeness to Him and this in a way that was not appropriate to the angel's nature, specifically in seeking their beatitude apart from God and thus in accordance with their own powers, and in seeking to have all created things subject to them, as these are subject to God Himself.[56] Given the nature of the angel, this pride is not something that developed over time as it does for the human person. Instead, it is something that manifested at once after the first instant of their creation, in the first free choice that they made not to be subjected to God as just described.[57] The effect of this choice was to render the will of the fallen angels inflexible, confirmed in their choice, again something that does not occur to the human person in one or even a series of actions but requires a lifetime of such decisions so as to confirm oneself in such a fashion.[58] The "quickness" and absolute nature of this confirmation is, again, a consequence of the very nature of the being in question. The will of the human person is changeable insofar as his knowledge is not firmly fixed, moving from one principle to the next, investigating the natures of things so that through this investigation and the discursive nature of his reasoning, he might attain to a better vision of the intelligible things to which he turns his gaze. As we have seen, however, on the part of the angel, its gaze is unimpeded by the

---

[54] ST. I. 62. 5.

[55] ST. I. 63. 1–3.

[56] ST. I. 63. 3. Envy is the other sin to which the fallen angels are subject. It follows upon pride insofar as they considered their "singular excellence" to be endangered not only by the Divine excellence itself, but by the excellence shown to and demonstrated by the human race, something that generated that sorrow over another's good which constitutes envy's description.

[57] ST. I. 63. 6.

[58] Ibid., ad. 3.

limitations and conditions under which human knowing is realized, beholding the very intelligibility of things with which the angel has been gifted in its creation. Since its knowledge is not progressive but complete in itself, the choice of the will consequent upon this knowledge is likewise complete, having been fixed in its choice from which it cannot be moved.[59] The difficulty that many experience in accepting this position was mentioned earlier, namely that in matters of free will, many today consider this power to be absolute, as something that is wholly under one's control and can thus be changed at a moment's notice under any circumstances. Such is not the view of Thomas, who considers the freedom of will to derive from its initial determination to the good, and is something that, together with the knowledge one has, the judgments that one has made, and, in the case of human beings the life that one has led, can be turned decisively to the good or to the evil and be confirmed habitually to one or the other, something that occurs in the first free choice of the angel, but only after a lifetime of choices have been completed by a human person at the time of his death.

Treatise on the Work of the Six Days of Creation (Questions 65–74)

In this treatise, Thomas deals with the material product of God's creative activity, and this in the context of a commentary upon the six days of creation as found in Genesis 1.1–2.4a. The teaching that is presented here is one that draws heavily upon two areas of ancient and medieval thought, namely, physics and astronomy/cosmology. In many respects, the developments of modern physics and cosmology have rendered much of what is contained in this treatise of interest only to the historian. Nonetheless, for the purposes of this work, we can attend to a few of its interests that may be relevant to the neophyte in his or her initial approach to the *Summa Theologiae*.[60]

---

[59] ST. I. 64. 2.

[60] If one is interested in pursuing these matters further, William Wallace, O.P. has supplied a number of excellent appendices to his translation of this treatise (pp. 171–234 of Volume 10 (1967) of the Blackfriars edition of the *Summa Theologiae*).

Although Thomas had dealt previously with the question of the creative act belonging exclusively to God, he affirms in Article 1 of Question 65 that all material things and creatures derive from God. This is to counter the view held by some Christians like the Manicheans that the material aspect of creation was evil, and that it had been created not by God but by some other principle itself evil in nature. In like manner, he argues again for the goodness of the material creation in Article 2. This time, he has the views of Origen in sight who argued that the inequality noted previously among the things of creation could only be explained as the consequent punishment meted out to spiritual creatures who had turned from God, the body thus being something not originally intended by God in His creative activities but the result rather of the sin of man. Not only is this view contrary to the very witness of the Genesis account (specifically the pronouncement by God that what He had created on each day was good), but also to the perfection that creation is, that the multiplicity, diversity, and inequality that it contains is the way by which the goodness that is God is represented, something that includes the creation of material things. When one beholds the unity and the relatedness of all things as each aspect of creation seeks its own proper good, that its lesser aspects are for the sake of its higher ones, that the totality of these relations is for the sake of the perfection of the whole itself, and that all of this is ordained to God as to its ultimate end and perfection, one cannot but accept the goodness of the whole of creation and of each of its parts, including its material and corporeal aspect. Lastly, in Articles 3 and 4, Thomas affirms once again that God alone is the principle from which all creation derives, and that the angels did not play a role in this activity, something that stood contrary to the views of the Arab philosopher Avicenna that enjoyed some influence in Thomas's day.[61]

Questions 66 through 73 deal with the particulars of each day of creation in light both of the physics and cosmology available to Thomas, as well as the commentary tradition on the six days of creation as found within many of Church Fathers, a tradition of which Thomas shows himself to be in solid possession.

---

[61] For these views, see Wallace (1967), p. 181.

The first article of Question 73 affirms the perfection of God's creative effort, a perfection that established the whole of the universe in its intended integrity and in its openness, so to speak, to its completion in "the perfect beatitude of the Saints at the consummation of the world," a consummation that is effected through the incarnation and the salvific act. As the response to the first objection states, there are, then, three consummations to be noted in God's creative activity, the first being the consummation of *nature* effected in the establishment of all created things upon the completion of the six days of creation, the second being the consummation of *grace* effected in the Incarnation of Christ, and the third being the consummation of *glory* at the end of time. The reply to the third objection notes that God's creative activity is restricted to these six days, that the multiplicity and diversity of creation, then, now and to come, were present implicitly in all that was brought forth in those six days. Lastly, the question of whether there were actually six days is entertained at Article 2 of Question 74. Thomas shows great caution here in the determination of this question insofar as the patristic tradition does not resolve the matter decisively. Nonetheless, according to Wallace, the tenor of the discussion together with various comments made throughout the treatise, indicate Thomas's readiness to accept Augustine's position, that is, of the simultaneous creation of all things, and that the reference to the six days in the Genesis account is reflective of the progression of the revelation of God's creative activities to the angels,[62] or, as Gilson states, the way by which the varied orders of beings are symbolized.[63]

Treatise on Man (Questions 75–102)

With this treatise, Thomas completes his consideration of God's creative activity, its culmination, if you will, in the human

---

[62] See the notes to this section of the text in Wallace's translation (pp. 155–159).

[63] Gilson (1956; 1994), p. 175. Gilson also suggests, backed by several quotations from this treatise, that the six days were a device by which Moses, the author of the first 5 books of the Scriptures according to the tradition of the time, explained these matters to the simple and unlearned people whom he guided.

person, that being which is both spiritual and material in com-position, a being in which the whole of creation is writ small (the human person understood as *microcosmos*), or in which the spiritual and the material meet (the human person understood as *horizon*). Given the importance of this treatise both in itself (as it summarizes Thomas's psychological views concerning the human person), and to the plan of the *Summa* (as it establishes a number of the principles and doctrines central to the matters determined in the *secunda pars* and for a number of discussions in the *tertia pars,* specifically concerning the human nature of Christ), a great deal has been written about it in the secondary literature. In the few pages that we can dedicate to this trea-tise, I hope to give an overview of its more important teachings, and will direct the reader in the appropriate places to works that offer a more detailed coverage of what can only be treated briefly here.

The treatise itself divides into two sections. The first deals with the nature of man himself (Questions 75 through 89), while the second treats of his origin or production (90 through 102). The first of the two has received the greater attention and con-stitutes what Torrell calls Thomas's "rational psychology,"[64] that is to say, his considerations concerning the soul of man, the powers that arise from it, and a general description of their varied activities with an emphasis upon the rational powers, leaving a consideration of the appetitive powers to the *secunda pars.* This latter decision may seem mistaken as it appears to leave this treatise incomplete in its breadth and depth. Nonetheless, when one recalls that the focus of the *prima pars* is not upon human agency, but rather upon God Himself and his agency, as the latter is manifested in His creative activity and the preservation and governance of all that He has cre-ated, one begins to understand the summary treatment that is offered here of the psychology of the human person, and why it is more appropriate to expand upon its voluntary and affective aspects in the *secunda pars* when treating specifically of human agency, that is, of his moral activity. It is for these reasons that Thomas also puts aside a detailed consideration of the body of the human person, leaving such an important and worthwhile

[64] Torrell (2005), p. 25.

investigation to its appropriate discipline, that of the medical or "experimental" sciences. The only considerations that Thomas entertains with respect to man's body are those that have a direct bearing upon the purposes of the theologian in these first two parts of the *Summa*.[65]

Questions 75 and 76 deal with the soul of man, and its union with the body. These two questions are quite difficult to appreciate and understand for a number of different reasons, three of which are of particular importance, namely Thomas's assumption that the reader has a good grasp of the Aristotelian psychology upon which his own views are based, second, that this treatise presumes a knowledge of the psychological controversies of the day in which he was involved, and lastly the tendency on our part, given the history of thought, to understand and interpret Thomas's psychological teaching and language in a distinctively modern way, something which does not coincide at all times with Thomas's own approach. To ameliorate these difficulties somewhat, let us begin with the metaphors mentioned above as descriptive of the human person, namely as "microcosmos" and "horizon."

Thomas probably understood "horizon" much as we do, namely as that "place" where the sky and the earth meet. He uses this notion as descriptive of the human person in three ways. First, that being human involves both a material or corporeal aspect, and an immaterial or spiritual one—body and soul respectively. However, "horizon" is neither the sky nor the earth taken separately. It can only be named and described in relation to their "union," the point at which both meet, and without this union neither aspect would exist as they are respectively named. In like manner, the human person is understood neither as his body nor as his soul. Instead, he is their union, that "place" at which both body and soul unite, that "place" where body and soul become realities without which there would initially be no such things. Lastly, "horizon" is used as

---

[65] This position is also strengthened when one recalls the audience and purpose for which the *Summa Theologiae* itself is written. For an assessment of Thomas's knowledge and use of the medical disciplines (and for other important related matters), consider Jordan (1988), pp. 233–246, and Ibid. (2006), pp. 33–59.

a way to compare the human person with the rest of creation, specifically that man in his nature occupies a "middle position" within creation, being both material and spiritual, related essentially to the things of earth and heaven, being both animal and image of God.

The danger with respect to this image and its application is that it can lend itself rather easily to interpreting Thomas's understanding of the human person in dualist terms, where the two aspects that make up the human person are radically opposed to each other in their natures, enjoying their own separate existences apart from their "union" in the human person, which union would be of the weakest kind, akin to a rider on horseback, or a sailor on a ship. The soul, in such a view, would be said to be housed in the body, to use it as its instrument. Finally, the body would be considered at the very least as secondary to that which is primary and essential to man's humanity, namely his very soul. To avoid these interpretations, one must note that although Thomas is clearly dual in his description of the human person, speaking of both material and immaterial aspects, body and soul respectively, nevertheless he stresses the unity of these two as being definitive of the human person. The human person is neither his body nor his soul alone. The body, for Thomas, is to be understood not as distinct from or radically opposed to man's nature, but rather as an intrinsic aspect of it. So intrinsic is the body to man's nature that Thomas considers the body as something that is brought into existence not only by, but also with, the soul. In like manner, he does not consider the soul as something that pre-exists a particular human person. Rather, it begins to exist in the first realization of a particular human person. Before this realization, then, there is neither soul nor body. To put this in more formal terms, "body" is to be understood as the material condition of the human soul, something that necessarily comes to be in the actualization of the soul and the human person himself. "Human person" is this particular corporeal rational being having the capacity to engage in all the powers proper to his humanity. "Soul" is the formal principle of the human person's existence. It specifies the kind of being that the human person is, and those activities and powers proper to him. This includes an essential and necessary realization of the body, its organization, and function within the whole of the life of man.[66]

From this initial description of "soul," it should be clear that it is not purely a theological term. It is a notion first developed by the ancient Greek philosophers and especially by Aristotle. In this pre-Christian usage, "soul" designated that which accounts for that most basic distinction between living and nonliving things; the former were said to have soul while the latter were not. In this usage, then, a thing's life arose from its soul. The term "soul" was also used to refer to the *kind* of living thing of which there were three traditionally designated, namely, plant, animal, and human. Finally, "soul" accounted for all the activities that characterized the kind of living being that one happened to be considering. Thus, an animal soul makes the animal itself to be alive, to be a certain kind of living thing, and allows for those activities that we commonly understand animals to exhibit. In short, "soul" is a vivifying, specifying, and actualizing principle, and includes within it the material, bodily and operational condition, powers, and activities so familiar to the human person's experience of a living thing.

Although this sounds very much like a dualist position, we have seen that this is not the case; the human person is that which is primary, not his soul. However, it is difficult to see why, in light of the importance of the soul and the dualist heritage with which we have been endowed, that one's focus should shift from the soul to the person. For it seems that in order for the soul to act in these capacities, it must pre-exist the body. How could it vivify, specify, and actualize the living being in question if it did not actually exist *before* this occurs?

When we consider the things of our direct sensible experience, we understand that each of them has a material aspect, the stuff out of which each is made. So, in the case of a house, we would say that its material principle is the bricks, wood, cement, nails, plaster, and other such things, all of which go into its construction. But while this material is necessary for the house's existence and description, it is not wholly sufficient;

---

[66] For a far more detailed exposition of this line of thought, please consider Chapter 6 "Forms and bodies: the soul" in Stump (2003), pp. 191–216.

there is something missing. What person would consider a construction company to have finished its job of building a house by simply delivering the materials to the work site? Clearly, there must also be an ordering principle, one that organizes these materials so that through this determination imposed upon these materials, the house actually comes into existence. Thomas refers to this organizing principle as a thing's formal aspect, or simply its form, that which makes the thing to be what it is.

The materials used in the house's construction possess their own characteristics and their own natures. The choice concerning which materials are appropriate is one made largely in accordance with the organizing principle of the house, something determined not only by the builder but also by the use to which the house will be put—different structures require different kinds of materials, and this is influenced directly by the reasons for which these structures are made in the first place. Thus, a wooden frame may be suitable for a one-story family dwelling, while steel is more appropriate for a high-rise apartment building. Again, if the house is to protect one from the typical rainstorms and winters common to the northeastern parts of Europe and America, one will not consider straw and paper as suitable materials for the roof and walls; wood and stone would be far more appropriate. Again, if a building is intended for habitation, different materials will be emphasized over those used in the construction of nonhabitable structures, such as warehouses. When these materials are brought together in the house's construction, they take on a nature and function in addition to those which they already posses as individual materials having definite natures and functions. Thus, a brick is no longer simply a brick, but an element within the "body" of the house, an element within a structural whole, now enjoying a new function in keeping with its nature (in this case, as part of a wall, which wall is important to the overall structure and realization of the other elements of the house that depend upon this wall and its integrity for their own functioning with respect to the house itself). This again is determined by the organizational aspect of the house. For it should be clear that these new natures and functions do not simply emerge out of the material themselves, but rather because of, and in union with, the organization conferred upon them by the house's form. Thus, one could say that the form of the house "gives rise to" or "causes" its material aspect, in this example, the "body" of the house, a "body" that only comes into existence through the activity of the form itself. Without this "body," the house would not really exist, and thus would not function as a house. The materials would still have their own respective natures and functions, but would not enjoy that nature and function that only the organizing principle of "house" could elicit from them. It is only in the completion of the ordering of the materials that the house is finally realized, that a new thing begins to exist, a thing having its own nature, qualities, and functions, something that can clearly and properly be called a "house." Until then, the form merely exists in the mind of the architect, and the materials at best lie about the work site waiting for their body to be realized. It is only the finished product that deserves the name of "house." To call a pile of materials at the work site, or that architectural plan on paper or in mind, "house" is to speak improperly or metaphorically at best.

In like manner can we understand Thomas's teaching concerning the human person. When we distinguish a living from a nonliving thing, we recognize that its material aspect alone is not sufficient to account for this difference. For if we assumed that matter were the only principle necessary for life, we would then have to explain why some material things live while others do not (if matter were the only principle necessary for life, then all things having matter should be alive. But clearly they are not. Therefore there must be something more). If we try to argue that life arises through a higher degree of order and complexity present in the matter of those things we call living, then we have admitted the position we are trying to argue against. For in this explanation, we no longer refer to the matter alone, but rather to its organization, its structure, its determination, its configuration—that is to say, to its formal principle. It is this formal aspect that gives rise to the kind of living thing we have before us and the activities appropriate to its kind. The form determines those materials appropriate to the living thing's realization, which when brought together provide for the material conditions that its very existence and functioning require. The matter of the living thing, then, is not just any matter, but matter of a certain kind, having a certain configuration, order, and determination. This material, so ordered and determined, warrants the special name of "body." It is in this sense, then, that we can say that the soul "gives rise" to the body, or that the body is the "material condition" of the soul, or that body "is caused" by the soul's activity, each expression being synonymous with the others. The human body, then, is necessary for the realization of the human person and the activities in which he engages. The human person does not exist prior to the soul's realization (matter may exist, but not body), and the soul itself only really exists in light of its material condition. What first exists, then, is the human person. All else is understood in reference to, and subordination to, him. Without this reference, there is initially no body and no soul.

Given that the body is the material condition of the soul's existence, and that consequently body and soul are not radically opposed to each other, there is no need on Thomas's part to speak of a mixture of the two, or to consider the problems that arise when one tries to explain their respective powers and the interactions that they enjoy, a great difficulty for any dualist position. Questions 77 through 83 consider the powers of the human person, specifically those that are of interest to the theologian. This interest is determined by the very plan of the *Summa* itself, namely those powers that are directly involved in the return that man makes to God, and specifically those powers that can be made most excellent in their operations in this regard, an excellence that is effected through the acquisition of the virtues, all of which is the subject matter of the *secunda pars*. Thomas treats of the powers in a general way in Question 77, and then considers in 78 those powers that serve directly the intellectual (79) and appetitive powers (80 through 83).

The powers of a living thing are rooted in the soul, but unlike the human person himself, many of them are not immediately manifested or actualized in the person's first realization. The powers are not the same as the soul, but rather are made possible by the soul's first realization in this particular kind of living thing that one has before one, be it plant, animal, or human. It is in this context that one can understand the classical definition of soul as the first form or act of a physical organic body having life potentially. This first act is the realization of that first perfection, namely the existence of a specific kind of living being, the human person in this case. It is consequent upon this first realization that the powers of the human person are established, but not in their full actualization. Instead, they are potential principles that admit of further realizations through the varied and many activities in which the human person engages consequent upon his first realization. The powers, then, constitute the further or second actualities of which the human person is capable, the state in which he finds himself to be, and to which he aspires, through his activity and that of others and society, to realize and perfect. Given the complexity of his nature, the human person has many and diverse powers, all of which require attention so that they themselves and the human person who possesses them might be perfected. In light of the destiny of the human person, some powers require greater attention than others. Thus, there is a hierarchy of powers discerned in the human person with the intellectual powers being the highest and thus definitive, since it is these which influence, direct, command, and transform all the other powers found within man, even though they are the last to develop and demand the greatest nurture and care. It is these that allow the human person to be free from the determinism of both his animal and what Thomas calls his vegetative aspect, which is responsible for the basic physiological processes of man's life.

Although the variety and multiplicity of powers that the human person enjoys is rooted in the soul, Question 78 shows that they are manifested in varying ways according to the degree to which they require the involvement of the body itself, the objects with which they are concerned, and their characteristic activities. The vegetative powers of the human person are the most emersed in the material condition of man, being wholly oriented to the integrity and care of the body, specifically with respect to its nutrition, growth, and reproduction. The sensitive powers are more extensive in their reach, being concerned with all corporeal bodies, and not just the one in which they are found. His intellectual powers encompass all manner of being, and not just those that are materially realized. With respect to his sensitive and intellectual powers, these are broadly collected under those that are cognitive and those that are appetitive. The cognitive powers make things that are external to the human person present to him, and are those that collectively are responsible for his varied activities of knowing. The appetitive powers serve to orient the human person personally to the very things that he knows. His appetition in this regard is twofold, following upon the mode of his knowledge. By his sensitive appetition, the human person is oriented to those particular material things that in some way he finds either suitable or not to him personally speaking. By his intellectual appetite, he is oriented to all beings, and not just to those that are materially realized, as they are understood to be good (or not) in themselves and not primarily in relation to him. By his appetitive powers, the human person is thus drawn to or averted from all the things that can be known by way of his cognitive powers. Lastly, there are those powers required for self-movement, those that are required to bring the human person into possession of those things that he knows and has judged to be suitable for him or as such, or to avoid those that are not.

Question 79 takes up the activities of the intellectual cognitive power, which especially characterize and define the soul and life of man.[67] Again, much of what is contained here will seem impenetrable to those who are not familiar with the works of Aristotle concerning intellectual cognition, not to mention the controversies, both ancient and medieval, that surrounded their interpretation. A brief presentation of some of the major points will be sufficient for our purposes.

Articles 2 and 3 state that the intellectual power has both a passive and an active aspect to it. This is something that is not specific to the intellectual power, but characterizes the cognition of man. With respect to his sensitive cognition, it is commonly understood that the human person stands as a passive recipient to the things of his surroundings. The active agent is not so much the person as it is the very thing itself which stands as something that can impress itself, so to speak, upon his five senses and the internal senses of memory, imagination, and the

[67] The sensitive cognitive powers are dealt with in a very summary fashion in Question 78, Articles 3 and 4, and this only according to the roles that they play in both intellectual cognition and more generally in human appetition. Greater detail on sensitive cognition can be found in Thomas's Commentary on Aristotle's *De Anima*.

like. When one approaches the things of one's experience, one discovers that things are not intelligible in themselves. If things were known intellectually simply by beholding them, then there would be no need for schooling, investigation, science, argumentation, or the reading of any book. Such, however, is not the case. Man must perform some kind of activity upon his sensitive cognitive knowledge so that it might reveal the intelligible content that is latent within it. For Aquinas, this is not something that simply requires hard work. There is a stage prior to this whereby the intelligible content that is latent in the things of one's experience must first be revealed if it is to become an object of one's intellectual consideration. In this revealing is found the active component of intellection, something performed by what Aquinas, following Aristotle, calls the *active* or *agent intellect.* This power takes what is passively received in sensitive knowing and "illuminates" or "abstracts" its intelligible content so that it can then be investigated by what is called the *passive* or *patient intellect.* Thus, what has been illuminated by the active intellect is "impressed" so to speak upon the passive intellect that then "beholds" what has been "illuminated" and can then begin to investigate that with which it has been impressed. The intellectual activity over which the human person has control is exerted by the passive intellect, the agent intellect being compared to a light that "reveals" the material that will occupy the passive intellect. The activity of agent intellect, therefore, is not creative, but is that which simply exposes what otherwise would have remained hidden. And what is exposed is itself something that needs to be clarified by the activities of understanding accomplished through definition, the discernment of the truth and falsity of the judgments we make concerning the things one has defined, and finally the validity and ultimately the soundness of one's syllogistic reasoning concerning what one has defined and judged. What is it that one attains through one's intellectual activity? Nothing other than the form of the thing, that which makes it to be the kind of thing that it is, as was described above. Thus, in one's experience of many men and women, one goes from the sensitive knowledge of "this man" to "man" through the activity of the agent intellect which makes the form "man" available to the mind so that it can then be penetrated further, revealing over time and through the engagement of many minds and the cooperation of intellectual communities and traditions, its very depths and riches, that is to say, the very nature or essence of "man." Herein is found the possibility of human language where words are used to point to what has been made available to the human person through the agent and passive intellect. When the intellect is turned to knowing without any view to the application of what has been discovered, Thomas refers to this as the *speculative intellect,* that is to say, the intellect working in such a fashion that it simply wishes to discover the essences and purposes of the things to which it is turned. When, however, it turns to the application of what it knows, either to the making of a product or to the doing of some action, he refers to the *practical intellect,* that is to say, the intellect working for the sake of the realization in one's doing or making what it has beheld in its speculative investigations. Nevertheless, it is the same intellectual power that acts in these ways, and not two distinct powers. In like fashion, intellectual memory is not a distinct power of the intellect but rather the intellect in its capacity of retaining the ideas or concepts that have been revealed by the agent intellect and impressed upon and investigated by the passive intellect. Lastly, conscience is again not a separate power of the intellect, but the name given to the reasoning process of the practical intellect as one decides how to act in a given moral situation.

Questions 80 through 82 deal with both the sensitive and intellectual appetitive powers of man. These are treated separately from the cognitive powers by reason of the fact that although knowledge is required in every act of appetition (how can one desire what one does not know?), nevertheless this knowledge alone is not sufficient to draw one into action; there must be some evaluation performed upon this knowledge in order for what is regarded initially as true, can be seen as good, which then can become the object of one's desire and consequently the cause of impulsion. Thomas explains appetition as an inclination on one's part that arises consequent upon some form. The most basic form that the living being enjoys is that of its soul, that first form which makes it to be what it is, and makes possible all the powers and the activities in which it can engage according to its kind. It is with the latter powers or potentialities that the first form of appetition, the *natural appetite,* arises, specifically insofar as each power is inclined by its very nature or constitution to something in which it will find its activation, actualization, and perfection. For example, if we take the sense of hearing, we understand that it is so constituted in its nature as to have a natural inclination to its proper object, namely to sound. In the presence of sound, hearing is activated, that is to say, made actual, and thus fully realized in its nature. Thus, one could say that hearing has a "natural appetite" for sound, that it "desires" or is naturally inclined to sound, and this for the sake of hearing's own act or perfection as a power. Natural appetite, then, is not about the actualization of the being who has these powers, but rather is about the actualization of these powers themselves, the natural inclination of these powers to those objects that will activate and complete them, an inclination that is rooted in and is a manifestation of the very nature of the power involved. Thus, this kind of appetite is purely passive, one that is necessarily oriented to a particular object and is necessarily activated in its presence. We might speak, then, of this appetite as being automatic or instinctual. This appetite is certainly part of the existence and definition of every power, and is something common to all forms of life.

The form that is central to sensitive appetition is that which is supplied by sensitive cognition, namely the individual material thing of one's experience. Now, how is it that the things of one's experience can be considered here as forms giving rise to the inclinations of sensitive appetition? This is a point of Thomas's theory of knowledge that requires more space than is available here to explain properly. To foster the reader's initial understanding of this, consider that in every act of cognition there is an acquisition, an interiorization, a uniting of the knower with the thing known. Clearly, the knower does not take on the matter of the thing to be known, nor the very existence of the thing in question. The matter and the existence proper to the thing to be known is its own, as is the matter and the existence of the knower himself. What is left, then, is the formal principle of the thing to be known, that which determines it to be what it is and to possess those powers appropriate to its kind. Cognition, for Thomas, is accomplished by taking on the forms of things and becoming them, not really but rather intentionally. In this, the knower does not know through the beholding of the images of things that flash by him, as if he were a patron in a theater watching a film. Instead, he is said to behold things as they are in themselves, and this as he has become them intentionally speaking. This is how Thomas understands Aristotle's declaration at *De anima* III. 8 that the soul is potentially all things sensible and intelligible.

Now the sensitive appetite is not a purely passive appetite, as was noted previously; the simple knowledge of things does not guarantee desire with respect to them. There needs to be some sort of evaluation performed concerning the object of one's knowledge, specifically that it is judged to be suitable (or not) to the one who is sensing it. Thus, for both the animal and the human person who both enjoy sensitive cognition, there can follow a sensitive appetition with respect to the things, people, and situations of their experience insofar as they are judged to be good for them personally speaking. Only insofar as this evaluation is made is the sensitive appetite supplied with its proper object, which then leads to its activation. Thus, the sensitive appetite is both active and passive; one is under no necessity to desire the things of one's experience *until* they have been evaluated as suitable for the one knowing them. In the animal, this evaluation is performed naturally and instinctively by what Thomas calls the *estimative* power, which operates in a like manner in the human person, but since this power can be influenced by the higher intellectual power as it exists within and arises from the intellectual soul, Thomas will call this power the *cogitative* to recognize this state of affairs.

Since there is the evaluation of suitability, the sensitive appetite manifests a more complex inclination in the manner in which it can direct the one who possesses this appetite to the things, people, and situations of its experience. Thomas speaks of a twofold manifestation of the nature of sensitive appetition. First, there is the striving to acquire those things judged as suitable for one's being and life, and the avoiding of those things judged as unsuitable to life and limb. Secondly, there is an active resistance exhibited in sensitive appetition when one seeks to overcome any difficulty that is associated with the seeking of the suitable or avoiding the unsuitable. Thomas refers to the former as the concupiscible aspect of sensitive appetition, and to the latter as the irascible aspect. The concupiscible appetite concerns those goods and evils in which there is little or no difficulty involved in their pursuit or avoidance respectively. The irascible moment of appetition arises once one adds the notion of difficulty to the good that is pursued or to the evil that is avoided. The concupiscible is thus prior to and more basic than the irascible, with the irascible arising out of and terminating in the concupiscible, acting as a helper, as it were, to the concupiscible when, as they say, the going gets tough. In situations where there is no difficulty in the pursuit of good or avoidance of evil, the concupiscible aspect is sufficient. More will be said concerning the sensitive appetite when we treat of the *secunda pars,* where it will be shown that the basic emotions that the human person experiences constitute a further manifestation of the architecture, so to speak, of sensitive appetition, where the basic emotions of both animal and man are the varied moments, if you will, of the concupiscible and irascible appetites, something that in man will become the very material upon which the virtues work, specifically the cardinal virtues of temperance and fortitude.

That these matters are so reflects the fact that the human person can manifest a certain rational control over his sensitive appetition, an issue that Thomas addresses directly in Question 81, Article 3. The nature of this control is not akin to the "despotic" rule that one exercises over one's own person. As stated earlier, the evaluation of suitability is not something that is wholly determined by reason itself, but is effected properly through the cogitative power, a power belonging to the sensitive cognitive powers. Thus, reason can influence sensitive appetition as it works through or in conjunction with the cogitative power to which the sensitive appetite directly corresponds, resulting in a "monarchical" rule of the affective life by reason. In this, Thomas suggests the image of a ruler exerting his power over his free subject, as opposed to the rule that one exerts over one's own property. This reflects the fact that the sensitive appetite has something of its own, a power of its own whereby it can resist the command of the higher power of reason. The importance of this lies in the fact that the concupiscible and irascible aspects of human sensitive appetition thus need to be properly guided and formed by the rearing and education that one receives, so that the sensitive appetite does not seek only that to which it is naturally inclined, but that it serves the greater and higher goals of the human person. Herein lies the main thrust of the ethical disciplines, to discern the good of the whole person and to align all aspects of this person so that this good might be achieved. The sensitive appetite seeks its own good, and is the basis for man's emotional life. But the perfection of this appetite is found only in relation to the one who possesses it. Thus, through the habituation, education, and training that can be received only through a community centered on the good of being human will this appetite cooperate in the ethical adventure of man. The proximate means whereby this is attained are the moral virtues, specifically temperance (perfecting the concupiscible aspect) and fortitude (perfecting the irascible aspect), as already noted above.

Questions 82 and 83 deal with the intellectual appetite, the will, and its role in free choice. We begin, once again, with the form consequent upon which the intellectual appetite arises. This is provided by intellectual cognition, and will thus deal with the intelligibility and universality of things, and not their materiality or particularity. And just as the sensitive appetite was engaged only insofar as its object was judged suitable (or not) for the one sensing, so too must there be some evaluation performed upon the object of intellectual cognition. This evaluation is in keeping with the nature of the form presented, namely that it is considered with respect to its goodness simply speaking, and not primarily as good in reference to the one considering it, as was the case with sensitive appetition. This constitutes the natural appetite of the will that it desires goodness absolutely considered in itself, and, as with all natural appetition, this inclination is definitive of the very nature of the will and is the condition of its existence and operation. This is the will's only determination; whatever it desires must be desired be reason of the object's goodness. The will, then, is moved necessarily only if reason can provide it with something that is perfectly or universally good, that is to say, goodness itself. However, if what is presented to the will is not perfectly good, then the will is not moved necessarily with respect to it. This is not to say that the will cannot be moved with respect to such things; it most certainly can. The point is that this inclination remains within the power of the person possessed of will. One has the choice whether to bind oneself to the good that is presented to one by the intellect. With respect, then, to any goods that are relative to or participate of an absolute good, the will is not determined to follow these in the same way that the sensitive appetite was in the presence of those goods that were deemed suitable to the one possessing this appetite. An example of an absolute good would be one's happiness; everyone, as Aristotle states at the beginning of his *Nicomachean Ethics,* desires to be happy—such is not an object of choice but a determination that is basic to man's being, that in which his perfection resides, that for the sake of which he does all that he does. The problem, naturally, is to discern that in which man's happiness consists, and then to select the means whereby this might be attained. These latter are indeed objects of choice, and are thus something to which one is not necessarily bound, but are those things to which one determines oneself freely, without coercion.

One can see, then, the difference between the desire of the sensitive appetite and that of the will. The former directs or orients the individual to things only insofar as they exist under the conditions of matter, as particular material things judged as suitable (or not) for the one sensing them. The latter, however, desires things as they exist apart from their materiality and according to their form alone. This is important, for it explains how it is that a human person can desire and love such things as truth, justice, and beauty, things that are only met and understood properly at the level of his intelligence. This is not to say, however, that the will cannot regard particular material things. It can and does, but not in the same fashion as does sensitive appetition, namely as they are particular and material goods suitable to one. Rather, the will can desire such things as they are instances or representations of a good to which the will is bound properly. Thus, if one thirsts for justice, then one can intellectually desire and love those particular actions that exhibit this quality, or people who embody this virtue in all that they do, or a political party or leader whose policies preserve, protect, and promote justice in one's country.

When one, then, considers the matter of free choice, one can see that it is a complex thing, extending beyond the reach of the will itself. That free choice or free will exists is, for Thomas, something that is evident from the life of man considered both in its individual and societal manifestation. For if there were no free choice, then "counsels, exhortations, commands, prohibitions, rewards, and punishments would be in vain," which is to say, all ethical endeavors at both the personal and communal levels. Being rational frees the human person from the sheer determinacy of matter, a determinacy that nonetheless manifests wholly at his physiological level but only partially at the sensitive. The human person finds that he exercises no direct control over the workings of his physiology. At best, he can influence it indirectly through exercise, diet, a healthy lifestyle, and other such activities that allow the body and its physiology to perform at an optimum level. With respect to his sensitive aspect, the situation is mixed, as we have seen. Unlike the animal, which is wholly determined in its estimation and its appetition, the human person can influence both of these in important ways, and these only insofar as his sensitive aspect is realized within his rationality, that is to say, as his sensitive aspect does not constitute the height of his being, but rather is an integral aspect of the realization of his rational soul, something that arises from, or exists within, or participates of, his rational life. It is not the case that human beings are simply animals with reason somehow tacked on, if you will. This approach is far too dualistic in nature to represent adequately Thomas's views on the matter. As was stated earlier, all that is found within the living thing is a manifestation of all that is implied in its kind, in its soul. Thus, once again, we do not find that dualistic opposition between reason and one's animality, but see, rather, that being rational, for the human person, manifests animality, an animality that is altered in such a way that our memory, imagination, estimation, sensation, emotions, and desires, although still animal in nature, manifest an activity that betokens their realization within the very life of reason itself, sometimes to the point of even warranting a change in name (as was the case for estimation in the animal, now becoming cogitation or particular reason in the human person; memory likewise receives the further name of reminiscence in man). Thus, the human person can importantly influence his estimations both prior to his sensitive appetition,

and also posterior to it. In like manner, although the movements of our animal desires and emotions are in some fashion
instinctual, they are not wholly so, since we can influence their
antecedent arousal, as well as how they play out once aroused.
In short, being rational allows the human person to have an
important control over what is a matter of sheer determinacy
in the animal; reason frees one from the tyranny, so to speak,
of one's animality, and allows, as was stated earlier, for the
establishment of a monarchy. All of this is possible only insofar as reason and will are not determined to anything other
than those things that allow them to be and to operate as the
powers that they are, the intellect to being and truth, and the
will to the good itself. Thus, although in a free choice, there
is an important role played by reason in its supplying of the
proper object of the will, an intelligible form whose goodness
reason has revealed, as something worthy of pursuit, nonetheless the pursuit does not arise simply from this knowledge but
requires another power, the will, so that this pursuit might be
realized. Thus, we have counsel on the part of reason, and the
act of acceptance of what has been counselled on the part of
the will. Free choice, then, is a desire proceeding from counsel,
the directedness that one personally and freely determines with
respect to the means whereby one might attain to some good
or end, as was discussed above. In this regard, one might consider free choice to be a refinement of one's willing the good,
a refinement that occurs insofar as the intellect is brought to
bear upon the good in view, and the many and diverse ways
by which it might be achieved. Thomas will talk in far greater
detail of the moments involved, if you will, in the properly
human choice later in the *prima secundae.*

Thomas turns his attention, in Questions 84 through 89, to
the activities of the intellectual cognitive power, specifically
how it understands things that are of a material nature, and are
thus unlike it (as it itself is immaterial—Questions 84 through
86), how it understands itself and what is contained within it
(87), and finally how it understands those things that are of
an immaterial nature (88 through 89). Given the introductory
nature of the present work, as well as its intended theological
audience, and having already offered a very general account
of cognition both here and earlier when treating of the human

person's knowledge of the higher things, especially of God Himself, I pass over this section and encourage the reader to consider the many and fine works that deal with Thomas's views concerning the processes involved in human intellectual knowledge.[68]

The second part of the treatise on human nature (Questions 90 through 102) treats of the creation of the first human beings (90 through 93), and the state of their persons prior to their fall into sin (94 through 102). With respect to the former, Thomas considers the creation of the human soul, the first man's body, and then that of the woman (90 through 92). These questions are of limited interest today in part due to the influence that the biology and science of the day have upon them, disciplines that were in their incipient stages at that time. Question 93, however, is of great importance. For it deals with the end point, so to speak, in the creation of man, that he is made "to the image and likeness of God," something that, among other things, will figure prominently in the transition from the *prima pars* to the *secunda pars*.

One should note, first, the placement of this question.[69] In dealing with the "end or term" of the creation of the human person, Thomas is drawing attention to something more than just the finished state of the being of man, that state consequent upon his creation. He refers to his first form or actuality, that which establishes him as a particular kind of being, ready to engage in all that has now become possible to his kind. Although this was treated in the first section of the treatise on human nature when he examined the soul and its nature, this should not be considered as an addition particular to theology, a contribution tacked on, if you will, to the so-called "philosophical treatment" of man in Questions 75 through 89. This, as was argued earlier, would mistake Thomas's intention and method of approach. For while it is an extremely worthwhile and viable project to consider (and even develop) his philosophical views concerning the human person, one must always begin with his own theological context and ordering of materials, as has been described in the prior

---

[68] For example, Part III of Pasnau (2002), and Chapter 8 of Stumpf (2003).

[69] In what follows, I depend in large part upon Chapter 4 of Torrell (1996; 2003), and Merriell (2005), pp. 123–142.

chapter and above, if one is to retain the fullness of his views concerning human nature and benefit from them in their modern applications. Thus, the questions that form the second part of this treatise contribute importantly to the matters dealt with in the first, with Question 93 supplying what is a "key concept in Aquinas' theological anthropology."[70]

The first article affirms the biblical testimony that the image of God is in man, a likeness expressive of his creator, albeit imperfectly (for Christ alone is the perfect Image of God). In trying to explain what "image" implies here, Thomas states, in Article 2, that an image is realized in a likeness of species, where this likeness is either based upon a similarity between two things of the same kind (thus the image of the father exists in his son), or is according to some accident that is proper to them, particularly, Thomas states, their shape (thus the image of the father is said to be in a painting or a sculpture). Utilizing the latter of the two (which effectively incorporates the distance between the exemplar and the image, as well as the creative aspect involved in the producing of the image), Thomas states that a thing is like God as it exists, lives, and knows or understands. It is with respect to the last of these, in knowing or understanding, that the image of God is best found in man. This image, however, is not manifested solely in what one might call a static manner according to his first form or actuality, as if one were to say that man's nature simply described as rational and volitional were descriptive wholly of what it means for him to be created in the image and likeness of God. Rather, this image is most perfectly realized as the rational creature imitates the dynamic intellectual nature of God specifically insofar as God actively understands and loves Himself. Consequently,

> we see that the image of God is in man in three ways. First, inasmuch as man possesses a natural aptitude for understanding and loving God; and this aptitude consists in the very nature of the mind, which is common to all men. Secondly, inasmuch as man actually or habitually knows and loves God, though imperfectly; and this image consists

[70] Merriell (2005), p. 124 referencing the work of twentieth century scholars, particularly that of Ghislain Lafont.

in the conformity of grace. Thirdly, inasmuch as man knows and loves God perfectly; and this image consists in the likeness of glory. Wherefore on the words, *The light of Thy countenance, O Lord, is signed upon us* (Ps. 4.7), the gloss distinguishes a three-fold image, of *creation,* of *re-creation,* and of *likeness.* The first is found in all men, the second only in the just, the third only in the blessed.[71]

But the human person also manifests the image of God according to the Trinity insofar as there is in him "a procession of the word in the intellect and a procession of love in the will,"[72] something that further emphasizes the importance of the realization of all that man finds himself to be, particularly in the intellectual, moral, and theological virtues, those means, which we shall soon see in the *secunda pars,* by which the human person not only perfects his nature, but also now, in light of the above, aspires to the image of God that he is. The rest of creation also manifests the Divine nature and the Trinity, not in image but in vestige, as an effect pointing to its cause, but in such a way that the effect fails to aspire to the representation afforded by the image. With respect, then, to the animals lacking reason, a trace of the divine intelligence can be found in what Thomas calls their disposition, presumably the determination of their natures which give rise to an activity not only particular to their kind but which seemingly involves order, purpose and thus some form of reason, albeit extrinsic to their type, but exemplified in the character of their behavior, what we might call instinctual activity. With respect to the trace of the Trinity in creatures other than those that are rational, Thomas states that

> the fact that a creature has a modified and finite nature shows that it proceeds from a principle; while its species points to the word of the maker, just as the shape of a house points to the idea of the architect; and order points to the maker's love by reason of which he directs the effect to a good end; as also the use of the house points to the will of the architect.[73]

[71] ST. I. 93. 4.
[72] ST. I. 93. 6.
[73] ST. I. 93. 6.

With regard to man, however, the case is far more direct: the image of the Trinity is found primarily in that way by which he imperfectly represents in his knowing and loving the processions of the Word and Love in God, and secondarily in the powers that give rise to this activity and the habits and virtues that perfect them. And the summit, if you will, of this activity and thus of the very image of God that man is, is found not just with respect to any sort of knowing, and the consequent love that breaks forth from it. It is found when it is concerned with the very object of which it is an image, namely God Himself. In the knowledge of God, then, man's contemplation generates that internal word most worthy to be pondered and most fitting to the nature of that which generates it, something which results in that most perfect realization of the very image of God that defines his nature: what begins with the natural constitution of the nature of man, is quickened in the lives of the just by the gift of grace, and fully realized in the blessed as they receive the very gift of God Himself in the beatific vision.

In these descriptions, one can readily discern their importance, at the very least, for the course that remains to the *Summa*. If man is made to the image and likeness of God, and that this implies specifically that he is the master of both his knowing and his loving, that he is "an intelligent being endowed with free-will and self-movement," then it is required on the part of the theologian to articulate the means whereby this image in man might be realized fully, that God might come to dwell in him.[74] This is something that is accomplished, in large part, by the *secunda pars* as it bears directly upon the way by which man might be oriented in the fullness of his being, acting, and feeling to the possession of God, in which his perfection and happiness exist. In like manner, the *tertia pars* provides, among other things, that perfect image of God, namely of Christ, as the way by which man might realize most perfectly the image of God that he is. At the foundation of these uses, however, is the fact that man is formed in the very image of God Himself, something that accounts for the human person's insatiable

[74] For a proper development of the themes of man's assimilation to the Trinity and the indwelling of the Trinity in him, see Merriell (2005), pp. 132–138.

thirst for God as his completion and happiness insofar as he finds himself to be ontologically and psychologically oriented to God at the core of his being, something that is well described by both Merriell and Torrell. The human person, then, from the theologian's perspective, is not simply approached as the philosopher might do so, namely in light of his "constant, unchanging nature," but rather in light of that "dynamic of movement from and to God," the *exitus et reditus* that was discussed above and in the first chapter of this work.[75]

Thomas finishes the treatise on man by considering the state of the race's parents prior to their fall into sin (94 through 102). This treatment is fascinating if only for the insight that it affords us into the pre-fallen operation of their persons, and by extension, of human nature, as God had created it to be. Thomas states that the first parents did not enjoy the beatific vision (for if they had, it would not have been possible for them to have fallen into sin—the same has been said of the angels consequent to their creation). Nonetheless, their understanding of God was greater than that enjoyed by man after the fall since their minds and wills were not troubled by the many and diverse things that afflict the fallen, especially a disordered affective experience. Right order and self-government existed in the person of man at all levels in the state of innocence, making their insight into God, through their experience of the things of creation, that much more precise and profound.[76] This depth extended to the things that they could know concerning the world, but was not perfect in detail or complete in scope.[77] The rectitude of their condition, namely of their minds to God, their sensitive and vegetative aspects to their reason, and their bodies to their souls, was a condition graced to them in their creation, and was not something implicit in their nature. The first of these subjections was key, giving rise to the other two.[78] This had a particular effect upon the range of their affective life. Since they did they not suffer evil, they did not experience those emotions that have evil as their object (for example, fear

[75] Merriell (2005), p. 123.
[76] ST. I. 94. 1.
[77] ST. I. 94. 2–3.
[78] ST. I. 95. 1.

and sorrow). Neither did they want for any good in a disordered fashion, thus avoiding the experience of concupiscence. Instead, they experienced their love and joy (with regard to the goods they had), and desire and hope (for those goods yet to come) in a way that was in complete conformity with their reason, and lacking, therefore, the disease and rebellion that characterizes fallen man's affective life.[79] In this rectitude, the first parents enjoyed every virtue in keeping with the perfection of their innocent state.[80]

Their mastery extended to all created things beneath them. All animals obeyed them, although among the animals there existed a certain "natural antipathy" insofar as those that are now carnivorous would also have been so before the fall, the sin of man not affecting their respective natures. However, the first parents had no need for the flesh of animals for their food, their hides for their clothing, or their bodies for their conveyance (they had food aplenty in paradise, no need for clothing, and bodies strong enough for their own transport).[81] While they did not exercise this mastery either over vegetative life or the natural forces of creation, they were able to use them "without hindrance."[82] As for the relations that existed among their own kind, there would have been inequality, specifically with respect to age, sex, parents, children, virtue, knowledge, strength, beauty, and other such things, since the first parents (or people in this question) would have enjoyed the full and free use of their faculties, and would have been subject to the principles of nature, giving rise to variation in all things bodily, but not to the point of giving rise to defect, as is the case in the fallen state.[83] Finally, there would have been a social order and thus a hierarchy of the governing to the governed in the prelapsarian state, a government that would have directed all toward their "proper welfare, or to the common good," and would have lacked all defects that are common to any and all governments since the fall itself.[84]

---

[79] ST. I. 95. 2.
[80] ST. I. 95. 3.
[81] ST. I. 96. 1, ad2 and ad3.
[82] ST. I. 96. 2.
[83] ST. I. 96. 3.
[84] ST. I. 96. 4.

With respect to his bodily condition, the first parents were immortal not by reason of something intrinsic to their nature, but rather by the grace that God gave to their soul "whereby it was enabled to preserve the body from all corruption so long as it remained itself subject to God."[85] In like manner, although material and therefore subject in nature to the reception of things both ill and good, the former would not have occurred to the first parents by God's grace (in the case of the unforeseen) and their own prudence (in the case of those things that they could foresee and thus avoid), while the latter would have happened, insofar as this would have been part of their natural activities and growth.[86] They would have taken food according to their need, something that, Thomas states, will not be the case after the general resurrection of the dead at the end of time, an indication that the heavenly beatitude cannot simply be described as a return to the paradisal state, but, rather, to something different and greater.[87] As for procreation, such would have occurred in the pre-fallen state, and this by way of coition, which, indeed, would have been pleasurable, but an experience in accord with the virtue they would have possessed, a virtue which would have prevented the reduction of this experience to that of the animals lacking reason, and deterred them from dwelling excessively and immoderately upon the pleasure involved and seeking it out in a wanton fashion. Thomas compares this to the experience of the temperate person who "does not take less pleasure in food taken in moderation than the glutton" but whose "concupiscence lingers less in such pleasures," where the pleasure is experienced rightly and to the full (and perhaps even more than the glutton is capable of), but all within the rule of virtue and reason.[88] Their offspring would very likely have been much like our own, being either male or female, and exhibiting the powers and activities that we would expect.[89] They would have enjoyed the same condition as their parents did, receiving the same graces, language and reasoning

---

[85] ST. I. 97. 1.
[86] ST. I. 97. 2 and ad4.
[87] ST. I. 97. 3.
[88] ST. I. 98. 1–2.
[89] ST. I. 99. 1–2.

abilities spoken of above, and these in due time according to the requirements of their nature.[90] Their final confirmation in righteousness, and that of their parents', would have been something attained only through the beatific vision of God's essence, something which, once gifted, would have caused them to "but cleave to Him Who is the essence of goodness, where-from no one can turn away." In this vision, they "would have become spiritual in soul and body; and (their) animal life would have ceased."[91] Until such time, though, the human race would have continued in the condition and manner described above, abiding in an earthly paradise, suited to their condition, pre-serving them in their immortality, and keeping them from all evil, a place that they could adorn with pleasure and in which they could become sanctified, "having attained to the spiritual life" and to then "be transferred thence to heaven."[92]

The portrait of the prelapsarian state is marked by its nor-malcy, that is to say, that it is recognizable and not something that belongs to the realm of the fantastic: man seeks out knowl-edge; exercises his will; engages in the pleasures of life; gets married; begets and rears children; engages in social activities; develops forms of governance; takes up his responsibilities in many and diverse areas; has an aesthetic sense; and seeks to know, to love, and be united to God. That this is so arises out of Thomas's view that "what is natural to man was neither acquired nor forfeited by sin,"[93] but was intended originally by God in the creation of the human person. Original sin[94] is something, then, that did not destroy the nature of man. Rather, it disor-dered his nature by destroying the harmony that was essential to his original rectitude, namely, between soul and body, rea-son and his animal life, and God and himself, with the latter being that upon which the prior two depended, as mentioned above. Thomas compares this to the situation where sickness introduces disorder into the body's nature through the destruc-tion of the equilibrium essential to its health. The sickness itself

---

[90] ST. I. 100. 1 and 101. 1–2.
[91] ST. I. 100. 2.
[92] ST. I. 102. 3, and 1–2.
[93] ST. I. 98. 2.
[94] dealt with at ST. I-II. 81–83 in the treatise concerning sin or vice.

neither creates nor destroys the nature of the body or the order that characterizes it. Instead, it impedes the proper functioning of the body by introducing something that disrupts the very balance of the varied systems required for its full and proper functioning.[95] The difference, however, is that, unlike the body, this equilibrium, so essential to the perfect life of man, was not an aspect of his created nature, but rather was gifted to him by God (for if this had not been the case then its loss with the fall of man would have meant the destruction of human nature). With the fall, this was lost. As Rudi te Velde states:

> Adam remained a human being, but what he had lost was the ability, by God's grace, to preserve in the actual exercise of his life the right order between the different parts of human nature. After his own disobedience to God, he felt "the impulse of disobedience in the flesh, as though it were a punishment." The life of the passions was no longer the obedient expression of man's self and of his rational freedom; instead, the passions seemed to act like another self. The same applied to the body, of which man became aware, no longer as a harmonious part of the human self, but as a loathsome burden which causes trouble and pain and is subject to sickness and death.[96]

This is a fitting way by which to complete the treatise on man, that is, with its culmination in Question 93 in the discussion concerning man made to the image of God, and then seeing how this manifested in his living before his fall, something that offers an affirmation of the goodness of man's very nature described throughout the treatise, but with an eye to the disharmony introduced by sin into his nature and life. The stage is set, then, to consider the means of return, the means whereby this harmony might be restored both through the activities in which he is called to engage as image of God, that is, as "an intelligent being endowed with free-will and self-movement," and the gift of his redemption effected through the person of

---

[95] ST. I-II. 82. 1.
[96] Velde (2005), pp. 158–159. The quote from Aquinas is from ST. I. 95. 1 and is a quote from Augustine's *De Civitate Dei* xiii.13.

Jesus Christ and His salvific act. In this, man is reoriented to that life in which he might find his perfection and happiness, a reorientation that begins to effect the healing of the disorder and disharmony that has afflicted his life since the fall, so that he might begin to live toward the very same thing for which pre-fallen man hoped, namely for the grace of union with God, his beatitude.[97]

Treatise on the Divine Government (Questions 103–119)

Having detailed the *exitus* of all things from God, Thomas completes the *prima pars* by considering God's governance over all that He has created. Not only is this a fitting completion to the *prima pars*, detailing how God, in light of all that He is in both essence and Trinity, governs all creation, but it also establishes the manner in which, generally speaking, we are to understand the *reditus* of all things to their Creator, a theme that will be taken up in a very definite manner in relation to the human person in the *secunda pars*.

The treatise divides into two parts, the first being a general consideration of the government of things (Question 103) and the second looking to the effects of this government (Questions 104 through 119). The first three questions of this treatise are central insofar as they deal directly with the manner in which the creation that God has effected is ordered, preserved, and changed. The remainder of the treatise offers details concerning the roles that the angels, man, and the material aspect of creation play in the governance of creation, specifically in light of the real causality that each of these exerts, the whole of efficient causality not being reserved to God alone but shared, by His will, throughout the whole of creation. And so, with respect to the angels, we learn of the various hierarchies or orders that exist among them, their relations with each other, their interactions with the corporeal universe, and their ministry to and guardianship of man (Questions 106–114). The influence of bodies is examined in Questions 115 and 116, while the action of human beings in general and their actual production are treated in Questions 117 through 119. Given that these latter

---

[97] For a more detailed treatment of this line of thought, consider Velde (2005).

questions suffer from the same characteristics that were noted in the above treatment on the work of the six days of creation, and that some of the details here, specifically those that concern the angels, are of limited interest, I will concentrate upon the first three questions of this treatise, and in light of them, make general reference to the treatise's remaining questions.[98]

Thomas's description of governance does not make primary reference to the absolute exercise of the power of God, but rather looks to this power as it provides the means whereby those governed might come to their true end and good, and thus the happiness of the governed might be attained and enjoyed. He sees clear signs of this in all the things of creation, most especially as they seek to manifest their natures through the pursuit of those goods that are appropriate to them. The fact that these natures have been so constituted so as to pursue their respective goods, which latter have been abundantly supplied and to which they are led readily for the most part, is for Thomas not only a definitive sign of the governance of creation, but also something that manifests ever so clearly the goodness of God the governor, a point that is especially emphasized as the governor provides for and leads all things to that good in which is found theirs ultimate perfection. Thus, the consequent order that is exhibited in the things of creation, their stability in both nature and operation, and the impulsion even of those things lacking knowledge to those goods in which they might manifest fully their nature all speak of the goodness of God and of His governance.[99] As He is the ultimate good, and therefore that from Whom all other things derive their goodness by participation, all creation is directed ultimately to Him as that in which all things under His governance find the perfection of their natures, the unity of their individual and collective being, and the realization of their purpose and peace.[100] In this,

---

[98] See Gilson (1956; 1994), pp. 168–173 for a summary of the distinctions among the angels, and the appendices to Volume 15 (1970) of the Blackfriars Edition of the *Summa Theologiae* for some of the matters dealt with in Questions 115 through 119.

[99] ST. I. 103. 1, ad. 1 and ad. 2.

[100] ST. I. 103. 2 and 3. One cannot but help recall the biblical verse that all creation groans in expectation of its Lord, yearns for its completion in His advent.

the creature, so ordered by God's good governance, becomes like Him not only in its being and nature, but also in the activity that it can effect, causing good in other things as good has been caused in it by its Creator. Thus, as God effects the preservation of things in their goodness and moves them so that good might be communicated to others, so too do the things of creation so constituted act as their respective natures allow.[101]

This gives rise to the question in Article 6: if all things are so governed by God, does He Himself immediately effect this governance? Or, do things other than God, things created by Him and having their own natures and their own respective activities, take an important role in His governance of the world? The objections argue the former as the latter position would seem to imply some defect on the part of God's ruling power. For

it seems to be imperfect in a ruler to govern by means of others; thus an earthly king, by reason of his not being able to do everything himself, and because he cannot be everywhere at the same time, requires to govern by means of ministers.[102]

In his reply, Thomas states that there are two things to be considered in every governance, namely, its design or plan and the execution of it. The first is something to be attributed to God alone who, in His governance of the whole of creation, is the only being whose knowledge extends to all aspects of creation, from its highest and most universal principles, to the lowest and most particular details of every single individual thing, in light of which knowledge He governs all things well, that is, to their good and perfection, and this immediately. However, in the execution of this design, God employs created things in the effecting of His governance of creation. For the good and the perfection of those things governed is something achieved when these things are allowed to become "causes of goodness in others" rather than just being good in themselves. Thus, Thomas states that "God so governs things that He makes some of them to be causes of others in government; as a master, who not only imparts knowledge to his pupils, but gives also the faculty of

[101] ST. I. 103. 4.
[102] ST. I. 103. 6. obj. 3.

teaching to others." In this imparting of the very nature of God's goodness to His creatures, so that they might act in imitation of Him from the natural manifestation of their natures up to and including the rational and freely effected actions of their intelligence consequent upon their knowledge of the highest of things, the good and the perfection of the universe is demonstrated and achieved. All things, from the angels down to the most lowly of physical principles, show forth the excellence of the Creator as they partake in the very causality that is implicit in the very being of God Himself, that is, in effecting goodness in their actions in conformity to and in service of the very design of creation itself. This very fact points to what Gilson describes as the immensity of God's goodness, that God, who could clearly effect the governance of creation through His own power, nonetheless determines that created things themselves should, for the sake of their own good and perfection, partake in the real governance of the universe that God has effected through His loving act of creation. God's governance of creation so described thus manifests, for Gilson, the way by which the infinite goodness of God is effectively communicated. In this, love becomes "the unfathomable source of all causality."[103]

A similar point is made in Question 104 concerning the first effect of the divine governance, namely the preservation of the being of all created things.[104] The first article argues that the entirety of a created thing's nature and being, and all activity that is consequent upon these, are preserved in their existence by the continuous and intentional exercise of the Divine power, in the absence of which a thing would simply cease to be. This is a direct consequence of the contingency of its being, the fact that it is not its own existence, but has this only insofar as it is participated, that is, gifted to it by that Being who is Being itself.[105] Is it the case, then, that the preservation of each and every

---

[103] Gilson (1956; 1994), p. 183. One should consider Gilson's whole discussion of the reality and importance of secondary causality in pp. 178–186 to gain the full impact of the teaching Thomas presents here.

[104] The second effect is the kinds of change that God can effect among his created things (105), something that, in light of the share that all created things have in the governance of creation, is extended to the angels (106–115), to physical things (115–116), and lastly to man himself (117–119).

[105] ST. I. 104. 1 and 3.

being is immediately effected by God Himself? Or, do created things play some active role in the preservation of other created beings? This is the concern of the second article of Question 104. Thomas responds that while God is the principal cause of the preservation of the existence of every thing, nonetheless having established an order among the things of His creation, an order which makes some things depend upon others for their preservation, it is the case that the created thing shares importantly in this effect of God's governance, something proper to Him according to His nature but shared with others as a consequence of His goodness instilled in all the things that He has made, as was argued previously. This preservation that the created thing participates is manifested in two ways, first indirectly, insofar as one removes or at least hinders the influence of some cause that threatens the life of the thing in question, and secondly, directly, insofar as one partakes of the causal relations involved in the very preservation of a thing's being. Thus, although one, in such a causal series, does not occupy the primary position reserved properly to God, nonetheless, according to the design of creation and the governance of it as established by God, secondary causes play an essential role in the manifesting of God's preservation of creation, in much the same manner as they do in His overall governance of reality. Such a point is readily understood in the gift of children within marriage, or as a teacher is entrusted with the formation of the minds and hearts of his of her students.

The second effect of God's governance is the change that creatures undergo. Thomas considers in Question 105 the change that is effected upon creatures by God, while the remaining questions of this treatise detail the changes effected by one creature upon another. These remaining questions exist in light of the prior considerations, namely as God has determined an important role that is to played by all things in the execution of His governance of creation, a fact that manifests His power and His goodness, and does not detract from these as some thinkers have argued.[106] In the earlier question concerning God's preservation of the existence of created things, His power is never

[106] See Gilson (1956; 1994), pp. 183–186, especially note 27 on p. 183, and his summation of this point on p. 184.

doubted; God could, if He so wished, turn His will from any created thing resulting in its annihilation—it is well within His power[107]—but He never does. For it is not only the case that all created things have natures that preclude total annihilation (immaterial beings have no potency in their natures for nonexistence, while material beings continue at least with respect to the preservation of their material elements which constitute the subject necessary for their generation and corruption), but that their preservation is a profound manifestation of both the grace, power and goodness of God. In this, we find the clear exhibition of the will of God, and of all the characteristics that we can possibly ascribe to Him, as detailed in the treatises on God and the Trinity. In fact, to argue otherwise might seem to preserve His power, but would in truth "hinder that manifestation, since the power of God is conspicuously shown in His preserving of all things in existence."[108] Thomas affirms, in Question 105, God's direct involvement in the changes effected in the formation of matter and the movement of all bodies.[109] Likewise does God effect the conditions that allow for intellection and volition to arise and their every act to occur.[110] These four questions, once again, raise the issue of the reality of secondary causality, something that Thomas addresses directly in Article 5.

He states that although God does work in all aspects of creation, it is impossible, and contrary to all appearances, to attribute all causality that we observe to Him alone. Not only would this destroy the order, reality, and truth of cause and effect among created things, and thus again imply a lack of power in the Creator to establish such, but it would also give rise to the question "to what purpose is the appearance of cause and effect instilled in the things of creation?" a question that would seem to imply no purpose whatsoever. Gilson puts the matter this way:

> The excellence of the work shows forth the glory of the work-
> man, and how poor indeed would be a world entirely bare of

[107] ST. I. 104. 5.
[108] ST. I. 104. 4. ad. 1.
[109] ST. I. 105. 1–2.
[110] ST. I. 105. 3–4.

efficacy! In the first place, it would be an absurd world. In giving the principal, no one denies the collateral. What sense would there be in creating heavy bodies incapable of moving downwards? If God, in imparting being to things, gave them some likeness to Himself, He ought also to have given them more of this likeness in imparting to them the activity which issues from being, by attributing to them actions of their own.[111]

It must be the case, then, that God works in all things in such a way that these very things have their own proper activities and exercise their own causality. In his explanation of this, Thomas considers the four causes, the material, formal, efficient, and final in light of this question. The material cause is not considered to be a principle of action, but rather is the subject that receives this action. The other three are indeed principles of action, but have a definite order among them: the end or final cause is that first principle that moves the agent or efficient cause to impose the form upon the matter so that the final cause, the reason for the activity of the agent in the first place, might be realized. Now, God acts in every agent according to finality, efficiency, and formality. From what has been written, it is clear that God is the final end of all that the human person does, the ultimate perfection to which all things aspire in their activities. Thus God is, in this sense, the cause of every activity, that is, as its end. Secondly, the fact that an agent acts efficiently is not something that it itself causes. Rather, it is capable of this only as it has been made to act as an efficient cause by some agent acting upon it in this manner. And just as there cannot be an infinite series of agents acting efficiently, but that in the end, all efficient agency is the consequence of that first efficient agent, God Himself, as the second proof for His existence has shown, it must be the case that God is the cause of every activity, that is, as that by virtue of which all things can act as agents or efficient causes. Lastly, the form of each thing, both with respect to its character and its very existence, is a consequence of God's creative activity, something that, as we have seen, is effected continuously by God's will throughout

[111] Gilson (1956; 1994), pp. 181.

eternity. Since all that a being does is dependant upon its form and the beneficence of God's will in its preservation, one can say, then, that God is the cause of its every activity, that is, as the source and the endurance of all that it is and does.[112] One can see, then, that although the work of God effects the work of man, and that man effects this very same work at the same time, it is not in the same respect that these occur, a fact that allows Thomas to avoid a contradiction. As Gilson states,

> When God imparts existence to things, He confers upon them at the same time their form, their movement and their efficacy. Nevertheless, it is to them that this efficacy belongs from the moment they receive it. Hence it is they who perform their operations. The lowest being acts and produces its effect, even though it does so by virtue of all the causes superior to the action it is subjected to and whose efficacy is transmitted to it by degrees. At the head of the series is God, the total and immediate cause of all the effects produced and of all the activity released therein. At the foot comes the natural body, the immediate cause of the proper action which it performs, even though it only performs it by virtue of the efficacy conferred upon it by God.[113]

Conclusion to the Prima Pars

Although it is clear that God governs His creation, and that His love establishes the reality of secondary causality, it is still undetermined how man who is made to the image of God, can effect practically the dynamism implicit in this image as he desires union with his Creator, and thus works toward his perfection and his happiness. Being rational could be described as a blessing and a curse. It is a blessing insofar as man, because of his reason, is freed from the sheer determinacy of his corporeal condition, is freed from the absolute control that his animal and vegetative aspects manifest in beings bereft of reason. As rational, he knows not only where he is going but also why. He is not restricted in his knowing to the individual, material things of his experience, nor to the judgment of the

---

[112] ST. I. 105. 5.
[113] Gilson (1956; 1994), pp. 182–183.

good by his own lights, but possesses the capacity to know the essences and purposes of all things, and to behold their intrinsic goodness. His nobility is clear, particularly in light of his status as *imago Dei,* capable of the processions of both word and love, a thing unique among all material beings in creation. However, the curse, so to speak, of man's situation is that his freedom caries with it the necessity and the responsibility to discover what and why he is, so that in light of this knowledge, he might most effectively orient himself to that in which his good and perfection lie. The nonrational animal has no such worry since it has no choice but to act in full accordance with its kind, determined in its judgments, feelings and behavior, forming an intimate bond with its world, being found quite at home within it. Man, on the other hand, is, by his very nature, not made for this world, as the animal lacking reason is. He is a *viator,* a traveler, whose home consists in God and the heavenly Jerusalem. But such is only generally indicated in his nature: he is free, but does not know precisely for what, his understanding of God and his desire for happiness both being indeterminate, and requiring clarification if they are ever to be attained.

The *prima pars* is admirable if only for the fact that it details this knowledge of God, this wisdom for which man thirsts, a knowledge for which he stands in need, for which the whole of his intellectual traditions strive, but which cannot be articulated adequately due to all the obstacles that were listed in the very first question of the *Summa.* There is, clearly, much more that could be said about the matters dealt with by the *prima pars,* particularly with respect to God's transitive activity in the establishment of His creation, something that will occupy the arts and sciences for as long as they exist. But, as Thomas states at the start of the *Treatise on Man,* only that which is required for the task of theology is treated, and particularly only those matters that contribute to the purpose of the *prima pars,* namely to speak about God both in Himself and as He is the Alpha and the Omega, the beginning of all things and their last end. Nonetheless, the purpose of the *prima pars* in its fulfillment, establishes the necessity of attending to that creature, the human person, who, made to the image of God, requires specific attention and guidance if he is to effect his return to his Creator as his last end. Thus, as Velde argues, the focus of the *prima pars* is now tightened, so to speak, upon one aspect of God's creation and government, namely the human person himself, specifically upon the work that he effects as image of God and thus as "created freedom," something that requires a finer focus upon what this entails on the part of both man and God, a focus that goes beyond the perspective of the *prima pars,* that is to say, of God, creation and His providential governance of it, and now lands upon man, this "special creature, whose freedom requires a new and different way of divine guidance which cannot be thematized from the perspective of creation."[114] It is this with which the *secunda pars* is concerned directly, and to which we now turn.

SECUNDA PARS

The *secunda pars* examines the activity that the human person can perform in his return to God, and thus constitutes what many, including Thomas, have described as the moral part of the *Summa*.[115] It is divided into two parts, the *prima secundae* and the *secunda secundae.* The former treats of the general principles of morality, those that govern or at least impact importantly human activity, while the latter offers a detailed examination of the virtues, both theological and moral, that help to achieve the rectification of human activity and the end of man himself. We proceed, then, as we did before, by dividing our considerations according to the treatises that comprise each section of the *secunda pars.*

Prima Secundae

Given the rational and volitional character of man's moral activity, Thomas divides his considerations into those that regard the end for which man strives, and those that regard the means whereby this end might be attained. The first is dealt with at the beginning of this part of the *Summa* in his *Treatise on Happiness* (Questions 1–5), a short but powerful articulation of what is central to the whole of Thomas's teaching on human morality, namely that it is established not upon obligation, law, rights, conscience, or freedom of will, but rather upon that in

[114] Velde (2006), p. 17.
[115] See, for example, Pinckaers (1993; 1995), p. 222.

which man's happiness consists.[116] The means whereby his happiness is attained is then approached, first, by examining the nature of the human act, and then the principles that govern it. The former is approached by considering what is proper to it (the *Treatise on Human Acts*: Questions 6–21), and then what it shares in common with the animals lacking reason (the *Treatise on the Passions*: 22–48). The latter divides into those principles that are intrinsic to the human person, and those that are extrinsic. The former is covered by three treatises, the first on *Habit* (49–54), the second on *Virtue* (55–70), and the third on *Vice and Sin* (71–89). The latter is dealt with by two treatises, one on *Law* (90–108) and the other on *Grace* (109–114). With these matters determined, Thomas will then pass to the *secunda secundae* wherein he will treat extensively of the theological and moral virtues, which together will present a vivid picture of the particulars that characterize a virtuous and graced Christian life in this world oriented to and anticipating the next.

Treatise on Happiness (Questions 1–5)

Thomas begins this treatise with the affirmation that the human person strives freely and intelligently for those goods that are proper to his nature. The question, though, has always been whether there is among all the goods for which man aspires, one that is above all the rest, one that rightly orders all his activity and constitutes the very end, good and purpose of his human living. As Aristotle before him, Thomas argues that there is an ultimate end for man, that for the sake of which he does all that he does, and that this end is something that is written, so to speak, into his very nature, that all that he seeks he seeks because of and under the description of this end and good, and that it falls to him, being rational and volitional, to discover that in which his ultimate end and good reside.[117] The problem, then, consists in making this determination; all people naturally desire to be happy, but disagree over that in which this consists. Question 2 rehearses the traditional answers that have been put forth in man's attempt to address this problem. The

---

[116] Consider Pinckaers (1993; 1995), Chapter 14 for these differences and their history.

[117] The reader should recall here Question 93 of the *prima pars.*

goods of wealth, honor, fame, and power (sometimes referred to as the goods of fortune or the external goods) are discounted as contenders for the human person's ultimate end and good for many reasons, including that they are all of them sought primarily for the sake of something further, as the means to some other end, something which cannot be the case for man's ultimate end as it is sought only for itself and not for the sake of something else. As for the bodily goods of beauty, health, strength, and pleasure, these too cannot be man's ultimate good and end, given their transitory nature, and the fact that although they do constitute various goods of human living, man's purpose is not something that can be satisfied merely in the preservation and the promotion of his bodily being. Rather, attention must be addressed to the entirety of his person, to his purpose, destiny and happiness, and not primarily to the partial good of his bodily condition. Again, the pleasures that man experiences cannot be his ultimate end and good insofar as these are fleeting, and are commonly pursued in relation to man's animal nature, both of which do not do justice to the nature of man's ultimate good. Nonetheless, pleasure is not something foreign to the happy life, but is intrinsic to it, specifically as it attends all activities that have been completely and well done by man. The emphasis, then, should lie upon the kind of activity engaged in rather than with its attendant pleasures, with the challenge to find that activity, and consequently that pleasure, which is most befitting to man's nature, purpose and happiness. Lastly, man's ultimate end and good do not consist in the goods that are proper to the soul itself. Thus, man's happiness is not found in his existence as a certain kind of being, nor in any of the virtues that he might acquire in the perfecting of his humanity. All of these, even the virtues, are for the sake of something higher, a point that is made even more evident in light of the discussion earlier in the *Treatise on Man* that the image of God is manifested in man to the degree to which he activates, if you will, this image in his rational and volitional activity, and this most perfectly as he strives dynamically to imitate the life and the activities of the Source of his very being (in light of which the *tertia pars* and its consideration of the model of models, Jesus Christ, become central to man's beatitude). In sum, no created good can constitute man's happiness, for none of these is goodness itself and thus does not have the capacity to perfect his nature and lull his appetite. Only that which is goodness itself can effect this peace, and this is found in God alone, man's ultimate end, good, and happiness.

The question then arises: if God is the very object which constitutes man's happiness, how can God, as infinite and uncreated, be subjectively possessed and enjoyed by he who is finite and created? Question 3 addresses this question. Thomas states that the acquisition of man's ultimate end and happiness is effected through an activity specific to his nature. Of all of these activities, only an intellectual one is capable of this. For, in light of the *Treatise concerning the Divine Essence,* God is not something that can be sensitively or physiologically attained, thus eliminating man's vegetative and sensitive activities. Nonetheless, the fact that man's intellectual activity acquires its material from the sensitive powers requires, on Thomas's part, a careful explanation as to how this natural condition of man's intellectual knowing can result in his acquisition of God Himself. A better part of how this occurs has already been explained in Question 12 of the *prima pars* where Thomas has detailed how it is that God is in man's knowledge, particularly with an eye to the beatitific state. In the remaining questions of this treatise, Thomas offers further details and completes what was left undetermined in Question 12.

From the various discussions on man's knowledge throughout the *prima pars,* it should be clear that there is more to man's intellectual activity than just its own operations of understanding, judgment, and reasoning. The *Treatise on Man* established that as a rational soul, the entirety of man's activity is permeated in varying ways and degrees by his rationality. Given that man's ultimate end is a person, and that this person is acquired subjectively in light of that activity which is definitive of man, one might describe this intellectual acquisition as in some way akin to the human situation whereby we most greatly appreciate, unite with, rejoice in, and acquire another person in all that he or she is, and this only as we bring to this relation the highest and the very best that we have, and these as they have been rectified as fully as they can be in light of all that is true, good and beautiful. Naturally, this analogy fails in light of its sensual component. Nonetheless, it does serve to give some indication of the personal aspect of this acquisition of God, and tempers what some have considered mistakenly to be an overly rationalistic account of man's meeting with God.

Thomas states that man's intellectual acquisition and enjoyment of God requires, first, that he know that he has attained God, and secondly, that he experience the delight or enjoyment that this knowledge brings. The order here is as we have seen in the *Treatise on Man*, namely that the will delights in something only insofar as one understands that it has been attained. We also saw in the *prima pars* that it is the will that initially directs man to that in which his happiness resides, but only in an indeterminate way. This fact serves to impel man to determine his understanding of the nature of this goodness to which he is oriented naturally so that he might act so as to attain it through the total sum of the actions of his life.[118] In doing this, man can achieve in this life what Thomas calls an imperfect happiness, something that anticipates its perfect realization in the next life at which time God's presence to him will most assuredly be known with the result that the will's yearnings will be wholly satisfied as he comes to rest in Him, the goodness for which he was made. The nature of this intellectual activity required for his happiness is speculative, that is to say, pursued just for itself and not as something that he will use or apply once acquired, as if his union with God were for the sake of some further purpose. In his speculative activity, he simply enjoys, contemplates, reverences, and wonders at God Himself, again, a most appropriate and beautiful way by which one addresses, respects, and loves another person. This knowledge of God can be anticipated, albeit imperfectly, as one engages in the speculative activity of philosophy and the wisdom to which it aspires in the study of metaphysics. However, since this knowledge is attained by only a few (as was explained in the first question of the *prima pars*), but is required nonetheless by all for their happiness, it is fitting that God made it available to all through His revelation and gifts of grace. In fact, every human discipline and thus every human power, both intellectual and moral, fall short of knowing the Creator and facilitating the kind of rela-

---

[118] One sees here the importance and the necessity of the material considered in the entirety of the *prima pars*.

tion and activity that are required for His acquisition. It is only through these gifts given by God to man, gifts that work in concert with all that he can effect in his return to God in both mind and will as He is Truth and Goodness Himself, that man can achieve his ultimate end and good, and take his rest in and enjoy that for which he was originally made.

Beatitude must result in man's delight, that is to say, in that pleasure that is proper to him as he is image of God, contemplating the very Source of being, truth and goodness. Would it not be strange if this experience were not in fact most delightful, that man's happiness was not pleasurable, especially as his desire had found its ultimate consummation and rest in the very good to which it was made? This delight, as previously explained, follows only upon the beholding of this highest good. However, this knowledge cannot be complete or all-encompassing. For God, being infinite, cannot be fully comprehended by a finite intellect. Thus, one's knowledge or comprehension will be imperfect. Nevertheless, Thomas states that the knowledge that man attains at that time will be sufficient for his happiness, something that is not that difficult to understand as a great majority of human knowledge in the present life is incomplete yet satisfactory to the varied tasks he sets himself and the desires that he had. In order to receive this knowledge of God, it is fitting that man's reason and will both be rectified before and after its attainment; before, insofar as one orders one's life, knowledge, actions, and loves so that they might wholly be directed toward this highest good Himself, anticipating His advent; and after, as the peace of one's will in the good attained is necessarily ordered to that in which it has found its rest, a condition of the repose itself. The former certainly does not cause God to give Himself to man in beatitude. Rather, one might consider this rectification as akin to the preparation of one's house for an invited guest, something that flows from the love and honor that the homeowner has for his anticipated guest. Even man's body is necessary for his happiness, something that is quite clear in this life as the body is so necessary to the activities of man's reason. With respect, however, to his perfect happiness, this does not strictly require his body, since after his death, he will be perfectly present to God in this disembodied state and will have attained his vision of Him. Nevertheless, Thomas argues that, in light of the good of man's nature, which is lacking in the disembodied state, man will only enjoy God, as God had intended him to be, that is, in the fullness of his person on the Last Day when he is reunited with his body in the general resurrection of the dead. At that time, in the very perfection of his being, which includes the rectification and transformation of his bodily condition, he will behold the face of God with his own eyes, as Job prophesied at 19.25–27.

The goods that man enjoys now in his imperfect happiness will not be required for the beatific vision. And although the same could be said for the society of one's friends (the friendship that one will enjoy with God being sufficient for one's perfect happiness), Thomas thinks that one's friends might conduce to the well-being of one's perfect happiness if only for the fact that they all "see one another and rejoice in God, at their fellowship." In the beatific vision, one person can indeed be happier than another insofar as one has disposed oneself more perfectly in mind, will, emotion, and body to the reception of God's gift of Himself, anticipating, as it were, this grace in one's present life. But as for the object itself, no one attains God more than another. All receive the same gift at the end of their labors, but some appreciate and enjoy the reward more than others. This is a happiness that is not usually attained in this life, but is something reserved to the next. Nonetheless, it could be given as the Giver so desires, as in the case of rapture, as was noted previously at ST. I. 12. Unlike his imperfect happiness, man's perfect happiness can never be lost once attained since his will at that time will be entirely at rest, and his person delivered from all that could harm it. This means that the desire to stray from good, to turn one's back, so to speak, upon the beatific vision so as to seek after other goods, will no longer be possible. We have here, once again, the view that the will is not indifferently directed by its possessor, or absolutely determined by him, but that it is what it is and performs freely only insofar as it is determined to and defined by the good itself. Man's freedom is enjoyed only insofar as it is directed to and satisfied by that which is perfectly good, something that is not encountered by him in his earthly existence, thus leaving him free to determine himself with respect to the goods that are placed before him. Once the will is in possession of its ultimate good, it reaches its fulfillment as a power and desists in its yearnings as it enters into the fullness of what it is in the presence of the good for which it was made. This is something that only God Himself can bestow on man, a pure gift that no one causes by that activity which is natural to him. Nevertheless, God requires of the human person that he act in such a way so as to prepare for the gift of Himself that He freely gives. This is what all desire, but have such difficulty not only attaining but even conceptualizing, something that requires all that was covered by the *prima pars* so that in light of it, one might be spurred to seek the means whereby this end might be attained through the loving disposition of one's person through one's own agency, and by the help that one receives from others in friendship and charity, and especially from God through His gifts especially of law and grace, both of which culminate, in the *tertia pars,* in the salvific act effected through His Son.

Treatise on Human Acts (Questions 6–21)

Because man's happiness has an essential reference to the activity that he performs, activity that defines his nature and of which he is master, it is most fitting that he understand the very nature of this activity so that he might strive most effectively for his beatitude. In doing this, he will be found ready and willing to receive the gift of God Himself, and avoid most carefully those activities that prevent this from occurring. As noted previously, Thomas has a twofold concern in the *secunda pars*, namely to defend and detail the position that human activity is undertaken for the sake of an ultimate end and perfect good wherein man's happiness lies, and secondly, to attend carefully to the means whereby man can attain this end, something that includes what he himself effects, and whatever help he receives from without, that is to say, those external forces of both a natural and supernatural origin, aiding and, in the latter case, making perfect, what he tries to effect through his own activity but is unable to do on his own. The first concern is all important and has been treated in the *Treatise on Happiness.* The second concern is what now occupies his attention here, and in the remainder of the *Summa.*

The *Treatise on Human Acts* is dedicated to an articulation of what is involved in man's voluntary activity with an emphasis upon the will, that power which, although described in the

Treatise on Man, receives its full and proper treatment here. There are four concerns in this treatise, namely to determine the nature of the voluntary (Question 6), the circumstances within which voluntary activity is realized (Question 7), the structure of the voluntary act (Questions 8 through 17), and finally how goodness and evil are said of this activity (Questions 18 through 21).

The nature of the voluntary act of man (Question 6)
Voluntary human activity arises from an intrinsic capacity on a person's part to direct his activities for the sake of an end that is known to him as an end. As stated previously, the voluntary is not defined as the bare capacity of the will to choose one way or another. Nor is the voluntary something that is isolated in the will apart from the other powers of the human person or any of the external forces that come to bear upon the realization of his activity.[119] We see, instead, that the will is determined to seek the good, to seek that in which man's end and happiness consist, and that it is aided in this pursuit by all the intrinsic and extrinsic powers pertinent to the attainment of his beatitude, all of which contribute essentially to, and certainly do not of themselves destroy, the voluntary nature of human activity. The common troubles presented by both the natural and the animal appetites to the realization of one's voluntary activity do not essentially affect its nature; it remains what it is, a principle of man's self-directedness toward an end known to him as an end that then gives rise to his understanding of those things that are related to this end as the means whereby it might be achieved. Even the direct intervention of God in man's life respects the voluntary nature of this activity (a point that will be made amply in the treatises concerning law and grace). Nonetheless, the voluntary nature of his activity can indeed by affected and even rendered involuntary, but this in only a few instances. Violence or compulsion visited upon one from an external source can indeed frustrate the commands that issue from one's will. But this frustration extends only as far as its external realization; the willing itself remains untouched, remaining in one's own control and no other's. Thus, while one might be frustrated in

[119] See Pinckaers (2005), p. 364ff for a succinct description of Ockham's notion of freedom, something that describes well the modern approach to this.

one's efforts to flee, being restrained forcefully by the authorities, nonetheless no violence committed by them can directly frustrate one's will to flee. As for actions done through fear and desire, they might seem, on the face of it, to be causes of involuntariness. Thomas, however, does not think so. In the case of the former, he states that although actions done through fear are involuntary insofar as they repugnant to one's willing and would certainly not be done were the situation different, nonetheless that they are willed so that a greater evil might be avoided makes them voluntary. Thus, the throwing of a ship's cargo into the sea during a violent storm is effected voluntarily to avoid the loss of the ship and the lives of its crew, an action that would not otherwise be taken, but is indeed decided upon and effected freely. In the case of compulsion and violence, however, the will does nothing of the kind, but continues in its wish to do whatever it is prevented from doing. Actions impelled by one's sensitive desire, however, are clearly voluntary insofar as one's desire draws the will toward the good that it has in sight, making this particular good agreeable to the will's inclination and, if pursued, lacking wholly the repugnance that characterizes those actions committed out of fear. It is quite a different thing to ascent to the throwing of a ship's cargo overboard in the midst of a storm than to take another drink when one has had enough. Only ignorance that precedes an action repugnant to one's will and could not have been reasonably anticipated and eradicated renders an action involuntary.[120]

The circumstances surrounding man's voluntary activity (Question 7)

The circumstances that attend one's voluntary activity are of concern to any moralist but particularly to the theologian for two reasons, first, as they directly contribute to the assessment

---

[120] In ST. I-II. 6. 7, Aquinas does consider the case where strong emotion drives one mad and thus incapable of using reason at the moment, or, in extreme cases, of destroying reason entirely. While such emotions can destroy the voluntary nature of an act, they do so by making it nonvoluntary, rather than involuntary, insofar as one of the factors of the voluntary has been destroyed, namely reason itself, something that alters the very essence of the nature of the activity in question, lowering it to that of the animal lacking reason.

of an act's goodness or badness, as well as its culpability, and secondly as they constitute the field, so to speak, wherein the acts of man are realized. Seven circumstances are set forth in Article 3, with the "why" and the "what" (that is to say, the motive of the agent, and the essential description of his activity) being the most important, all other circumstances being subordinated to these two in varying ways.

The structure of the voluntary act (Questions 8–17)
His examination of the voluntary act and its structure is divided into two parts. The first regards those acts that arise within the agent and find their completion therein (his intransitive activities: Questions 8 through 16), while the second considers those that result in the practical actions that the agent must take if he is to realize the former's intention and goal (his transitive activities: Question 17). With respect to the former, Thomas first considers those that directly regard the end (Questions 8 through 12), and then those that regard the means to this end (Questions 13 through 16).

With respect to the end, there are three intransitive activities that belong specifically to the will, namely, volition, enjoyment, and intention. *Volition* (the subject of Questions 8 through 10) is the first and most basic orientation of the will to good. As discussed previously, this orientation is not something that is chosen, but constitutes the natural inclination of the will to its proper object, its ultimate end, that in light of which it desires everything that it desires. Reason plays a vital role here insofar as it presents whatever it knows to the will under this very description of a thing's goodness. For the will is not moved by either the being or the truth of a thing, both of which constitute the proper objects of reason, those to which it is naturally inclined in its nature. It is only in light of the thing's goodness, something that reason reveals through its investigations, that the will has something to regard, which, if the will so desires, can result in an act of volition, or wishing as it is sometimes called. At the root, then, of every volitional act, there is an intellectual understanding of something that can occasion the volition of the will as what is known has been revealed to be good and presented as such to the will, and then to which the will initially binds itself freely through this act of volition. And so, if reason discerns the goodness of wealth, this may occasion the simple wish on the part of the will for this good, but without anything further implied than the will's decided inclination toward this good.

The will's volition is something that may be influenced by the other powers of the soul, even though the will exercises dominion over them all, as was described in the *Treatise on Man*. This occurs, however, only as these other powers work within the parameters set out above, specifically by influencing the way by which reason discerns the goodness of what it knows, and this by working upon man's sensitive cognitive and appetitive powers, and even his corporeal condition, as they can influence reason's operations in varying ways. The movement of the will, nonetheless, remains its own, no matter what influence is brought to bear upon it. Indeed, God can directly affect man's volition but this only insofar as He is the will's Creator and is that perfect goodness in which the will finds its ultimate rest and completion, that which it wills of necessity and to which it is directed in all that it does. It is because of this that the agent wields his will freely insofar as he finds nothing in the world that is perfectly good, but good only to a degree, specifically, to the extent that it participates of the source of all goodness. Thus, man necessarily desires his ultimate good and happiness, doing all that he does under this description. But given reason's role in volition, and the other factors that can influence reason in its operations, man not only can be mistaken concerning that in which his true good and end lie, but he also has the capacity to frustrate his search for his true good and end by actively not searching for it at all, such is the extent of his freedom. God can wield His influence over man's will, but always in such a way that he respects his freedom, allowing man to be what he is, namely made to His image which includes being the principle of his own actions, a fact that, together with salvation history, gives rise to the investigations of the *secunda pars* but especially the *tertia pars*.[121]

Question 11 constitutes the other end, so to speak, of the voluntary act, namely that activity whereby the end, which first activated the will in its volition, has now finally been attained, effectively completing the voluntary act. In this attainment, the will experiences the fruit of its labor. It rejoices in that for which

[121] ST. I-II. 8–10.

it has striven, and experiences an *enjoyment* or delight proper to it as it reposes in the object attained. This requires both a cognitive and an appetitive activity on the part of the agent, the former as he understands that that which he desired and for which he worked has been attained, and the latter as the will rests in this, a rest that is characterized not only by the cessation of its movement, but also by its active enjoyment of or delight in what it has attained. If, however, the end and good attained are not man's ultimate end and good, then the repose and enjoyment of the will are but temporary (one need only reflect upon the fleeting nature of the enjoyment one derives from the varied goods of this world to understand Thomas's point). The true fruition of the will, that by which its movement is quelled completely and its activity fully realized, is found in God alone, as Thomas described previously in the *Treatise on Happiness.*

Question 12 deals with the last of the will's actions with respect to the end, namely that of *intention.* Up to this point, Thomas has considered the initial and terminal movements of the will, volition, and enjoyment, respectively. Clearly, the activity of the will must be further specified if choice is to result. This specification occurs, first, in the will's intention following upon what reason has presented to it as good and for which the will simply wishes. It is one thing to speak of the will having a wish for the goodness of what has been presented by reason, but another to bind itself in a more definite way to this good as something that it intends. Thus, we recognize many things to be good and for which we experience a general wish or volition, but go no further in our acts to possess them. For example, one might consider an education to be good but not something that one pursues actively. What is lacking is the intention of the will to pursue that which has been recognized as good, a focusing, so to speak, of the will, a determining of it, a resolution to proceed in a more concrete fashion than was experienced in the initial volition for the good in question. For this to occur, there must be an important contribution made by reason, namely that it judge whether the end and good so wished can in fact be attained. Without this judgment, one cannot move to the next stage wherein one determines the means by which this end can be achieved. Thus, one might consider an education to be a great good and highly desirable. But because of one's social or economic situation, it might be judged as something that is beyond one's reach, and consequently is not considered seriously beyond the wish that one has for this good.[122]

The intention of the end constitutes the height of those activities that regard the end itself. Questions 13 through 16 address the means whereby one's intention can be achieved. He deals first, in Question 13, with *choice* and the most proximate activity of reason that is required for this, namely a practical decision made by reason concerning which of the many and desirable means whereby the end and good in intention might be achieved is best. Question 14 considers the activity of *counsel* whereby these many and varied means are collected, while Question 15 regards the will's *consent* to this collection as suitable avenues that it may pursue. To illustrate this structure, consider the situation where one might understand that health is good, something for which one readily wishes. Upon further examination one considers it to be well within the realm of possibility. Intending this end, one takes counsel as to the many and varied means whereby health might be realized. The result is a fairly good number of options from which to choose, to which one gives one's consent. However, if the end is to be realized, one must determine which of the options will best achieve it. Once this practical judgment has been made, one must bind oneself personally through choice to this decision, something that then sets the stage for the execution of those acts whereby the end and good of health might really be attained.[123]

Choice is clearly something that demonstrates a complex intermingling of both reason and will, something that goes well beyond a mere influence of one upon the other. Nonetheless, the act of choice is more properly associated with the will insofar as "choice is accomplished in a certain movement of the soul towards the good which is chosen,"[124] something that

---

[122] Thomas considers this judgment of reason at ST. I-II. 13. 5 where he distinguishes between the will's activities with respect to means and end. Thus, intention considers the end as possible, choice, on the other hand, will consider whether the means are possible. However, one should also consider ST. I-II. 12. 4.

[123] The intent here is to demonstrate the structure of the voluntary act, and not to argue that this process is strictly followed in a chronological way.

[124] ST. I-II. 13. 1.

does not follow necessarily from reason's judgment that this particular means is the best way to realize the end and good in intention. It bears repeating that choice does not regard the end itself but rather the means by which the intended end and good can be achieved. Choice, then, is understood intimately and essentially in relation to the practical activities that are to be performed by a person if the intended end and good are to be realized. It regards only those means that are possible. For one does not intend, take counsel, make decisions, and effect choices concerning those matters that are beyond one's practical attainment, and thus do not conduce to the ends and goods for which one wishes and intends. But for those things that are within one's practical grasp, one chooses freely and not from necessity. Only man's perfect good, his happiness, determines his will necessarily, but this not with respect to the means, but only in its first and basic orientation to the end itself, something that it does not choose, as stated earlier.

Since choice deals with the means whereby one's intended end and good are achieved, *counsel* becomes necessary insofar as great uncertainty usually accompanies one's turn to the every day things and people with which one's actions are concerned in one's progress toward one's intended end and good. The difficulty has always resided in the determination of what ought to be done here and now to realize one's intended end in the best and most moral way. It is little wonder, then, that there will be a virtue, that of prudence, associated intimately and importantly with counsel and the other aspects of the determination of the best and most moral way by which one's actions in the present can speed one to the attainment of an intended end.

Consent, as mentioned before, follows counsel as the will's movement toward the many and varied means that counsel generates. In consent, the will draws these means to itself as so many particular ways by which one can be sped along the road to the decision and choice that one must ultimately make if the end and the good are to be realized. Choice, then, is the final focusing of the will upon one of the many options generated through reason's counsel and to which the will has previously consented.[125]

---

[125] See especially ST. I-II. 15. 3. ad3.

Having determined through one's choice a specific way by which to attain the end that one intends, one is left with the practical actions that must be taken up if the immanent activities described previously are to issue in the fruition spoken of in Question 11. While this is the focus of Question 17, Thomas anticipates this with an examination of the means that are within the will's control as it applies all that has preceded to those practical actions required for the end's attainment. With this in place, Thomas can then finish his examination of the structure of voluntary activity by considering the actual command wielded by will and reason in the pursuit of the agent's end and good.

Because the particular goods of the voluntary agent's every power are included in the good of the will, the will is said *to use* these powers in its practical activities to realize that which has been chosen. This *use* implies the cooperation of reason as it guides the will in its use of the powers so that it might apply one thing to another in the particular, contingent realm for the sake of the realization of the chosen end. Thus, use follows after choice. There is, however, a sense in which use precedes choice, namely where the will impels reason to seek after all that is required of it in the realization of the voluntary act. Thus, even the *command* that is exercised by reason with respect to and consequent upon the choice that has been made, presupposes this sense of use where the will impels reason to its activity of commanding what has resulted from the act of choice. But from the perspective of the execution of the particular activities required for the realization of the intended end, use follows the command of reason, just as the use of a stick to defend oneself from attack follows upon the command exerted by reason to do so. In this view, then, we have the choice of will, followed by the command of reason, and will's use of the powers required for the fulfilling of reason's command as manifested practically in the varied transitive activities performed so that the end and good intended might really be attained and thus enjoyed.[126] To return to the example of health, if the decision and the choice made for the sake of health involved cycling

---

[126] See especially ST. I-II. 17. 3. ad1 for the series of immanent and transitive acts involved in execution.

10 miles every day, then one would have to effect the particular actions whereby this actually occurs; of commanding that this be done, the actual putting into effect of the varied and many powers whereby this might be attained, and then, returning to Question 11, the recognition, at some point in the future, that health has been attained, and the delight or enjoyment that follows upon this awareness.[127]

How goodness and evil are said of man's voluntary activity (Questions 18–21)
The last matter addressed in this treatise is the goodness and evil of voluntary acts. He divides his considerations into two areas: first, how it is that a human act can be good or evil and secondly, what results from the human act so described (Question 21). The former divides into three parts, namely the goodness and evil of human acts generally considered (Question 18), and then this in relation to man's immanent and transitive activity (Questions 19 and 20, respectively).

The first article of Question 18 recalls the discussions in the *prima pars* concerning the nature of goodness, where "good" was said of that which conduces to the fullness of a being's nature, and "evil" of that which deprives the thing in some way of this fullness. Thus, for the human person, sight is considered to be good insofar as it conduces to a certain fullness or perfection of his nature, a realization of what is potential to his humanity, while blindness is considered evil as it denotes a privation of his being, a lacking of a certain perfection which by nature he is supposed to enjoy. These terms are applied in like fashion to human activity. Thus, an action is considered to be good as it conduces to a certain fullness or perfection of a person's nature, and evil as it deprives him of this. He then specifies this generic description in the articles that follow.

[127] The reader may wish to consult a traditional chart of the structure of the perfect human act provided by Thomas Gilby O.P. in Volume 17 (1970) of the Blackfriars' translation of the *Summa* (Appendix 1, p. 211). The reader should attend to his *caveats* concerning this scheme on p. 212, particularly that they do not necessarily follow the neat description that has been offered here, but is far more complex in it realization. One should also note his example of all 12 stages as applied to a voluntary act on p. 214. See also Gilson (1956; 1994), pp. 252–256.

First, the assessment of the goodness of an act requires that there be an attention to the object with which it deals. This object determines what kind of act one is performing, that is to say, its species, and the act's goodness is determined in relation to its object insofar as this object is suitable, or evil if it is unsuitable. Thomas offers the example of making "use of what is one's own," and of taking "what belongs to another." In both cases, the activity, from a material perspective, is the same: making use of something. They differ, however, in the objects with which they are concerned, namely with what is one's own, and what is another's. These determine the form that the activity takes on, their respective descriptions and the consequent moral assessment to which each is subject, and is analogous to the way that the soul determines the kind of living being that is realized in this particular material or bodily manifestation, where the material in both man and beast is alike, the difference being located in the form, the ordering or determining principle, the soul, as was described in the *prima pars*. Secondly, the assessment of the goodness of an act must regard the circumstances within which it occurs. Although circumstances do not stand as formal and thus determining aspects of an act (as the object did), nevertheless, they contribute greatly to its fullness (or lack thereof), again, as do the varied accidents attached to the soul of a living thing. Thus, just as one's shape, size, physical disposition, weight, and other such things have a great bearing upon the fullness of a living thing's being, so too do the "who," "what," "where," "by what aids," "why," "how," and "when" bear importantly upon human activity and its moral assessment. Finally, an act derives its goodness from its end, that to which the act is oriented so that the fullness that the agent lacks might be achieved. Thus, an act of charity performed for the sake of one's love of one's fellow man and of God Himself is good, while the same act done for the advancement of one's own glory is not. In order for an act to be evil, it must lack in only one of these factors. But for an act to be judged as good, it must have all of them.

The nature of these factors, together with the discussion concerning the structure of the voluntary act, indicate clearly that reason is central to their determination and realization. Indeed, the will impels reason to do the things that it must do so that the end to which the will has bound itself in intention might be realized through the external acts that the agent performs. But reason provides at every stage the cognitive operations required by the will so that it might engage in its activities with respect to the end, beginning with the presentation of what reason knows under the description of good, to the assessment of its possibility, the discernment of the many and varied means to attain it, the judgment of which of these best achieves it, the command to effect what practically has been done, and lastly in the recognition that it has been attained. The will may be determined to goodness and the ultimate good by its nature, but it is reason that guides the will in the specification of and orientation to that in which its ultimate good consists. The consequence of this is that it is essential to voluntary human activity that it be in accord with reason. For reason is that which determines what is suitable (or not) for the human person, that which determines the means whereby this is achieved (or avoided), and that which guides the human person in its practical realization (or avoidance). Its reach is universal, extending not only to the entirety of one's person, but also to the larger context within which this activity is performed, and even larger still, in the context of those goods and ends that are most high for man, the family, society, and reality itself, all of which are directed ultimately by that good and end which is first and final. For morally good activity to be realized, then, it is clear that reason must be not only that which determines these matters, but that its determinations be rectified by what is true and in conformity with what is really good, the latter of which constitutes what it presents to the will for the sake of the immanent and transitive activities discussed in the prior questions of this treatise.

The goodness (or evil) of the will's immanent activities is determined in relation to its end. One must be careful, however, to make a distinction between the end to which the will is determined naturally, namely the good itself in light of which it seeks whatever it seeks and how this is realized in its intention. While it is true that the will seeks all things under the description of the good presented to it by reason, nonetheless it could be considered evil insofar as the good it intends is not truly good, but only apparently so. The latter "which has indeed some measure of good," without which it would in no way be pursued by the will, is nevertheless "not of a good that is simply suitable to be desired,"[128] which is to say that it is not in accord with reason itself. Thus, the activities that flow from the will, although always oriented to and intending the good itself, are not always suitable to the nature and end of man, and thus are considered evil. As long as the good presented to will by reason is in accord with reason, as discussed in the prior paragraph, then the activity that issues from the will "enters the moral order and causes moral goodness in the act of the will."[129] That reason acts in this fashion with respect to the will is effected by the eternal law. Reason, then, is appointed, so to speak, to determine what is truly good and worthy to be presented to the will for its intention, and this not arbitrarily, but according to its discernment of whether it is suitable for the agent or not, particularly with respect to his ultimate end, something in which reason is aided through an appeal to the external forces pertinent to his voluntary activity, specifically those of law and grace, to be examined at the end of the *prima secundae*. The will, then, derives its goodness from the end that it intends following upon the goods that are presented to it by reason, something determined by the eternal law which has so ordained reason to act as it does. In this, the agent has the opportunity to conform his reason to the highest truths that it can attain, which then redounds to the will, allowing it to be presented with, and to intend the greatest good available to it, that which will fulfill the end to which it is naturally oriented. In short, the true and best good for man is found in taking on the mind and will of God in all that he thinks and wills, placing him in the situation where his doing and his making might be most good as they derive from reason and will so perfected.[130]

As for man's transitive activities, good and evil can be said of them either on the part of the act itself and the circumstances that surround it, or in the act's relation to the end. Thus, the giving of money to the poor for the sake of their sustenance and

---

[128] ST. I-II. 19. 1. ad1.

[129] ST. I-II. 19. 1. ad3.

[130] The reader should consider Articles 5 and 6 of this question that deal with matters associated with conscience and its binding force, something that demonstrates how important it is for the will to be in accord with the determinations of reason.

well-being is good, but becomes evil if done for the sake of one's own glory and reputation. In the latter example, the evil that is in the will passes into the external act itself, as the transitive act manifests the intention of the will for this less than suitable good. In the former example, on the other hand, its goodness derives from the order established by reason concerning both the determination of the act to be done and the circumstances that are to be observed so as to maintain the suitable nature of the act to be done. It is to these determinations that the will consents and observes in its choice and the playing out of the external actions seeking the end intended, desiring that the goodness of the intransitive activities that the agent has undertaken so far may be embodied and preserved in the transitive activities to which the former have given rise. Once again, for an external act to be good, all these factors must be satisfied: the end must be good, as well as the nature of the act and its circumstances. If there is a defect in any one of these, this renders the act evil.

Thomas completes his examination of the voluntary human act by looking to the consequences that follow their goodness or evil. In brief, the rectitude of an act or its sinful nature derives from the former being in accord with the order of reason and the eternal law, as was described previously, and the latter when it turns aside from these. As these acts either conduce to man's good or do not, they deserve praise or blame respectively insofar as the righteous or sinful act can be imputed to the agent insofar as he acted voluntarily. As for the recompense that is to be allotted to one who commits such deeds voluntarily, this is a matter of justice that discerns in the situation what is due to the person who has so acted in light of the nature and extent of the benefit or harm done to another.[131]

This examination of the structure of human voluntary activity details not just the nature of man's freedom, but this as it is perfected in the dynamism implicit in realizing the image to which the human person has been made. The principles

---

[131] There are many excellent accounts concerning the principles of morality as they are applied to the nature of the human act. For these and a fuller treatment of their doctrines and issues, the reader might begin with the appendices to Volume 18 (1966) of the Blackfriars' translation of the *Summa.*

developed here will be vital to the subject matter of the remaining treatises of the *secunda pars*, and provides great and very useful insight into the order or structure to one's voluntary activity, a structure that should not be understood as something realized chronologically, as noted earlier,[132] but should be seen rather as the cognitive and appetitive interplay that is required in any and every properly human voluntary act, an interplay that if not understood can give rise to very specific defects in the moral life, something that is amply demonstrated in the descriptions offered in the *secunda secundae* of the vices that harm the moral life.

Treatise on the Passions (Questions 22–48)

Having considered those activities proper to man's nature, Thomas now takes up those that are important to the realization of man's happiness but which are shared in common with the animals lacking reason, namely the passions. One should note from the start that the word "passion" is a transliteration of the Latin *passio,* and is not intended to denote accurately the phenomenon with which Thomas is concerned here, there being no word in our language sufficient to the task. At the very least, it is a mistake to consider this treatise to deal only with what is commonly represented by the word "passion." While this is included in Thomas's treatment, his understanding of *passio* is far more extensive in scope. It is, perhaps, closer to the mark to refer to the passions as emotions, especially in light of the discussion of the 11 passions that occupy the majority of this treatise, passions that we commonly understand as emotions. Nonetheless, there is a wide variance, and even much confusion in the minds of many people, concerning the nature of an emotion which makes some translators of this treatise hesitate to use it with the concern that they might import or at least suggest modern meanings that are not intended by Thomas in his treatment. For lack, then, of a suitable word, let us use the term "passion" to denote the phenomenon in question, and, following Thomas's treatment, allow it to be defined by his use.

The treatise divides into two parts. The first considers the passions in a general fashion, being concerned with their

[132] See also Pinckaers' comment on this (1993; 1995), p. 224.

definition (Question 22), the differences that exist among them (Question 23), how good and evil might be predicated of them (Question 24), and how they are related to one another in the human experience of them (Question 25). The second part is quite extraordinary insofar as Thomas treats in great detail the particularities of each of the 11 passions so defined in the first part, something that is quite unique in the theological literature of the time. By these, we not only arrive at a well-articulated understanding of those passions central to the moral life, but we also begin to see the means whereby these passions might be harnessed so that they, together with the volitional activity that is properly man's, might most effectively be oriented to and strive after man's ultimate end and good.

As was noted in the *prima pars,* the passions belong to man's sensitive appetition, that appetite which is specific to and rooted in his animality, that which he shares in common with the animals lacking reason. Unlike man's intellectual appetite, his sensitive appetition, being essentially associated with his animal and corporeal condition, does not arise without a change in his bodily state. This and the causal relations involved in a passion are central to its definition. On the one hand, the body might cause the movement of man's sensitive appetite, as in those situations where one finds oneself natural disposed to anger, fear, desire, and the like. While this is important to Thomas's determination of the nature of passion, they do not constitute his primary concern. Rather, the phenomenon that he has in sight is that which arises because of an evaluation made by the one possessed of sensitive appetition concerning the good or evil of some particular concrete thing before him, specifically whether it is suitable or not for him personally considered, and not universally as the rational appetite so acts. This evaluation is something that is performed by the sensitive cognitive power of estimation in the animal, and cogitation in the human (the change in terminology reflecting the influence of reason upon the power itself, something to which we shall return shortly). This gives rise to the change within the body, a change that is part of the description of passion itself without which one would not have the phenomenon in question. Thus, fear is something that arises insofar as one discerns that there is some evil that approaches that one cannot readily or easily avoid. This passion is made manifest in the alteration that this assessment has upon the bodily condition, a change with which we are familiar. The causality, then, of this phenomenon is not of the body in relation to the soul, but rather of the soul in relation to the body where the bodily reaction constitutes the material element of the passion, and the evaluation made is its formal element, both of which together make what Thomas calls passion a reality. What follows from this is that passion is not something that is particular to the human person, nor is it something that defines his humanity. Nor is it something that is implicit in man's status as having been made to the image of God. It is something that attends his corporeal and animal condition on this earth. And while it is the case that an analogous experience of the passions is had at the level of man's rational appetition, Thomas's central concern here is the experience that man shares with the animals, how to describe it, and most importantly that it be brought specifically under the virtues of temperance and fortitude.

Just as we were given a detailed account of the structure of the voluntary act in the prior treatise, so too are we offered in this treatise an examination of the structure of sensitive appetition. Thomas begins, in Question 23, with the distinction of sensitive appetition into its concupiscible and irascible aspects, and then offers details concerning their interrelations in Question 25. The concupiscible is the more basic of the two as it regards particular good and evil in a simple and personal fashion where one is drawn toward that which has been evaluated as good or suitable for one, or repulsed from that which is evil or unsuitable. With respect to the suitable, we have the three moments of concupiscence, namely of love, desire, and joy, love being that first binding of the person to that which he finds to be suited, fitting or good for him, desire being the going out of the appetite to that which is loved but not possessed, and joy being the rest or fulfillment of the appetite in that good when finally possessed. With respect to evil, we have the contrary moments of hatred, aversion, and sadness, hatred arising only insofar as one loves something, as it is that passion one experiences in the face of that which is opposed to one's love. Aversion is that natural appetitive movement away from this hated thing, and sadness is the fulfillment of the appetite in that hated thing if by chance it comes to rest in one's life. For example, one can have a personal love for the countryside in its pristine, natural, and verdant condition. This gives rise to the desire to walk, perhaps, among its meadows, valleys, and mountains, something that culminates in joy as one actually does these things. One's hatred arises in relation to those things that are contrary to one's love, desire and joy. And so, one might hate, for example, urban sprawl which leads to the invasion and possible destruction of these natural places. One avoids this in one's search for greener meadows. But if one cannot avoid this development, and finds oneself bereft of the country that one loved, desired and enjoyed so in former times, then sadness befalls one. These describe the moments, so to speak, of the concupiscible aspect of man's sensitive appetition, one's basic comportment to the things, people and situations of this world in a personal, animal and individualistic fashion, regarding the good and the suitable with respect to one's own lights, and not as they are in themselves.

The irascible aspect, on the other hand, regards a more complex object. It too considers both the suitable and unsuitable in things. However, it regards these insofar as they present some difficulty in their attainment or avoidance, and not simply as the concupiscible aspect does. Clearly, the irascible passions are necessary to man's life in the world, since most of its goods and evils are not simply acquired or avoided. Thomas thus speaks of the irascible passions as coming to the aid of man's concupiscence, helping him to overcome the difficulties that frustrate his concupiscence. The irascible passions are distinguished according to what aspect of the complex object they regard primarily. In the face of an arduous good, one can regard the goodness itself over that of its arduousness, and thus be drawn toward it in the passion of hope. On the other hand, if one regards the arduousness over that of the good, one is repelled from it by the passion of despair. With respect to the arduous evil, if one regards primarily its evil aspect, one experiences the passion of fear. If, however, one regards the arduousness involved, and assesses that one can overcome it, then one turns toward this evil in the passion of daring so that one might escape this evil by facing it, doing battle with and destroying it. Lastly, there is the passion of anger, what one might consider to be the last stand in one's passional defense against an evil that afflicts one, that has come to rest in one's life, and concerning which one must then make a choice, either to succumb to it and thus experience the sadness that this would cause, or to attack it in the passion of anger so as to eliminate this evil from one's life and avoid the sadness it brings. So, as the passions of the irascible appetite are an aid to one's concupiscence, they can be said to arise out of and to resolve ultimately into the passions of the concupiscible aspect. In other words, every sensitive appetition is rooted in love and resolves ultimately into either joy or sadness, with all the other passions described above playing their subordinate roles as is more fully described both in Question 25, and in the second part of this treatise where Thomas offers explicit details concerning each of these passions. Completing the example offered above, in the face of the difficulty of fulfilling one's desire to enjoy an unspoiled countryside, one regards either the good or the difficulty presented by this. With respect to the former, one experiences the hope that allows one to seek out the ways by which this might be realized. Perhaps one might become involved with civic government and seek to enact laws so as to protect these places. Or, one might engage in all the difficulties involved in moving to a more isolated area. However this plays out, the hope is the same, namely that impetus to chase after the good loved and desired yet difficult to attain. If, however, after due consideration, one discovers that one simply does not have the wherewithal to overcome the difficulties involved, despair sets in, a despair that still regards the thing loved and desired as good, but now out of one's seeming reach. With regard to the difficult evil that such a situation may present, one may focus upon the evils that threaten the countryside and experience a fear for its future. Focusing, however, upon the difficulties brings one to face these fearful prospects by, perhaps, doing battle with the developers, fighting city counsel, or other actions of a daring nature. Finally, there is anger that might be experienced in the face of a defeat at the hands of the counsel or the developers, a defeat that one refuses to accept, but decides to fight against even more obstreperously. One can see how these might resolve at any moment into either joy or sorrow, or how they can interact one with the other depending upon the situation as it changes, thus making it difficult to be precise concerning their arousal, continuance, and termination, something that also afflicts the account offered by Thomas concerning the 12 stages of the voluntary act. This difficulty should not dismay one since the accounts here are not offered as strictly sequential, but rather as explanatory of the complexity of the many and interrelated moments of appetition both sensitive and intellectual, and this for the sake of the material to come concerning their moderation and perfection through virtue.

Question 24 deals with the morality of the passions, how good and evil might be said of them. Insofar as the passions arise from the natural judgments that are made by the estimative and cogitative powers of the sensitive aspect, they are neither good nor evil in themselves, being movements of the sensitive aspect of man apart from the order of reason that is required to make something assessable as either good or evil, as was discussed in the prior treatise. It is only as the passions themselves come under the rule and order of reason that one can attribute the descriptions of good and evil to them. In this way, then, the passions will have a share in the voluntary activity of man insofar as they can be controlled in a certain respect, or at least checked, by the will (in the capacity of its use, as described in the prior treatise), and influenced by reason as it can come to bear upon both the activities of the will with respect to the passions, and its own activities with respect to the cogitative power, an influence that allows Thomas to refer to cogitation as particular reason. It is through reason's action upon the passions, moderating them so that they might be turned to the ends and goods that reason so ordains, and this in a habitual way through virtue, that the passions become not only good, but are effectively moderated with respect to the clear influence that the passions can have upon reason and will in their respective and joint activities.

Questions 26 through 48 constitute the second part of this treatise. It offers detailed expositions of each of the 11 passions, centering upon the nature of the passion in question, its causes and effects (and, in a few cases, the remedies for it, and the goodness and badness that attach to it). Overall, these descriptions are remarkable if only for the fact that one acquires a better sense of how what is shared in common with the animals is qualified in light of being manifested within the rationality that defines the human person. Thus, although we share all 11 appetible moments with the animals lacking reason, the experience of them is broadened and deepened in light of man's rationality, remaining all the while something rooted in man's animality. One can see this also with respect to man's sensitive cognitive powers. Although these are generically the same as those possessed at least by the higher animals, they become broadened by their presence to reason. The memorative power is one example where for man it deserves to be called "reminiscence" insofar as it is receptive of syllogistic techniques whereby man can seek "for a recollection of the past by the application of individual intentions."[133] The nature of the power does not change; it is still a "storehouse" of those things met in the past or derived from one's estimation. However, it can now be developed and manifested in a qualitatively better way as it partakes of that which is highest in man, his rationality. The result, then, for man's sensitive life, both in its cognition and appetition, is a lifting up, so to speak, of what is animal into the rational wherein, while remaining what they are and directed to whatever they are naturally set, they now manifest an activity which can partake of and obey the rational life to such a degree that they now become subject to the determination that the virtues themselves can effect. Since it is well beyond the purposes of this book to examine each of the passions in detail, let us restrict ourselves to one of them, namely the passion of fear (Questions 41 through 44).

As we saw above, fear is that irascible passion that constitutes one's withdrawal from an evil that is immanent and cannot be opposed or avoided. In its basic form, it usually concerns those objects that threaten or endanger one's person, thus running counter to the basic good of one's life and the desire to preserve and promote it. Both man and beast alike experience this. However, because of man's reason, he is able to experience a broadening of fear beyond those concerns that he shares with the animal lacking reason. He has the ability to consider a far greater range of things as being impending unavoidable evils

---

[133] ST. I. 78. 4. See Yates (1966; 1992) and Carruthers (1990) for the extent to which this can be effected in which lies the basis for mnemonic techniques.

and these both as they extend to more concerns than just that of one's immediate corporeal well-being or individual life, and as they can be intensified (or mollified) by the additional contributions that reason can bring to bear (directly and indirectly, that is to say, in its own considerations, and in the way that it can influence the other sensitive powers in their contributions to the passion of fear). Thus, while man and beast both fear the bear that charges at them, only man can have a fear of bankruptcy, uniformed officials, speaking before a group of one's peers, certain political ideas or parties, and a whole range of things as he can discern an evil in them that somehow threatens him and cannot be avoided. Man can intensify any one of his fears to the point that he becomes paralyzed by it, rendering himself unable to consider what to do and even in some cases unable to move himself at all. On the other hand, he can also mollify his fears, learning how to deal with them so that he might be able to function effectively in the face of these situations, and even, in some cases, effectively eliminate his fear. The idea at work here is that unlike the animal, man has a definite contribution to make both before and after the arousal of his fear, the former insofar as he can influence in many ways the way by which he assesses naturally the evil of the things, people and situations of his daily life, and the latter insofar as he is not impelled automatically by his fear to the action that it demands, but retains, instead, his freedom to consider and choose what to do by reason again of his intellectual faculties. Being rational frees one, then, not only from the sheer determinacy of matter, but also from the utter control that the passions exert over the animal lacking reason. The idea here, then, is to mold one's appetitive life in such a way that one fears rightly and virtuously, and not be subject to the impulsions that arise from the limited regard that one's sensitive appetition has, something that is not directed to the good of man but rather only that of the individual himself.

Thomas discusses six kinds of fear to which the human person is subject. These six divide into two groups. The first regards those evils in men's actions. Among these, first, there is *laziness* that Thomas defines as the fear of too much toil. Here one judges this labor as an excessive burden to one's nature and is thus something from which one shrinks. Secondly, there is *shamefacedness*, the fear of damaging one's reputation through disgraceful actions that one is about to perform, while the third, *shame*, fears the same thing, but now in relation to those actions that one has already performed. The second group regards those evils that are encountered with respect to external things that exceed an individual's power of opposition. A thing can exceed in this fashion by its magnitude wherein one is unable to gauge it properly. This fear is called *wonder*. A thing can overwhelm, secondly, by being unusual, something to which one is not accustomed. This fear is called *stupor*. Finally, a thing can overpower by reason of its being unforseen or unexpected. This fear is called *anxiety*.

Two points concerning this list. First, while anxiety is understood commonly to be a kind of fear, the other five often come as a surprise to many, especially wonder, that phenomenon that Aristotle and the scholastic theologians considered to be central to philosophy and the intellectual life in general.[134] In wonder, one is struck by some object of cognition that has overwhelmed one's sensibilities and capacity to understand and explain it. Wonder is a kind of fear insofar as one, in the face of the wonderful, shrinks from immediately forming a judgment about it by reason of the fact that one does not wish to dishonor the wondrous thing by offering an account that would very likely fall far from the truth. Instead, one reserves one's judgment until one has investigated the matter as carefully as is required, thus respecting the object itself, the pronouncements made about it, and the integrity of the truth itself. Stupor, on the other hand, centers not upon the wondrous object but rather upon the subject himself where, because of the unusual or unfamiliar nature of the wondrous thing, he not only offers no judgment concerning it, but does not even enter into an investigation so that the truth might be known about it. Stupor, then, is a major impediment to any intellectual endeavor, while wonder is the beginning of all wisdom.[135] The second thing to be said here is that these species of fear are not necessarily all to be shunned. While stupor and laziness have no redeeming value, the same could not be said for the other four fears whose

[134] For Aristotle, see *Metaphysics* I. 2. 982b11–29.
[135] See ST. I-II. 41. 4. ad5.

intellectual and moral benefits are clear. Even anxiety, when moderated appropriately, has the effect of making one ready in mind, will and body to await, consider, meet and hopefully repel the evil that threatens. Many have experienced the centering and clarifying effect that a moderate degree of fear has upon one's person, something, however, that is nullified when the fear becomes too intense and overwhelms. The control of this is found in the virtuous life whereby one can experience the passions, in this case, fear, in the best possible way, that is, as they can be brought to bear upon those actions that we perform for the sake of our end and good.[136]

Finally, as stated previously, one must include the physical aspect of the passion under consideration as this constitutes an essential part of its description. First, it is interesting to note that Aquinas considers the bodily change and the passion associated with it as mutually complimentary insofar as the former resembles and takes on the defining characteristics of the latter insofar as this is possible within the context of the corporeal. In other words, the withdrawal of the sensitive appetite, that movement definitive of fear, is mirrored by a general contraction or shrinking in the body, wherein the comportment that one takes to the immanent danger turns inward and is expressed in the bodily reactions that are definitive of fear. Thomas offers a list of these: the heat of one's body withdraws from the extremities, resulting in cold hands, cold feet, and shivering; the loss of the ease with which one performs one's regular activities, such as the ability to speak, one's general coordination, and the regularity of one's natural bodily functions, particularly that of the heart, one's bowels and bladder; the hindrance of reason and will in performing their proper activities, particularly those detailed in the prior treatise concerning the voluntary act. Such things should not be a surprise if one understands that these bodily manifestations are the material condition of the realization of the formal element of the passion itself, which when taken together denote the actual passion itself so described. This is a direct consequence of a hylomorphic theory of human nature, as was described previously in the *Treatise on Man* when the relation of body and soul was discussed.

[136] See ST. I-II. 44. 2 and 4.

Much more could be said about both fear and the passions. However, what has been presented gives a good sense of the importance of this treatise, namely as an examination of the nature of the passions themselves, and of the role that they play in those actions that aspire to man's end and good. For these, together with the powers of reason and will, importantly define the extent of human activity important to the realization of human happiness.[137] What remains to be examined are the principles that can be applied to this activity so that man might act most effectively in his pursuit of his ultimate end and good. It is to these matters that we now turn and that will occupy Thomas's attention for the remainder of the *prima secundae*.

Treatise on the Habits (Questions 49–54)

Thomas deals first with those principles that are intrinsic to the human person (Questions 49 through 89), and then those that are extrinsic (Questions 90 through 114). The intrinsic principles of human activity are the powers of his soul and the habits that can be applied to them. Having dealt with the former in the *Treatise on Man*, he begins with the ways by which these powers might be subjected to habituation and, consequently, determined to a particular way of acting. He deals first with the habits in general and then considers their perfection in the virtues (Questions 55 through 70) and vices (Questions 71 through 89).

The translation of *habitus* by "habit" is another transliteration commonly used by translators in the face of the lack of a word in our language that appropriately signifies the phenomenon about which Thomas writes. At the very least, one should not equate the common understanding of the word "habit" with what Thomas describes here in this treatise, especially as this common use limits its application to a static and mechanistic determination of a person's sensitive appetites or to some repeated basic activities where reason and will are no longer importantly operative. Instead, "habit" denotes something quite different. It is, in Torrell's words,

---

[137] At the very least, one should consider Pinckaers' essay "Reappropriating Aquinas's Account of the Passions" in (2005), pp. 273–287 for a more extensive treatment of some of these points.

the capacity of adaptation and extension to the ever new, which perfects the faculty in which it arises and gives it a perfect liberty, a source of true delight in action. *Habitus* is thus the sign and the expression of the full flowering of nature in a certain direction.[138]

What this implies must be explained carefully.

Thomas defines habit as something that qualifies man's varied powers and activities, disposing them in such a way that they (and man) are directed well (or badly) in relation to his nature and his end. If man is directed well with regard to these, the habit is considered as good, and if badly, then as evil.[139] In light of this description, habit covers a very wide field, extending across the entirety of man's activity, particularly with respect to those activities that are proper to him, or at the very least, amenable to the command and guidance of reason. Thus, if man has the capacity, for example, to learn theology, be temperate, or engage in carpentry, then doing these well demands that he acquire the habits that are dispositive to each and this, not just for their own sake, but also for the sake of those ends and goods particular to his nature, which contribute ultimately and importantly to his happiness. The perfecting, then, of man's nature and the activities that flow from this in his pursuit of his end is importantly effected through the many and varied intellectual, moral, and productive habits available to him through those areas of his culture wherein such are developed, preserved, and taught. One can understand, then, why it is that Torrell considers the habits as signs and expressions of the full flowering of man's nature accomplished only as he strives for his end and good, and this within the cultures of which he is a member.

The necessity for the habituation of man's nature, powers, and activities arise from something that was discussed earlier in the *Treatise on Man*, namely that although man's powers are established in their existence and nature by the soul, nonetheless as powers they are ordered to perfections that the soul itself does not provide. The existence of man as a certain kind of being is consequently not sufficient to the perfection and

[138] Torrell (1996; 2003), p. 264.
[139] ST. I-II. 49. 1.

happiness that is possible to him. Man is complete and happy only insofar as he strives by his activities to realize all that is implicit in his nature and this, ultimately, for the sake of acquiring that for which he was made, his happiness, a point amply demonstrated in the *Treatise on Happiness*. It is the nature of man and of his powers, then, to be oriented to and receptive of what Thomas calls their proper objects, those things for the sake of which they were made, those things in which they find their "second actuality" beyond the first actuality they receive as specified by the soul. Herein is found the first condition for the necessity of a habit,[140] namely that there be a distinction of potency and act between that which is disposed and that to which it is disposed. For example, the sensitive appetite exists and has the nature that it does by reason of the human soul. However, its activation, so to speak, is found in the sensitive things of this world as they have been evaluated as good or bad for the one who senses them. Again, reason exists and has its nature from the soul itself. However, it is only in the experience of things themselves, specifically with respect to their being and their formal principles, that reason activates and begins to realize that for which it was established by the soul in the first place. The second condition for habit's necessity is found where that which can be disposed by a habit is capable of this in several ways and to various things. Consequently, something that is disposed in only one way is not properly said to be the subject of a habit but rather is simply said to be determined by the nature or form specific to it, the notion of a habit over and above this determination being unnecessary. A person's life, for example, is something implicit in his nature and is not something to which he is habituated consequent to his initial realization as a living being. However, his intellect can be disposed in several ways and to various things, thus giving rise to the necessity of being habituated rightly if it is to reach the fullness that belongs to it (and to man) potentially speaking. The third condition of habit's necessity is found consequent to having set out upon one of the ways by which the thing in question can be determined, namely that there has to be a coordination of many and varied things for the realization

---

[140] Found at ST. I-II. 49. 4.

of the power or act in question, a coordination that determines whether the thing so disposed is disposed for better or worse. For example, there are many and varied ways by which the habit of biology can be realized. But in the determination to one of these ways, there must also be a determination or coordination of the many and varied facets that go into the realization of this habit without which this disposition would not be realized.

The necessity and the dynamic nature of habit is clear, as is its distinction from our common use and understanding of it. It disposes and thus determines not only the power and the activity in question, but also these for the sake of the activity that man himself must engage in for the sake of his happiness. Indeed, herein is the full flowering of man's nature under the phenomenon of habit, an adaptation and extension of his nature to the ever new that is in itself delightful, the means whereby his freedom as a rational being is both revealed and appropriated (and in which lies one of the great purposes of a truly liberal education). In light of the conditions which necessitate habituation, it is clear that the body itself is not properly the subject of a habit so understood, specifically as the body's processes are autonomic in nature, and thus determined to one mode of activity alone and not to many. Thus, one would not speak of applying a habit to digestion, something made quite clear when one considers the means by which a habit grows (one does not become better at digestion by eating). Instead, habit is said principally of the soul, both with respect to those activities that characterize man's nature (namely his rational and volitional activities), and those that he shares in common with the animals lacking reason (specifically the cognitive and appetitive activities of his sensitive aspect). These powers require habituation if their activities are to realize what is potential to them and to the nature of the one who possesses them, habits that are in the soul as they dispose man's powers and activities that fall under the three necessities described above.

The sensitive powers of man are habituated only insofar as they are susceptible to the command of his rational powers. Thus, although man's sensitive appetition is directed to one thing by his soul, namely to seek naturally those particular things that are suitable to it and to avoid those things that are not, nonetheless as this can come under reason's influence, it can share in the life of reason and thus be ordained by reason to many and diverse things beyond that of which the power itself is capable, and this for better or worse, as was discussed earlier in the *Treatise on Man*[141] and *on the Passions.* His sight, on the other hand, cannot be habituated in this manner as it is determined fully to its operation by the soul, being entirely passive to the formation that it receives from the soul in its establishment as a power, and in its full activation by its proper object; it effectively has nothing of its own which allows for the further development of its act, and thus no disposition for better or worse that can be applied to it by reason and will. However, the intellectual and volitional powers of man clearly by their very natures present themselves as being in need of habituation.

Questions 51 through 53 deal with the formation, growth, diminution, and corruption of the habits. Concentrating upon the habits that dispose the powers of the soul and their activities, Thomas states first that these powers admit of a certain natural formation, which is to say that they are inchoate to the individual insofar as they arise from one's nature and as they are impacted by the corporeal constitution that an individual happens to possess. Nevertheless, the formation of these is not wholly the result of the action of the soul in the establishment of both man's nature and the powers that belong to it. There is an important contribution made by forces external to the agent which differ according to whether we have in view the cognitive or appetitive powers, and again whether we have in view the nature that gives rise to such, or the individual possessed of this nature. With respect to the former, the intellect is disposed naturally to its foundational principles as it encounters the intelligible forms of things generated by the agent intellect acting upon what has been received through sense cognition, as was discussed in the *prima pars.* Thus, reason's habit of understanding first principles, for example, is something that arises both because of the soul's action in the establishment of reason's nature and operation, and the intelligible forms that it abstracts from the sensible things of a man's experience. The natural habits of one's intellect, however, are also engendered

---

[141] See ST. I. 81. 3. corpus and the replies to the objections.

by the physical constitution of the individual in question, some, for example, having a better sensitive cognitive apparatus than others, thereby allowing for a better grasp of the first principles of human understanding and their consequent application. With respect to the appetitive powers, the will does not possess a natural habit in the same fashion that the intellect does. Instead of possessing natural moral habits, it possesses naturally those principles that govern the manifestation of human activity and lead to the development of these habits. Thus, the will in its very nature is inclined to goodness itself, but is not determined habitually to any one thing, both in its nature and as it is possessed by an individual; that good is to be pursued and evil avoided are principles from which the moral virtues arise as man determines what is indeed good and evil, and habituates himself to these accordingly. However, on the part of the sensitive appetite, there may very well be natural habits there insofar as one's bodily constitution inclines one, for example, to chastity, meekness, anger, intemperance, and the like.

For the most part, however, the formation of habits is attributable to the activities that one performs repeatedly over time by powers whose constitutions are both active and passive, that is, of a definite nature and actuality which opens them to further realizations, as was described above in Questions 49 and 50. In the repetition involved in these activities, the power in question is conformed to the object with which it deals, the latter leaving its mark, so to speak, upon it. In only a few cases is this habituation effected by one act.[142] It is far more common that the stability and determination that is essential to habit are imprinted upon a partly passive power as the activities in which one engages eventually overcome, so to speak, the potentiality of the power and form it to their actuality. And so, in the intellectual life, although the intellect is initially formed or made actual by the soul and habituated naturally to its first principles in its encounters with the sensible world, it is activated and habituated primarily in accordance with activities that it itself undertakes and these repeatedly and over an extended period of time. For example, take the capacity to speak another language. This habituation is something to which the intellect is potential,

---

[142] See ST. I-II. 51. 3.

but is something that is not simply caused by the wishing or good intentions of the agent, or even by one or a meager collection of efforts to engage in this undertaking. It is something at which one arrives, a stability or permanence that one acquires, only through practice and repetition over an extended period of time, factors which differ for each person according to the fitness of their natural disposition in body, intellect, and will to this sort of activity, and other internal and external factors.[143]

As to the diminution and corruption of habits, this is effected by the acquisition of that which is contrary to them. For example, the habituation to biology could be corrupted through entertaining propositions of a nature that are contrary to and thus destructive of the foundational principles of the discipline itself, or through engaging in a faulty application of the scientific method whereby it engages the intellect with the objects specific to this discipline. Again, one's temperance could be corrupted as one considers judgments that are contrary to the nature of this virtue, judgments arrived at through ignorance, passion or the deliberate choices that one has made. The diminution of habits (Question 53) occurs insofar as one takes up those means contrary to their growth, that is, as one ceases, at the very least, from application to those things which bring the powers in question from their potential to an actual state. The powers are then left either to decay, so to speak, from their former condition, or are formed by whatever external factors impress themselves actively and repeatedly upon the individual. The latter might include the moral views of a culture, for example, that are impressed upon one, where one's intellect is formed by judgments made by others in the absence of doing this for oneself.

It should be clear from this treatise that the habits address and dispose all properly considered human activity that involves reason and will, from the theoretical and practical operations of man's intellect and volition, down to the "political" rule that reason and will exert over the concupiscible and irascible aspects of his sensitive appetite,[144] and all of this for

---

[143] Consider ST. I-II. 52 for greater detail concerning the growth of the habits.

[144] For the latter, see ST. I. 81. 3. ad2 and ST I-II. 56. 4. ad3.

better or worse, something assessed according to whether the disposition that is established in these activities is suitable to the nature and/or the end of the agent. Thus, insofar as the habits are principles vital to the good functioning of those powers involved directly in man's voluntary activity in the pursuit of his end and good, the habits become subject to moral evaluation and are indispensable means whereby man might achieve his happiness.[145] What remains are the details whereby the habits act in this way. This is the subject matter of the next two treatises on the virtues and the vices, respectively.

Treatise on the Virtues (Questions 55–70)

Simply put, virtue is a good habit, one which perfects a power of the soul in its activity that is directly contributive to the voluntary activity in which man engages for the sake of his end and good.[146] Specifically, virtue properly addresses and perfects man's intellectual, volitional, concupiscible, and irascible powers in their activities. It qualifies the intellect powers so that they are prone to work well, while the other powers receive this aptness as well as the right use of the virtue itself, the latter of which is not found in the intellectual virtues. For example, while one might possess the virtue of grammar, this in itself does not make someone speak or write correctly. However, the virtue of justice not only makes one apt to do just actions but also makes one act justly. This basic difference explains why habit and virtue are more commonly associated with man's moral activity than with his intellectual activity, insofar as our general understanding of virtue is directed more to the perfection of the activity performed and the agent that performs it rather than the predisposition to do such. One must also consider that the aptness of the intellectual powers to perform well does not of itself make the person good, something, again, that is contrary to our common understanding of virtue, which makes not only the act good, but the agent that performs it as well. Nonetheless, given that the intellectual powers admit of the perfecting qualification that is virtue, particularly as these powers contribute directly and essentially to the realization of

---

[145] See ST. I-II. 54. 3.
[146] ST. I-II. 55. 4. See the other articles of Question 55 as well as 56. 1.

the voluntary act, these intellectual dispositions are referred to as virtues. Limiting ourselves, first, to the virtues that man can acquire by his own agency, there are three that perfect the intellect's speculative activity, that of *understanding, science,* and *wisdom,* and two that perfect its practical activity, that of *prudence* and *art.*[147] With respect to the will, there is *justice,*[148] while the irascible and concupiscible powers are addressed by *temperance* and *fortitude,* respectively.[149]

As stated previously, it is the nature of the intellectual virtues to make one prone to the good work of the consideration of reason's very object, namely truth itself, and this either in itself or in relation to another. The former is perfected through the virtue of understanding that good habit that makes the human person prone to grasp the basic principles that lie at the foundation of all human reasoning, both speculative and practical, while the latter is perfected through the virtues of science and wisdom. The virtue of science perfects man's reasoning as it regards some particular area of reality to which man's mind is turned and investigated by means of a method that is appropriate to it. For example, one might acquire the virtue of physics as one acquires a deep and profound knowledge of the causes and principles that lie at the heart of the nature of material things and the universe itself. The virtue of wisdom, however, perfects man's reasoning not with respect to some particular aspect of reality, but rather with reality taken as a whole wherein its highest governing and determining principles are discovered and understood to the degree to which man is able to behold such things. The philosophical discipline of metaphysics has traditionally investigated these first and ultimate causes and principles of reality, but is also something that is regarded by theology, albeit in a different fashion, as was discussed in the first question of the *prima pars.*[150] Through these virtues, man's reason is made capable of appropriating the truth of all things.[151]

---

[147] ST. I-II. 56. 3.
[148] ST. I-II. 56. 6.
[149] ST. I-II. 56. 4.
[150] ST. I-II. 57. 1–2.
[151] To understand the implications of this last statement, one might wish to consider Josef Pieper's essay "The Truth of All Things" in (1966; 1989), pp. 11–105.

The practical intellect is a somewhat different matter insofar as its considerations are oriented to knowing not for its own sake, as was the case with the speculative intellect, but rather for the sake of application. There are two forms that this application can take, either in man's making or in his doing. The virtue of art perfects man's reasoning as he brings it to bear upon the making of certain things. Thus, the master carpenter is said to possess the art of carpentry, the virtuoso, the art of musical performance, the master chef, the culinary art, and so on. In each case, man's reasoning has been so perfected by the virtue in question that it has taken on the very art involved, making him ready to execute well all that is required by his activity so that a product might be well made: the beautiful chair, the perfect performance, and the exquisite meal, respectively. In the end, the quality of the product in relation to the criteria specific to the art in question determines whether the virtue exists or not in the person, and who, by consequence, deserves to be called a master carpenter, a virtuoso, or a master chef.[152] Prudence, on the other hand, perfects man's reasoning as he brings it to bear upon those things to be done, something that differs from making insofar as making finds its completion in the product that is made, while man's doing terminates in the action itself, something that importantly denotes his immanent activity which itself has a direct and necessary bearing upon how he manifests this in what he does in the world, something that has been discussed in great detail in the *Treatise on Human Activity*. Among the intellectual virtues, prudence is the only one that confers both aptness to do good work, but also the right use of this disposition. In this, prudence considers both the intellectual and appetitive activity of the human person, that he be well-disposed to the end and to the practical means whereby it might be chosen and attained, and to actually effect activity so that reason's deliberations about such matters might not remain in the speculative realm but be realized in the practical. In this, prudence has the nature of both an intellectual and a moral virtue insofar as it rectifies the considerations of

---

[152] ST. I-II. 57. 3. Many other matters are essential to this virtue, which cannot be suggested adequately here. One might wish to consider Gilson (1957) and (1965). Pieper (1988; 1990) is also recommended.

both reason and will, regarding the truth of the matter at hand and the good to which one is directed, applying what is true to the pursuit of what is good, rectifying the entirety of a man's voluntary activity with respect to the attainment of his end and good. In light of this, the necessity of prudence is clear, namely that it is by this virtue that all that a man must do in order to be well inclined and to choose well with respect to the means whereby his end is attained is addressed, a virtue that effects a unity, so to speak, of the appetitive and the intellectual so that all that is at one's disposal may be brought to bear most effectively upon the attainment of one's happiness.[153]

The moral virtues address the appetitive aspect of man in both its intellectual and sensitive manifestations. The nature of man's appetition inclines him to that which is good, namely that which perfects or completes him with respect to, at least, his powers, and at most his very person. The moral virtues are such that they not only readily dispose him to do this well, but they also bestow the right use of the disposition that they effect. And so, for example, the virtue of fortitude will not only make man prone to doing courageous deeds, but it will also make him act courageously.[154] That such a morally good act (or any moral act for that matter) is realized in the first place requires the presence of both the intellectual and moral virtues, something that is explained in light of what has been said concerning prudence and the nature of the voluntary act, where both the cognitive and the appetitive aspects of man must act in concert in a rectified manner so that a morally rectified act might occur. For the goodness and thus the rectification of man's appetitive aspect consists in its conformity to reason, wherein the moral virtues can then arise, either as they are directly involved in the voluntary act (in the case of the will) or participate in its life through obedience and conformity to it (in the case of the irascible and concupiscible aspects of his sensitive appetition).[155] This conformity is effected at the very least by the virtues of understanding and prudence without which there would be no moral virtue. For it is through understanding that

---

[153] ST. I-II. 57. 4–5. See also ST. II-II. 47.
[154] ST. I-II. 56. 3.
[155] ST. I-II. 58. 1–2.

one acquires those principles foundational and essential to all human reasoning and acting, something that then allows for the possibility of the discernment, through appropriate counsel and judgment, of the means whereby the end that is intended might be realized in those commanded practical activities that follow upon choice. Prudence, then, inclines one well to an end which is truly good, and marshals, moreover, all that is required on the part of the means whereby this end might be attained, something that gives rise to all other practical activities and the virtues that perfect them. A consequence of this is that one could be morally virtuous without having acquired the intellectual virtues of science, art, and wisdom. In a like manner, one could also possess the virtues of science, art, and even wisdom but not possess moral virtue, experiences that are common enough but which are nonetheless remarkable given the clear advantages that the intellectual virtues afford one in one's quest to be morally upright, and likewise the advantages bestowed on one who is morally virtuous to engage in the acquisition of the intellectual virtues. Be that as it may, for one to be called prudent demands that one have not only the virtue of understanding, that whereby one acquires an understanding of the universal moral principles that govern one's activity, but also the other moral virtues as well so that this intellectual virtue may not be overcome by one's passions, specifically by one's desire for sensual goods, and one's fear of the difficulties that attend the many goods of this life.[156] By this very fact, it is clear that the moral virtues cannot be identified with the passions, but are rather the means whereby the passions are brought into conformity with the life of reason. In this conformity, moral virtue does not destroy the passional life of man. Instead, it directs this aspect of his appetition to the good that has been discerned by his reason, at the very least moderating its impact upon the voluntary act (when it impels one contrary to what one should choose), or at most conforming it to the life of reason so that one might experience the passions in full accord with what reason and will command. In this way, the passional life of man is perfected by the moral virtues, allowing not only for their full experience, but this in the right way, at the right

---

[156] ST. I-II. 58. 4–5.

time, to the right degree, with the right people, and so on. For, as Thomas states, "it is not the function of virtue to deprive the powers subordinate to reason of their proper activities, but to make them execute the commands of reason, by exercising their proper acts."[157] In this way, virtue directs the passional life to its properly full and regulated expression, something that was enjoyed naturally by man in the prelapsarian state and for which, in his fallen condition, he strives insofar as this is possible.

Not every moral virtue is concerned with the passions. There are many that qualify and perfect those activities over which the human person has a direct control, virtues that are distinct from those that regard the activities of man's sensitive appetition, over which reason and will exert only an indirect influence and command. The former are collected under the virtue of justice, that virtue whereby the intellectual appetite, one's will, is rectified in its relations to other people, individually or collectively considered, as it renders to each one what is due to him. The latter, however, are not directed primarily in that fashion, but regard, rather, the individual himself, as he requires an ordering of his passional life so that he might act effectively not only with regard to others in justice, but especially in all those activities, both moral and intellectual, that are required of him if he is to achieve his happiness. The passions of one's sensitive appetition are not collected under one virtue, if only by the fact that the passional life itself is divided into its concupiscible and irascible moments. The virtue of temperance does indeed collect within it all those virtues that perfect man's concupiscence. However, given the complex object of his irascibility (namely, the arduous good or evil, and the regarding of one or the other in one's approach or withdrawal, as was described in the *Treatise on the Passions*), the virtues that perfect it are diverse, specifically, fortitude (concerning fear and daring), magnanimity (about hope and despair) and meekness (about anger).[158] Nevertheless, Thomas treats fortitude as many others did before him, as addressing the irascible aspect as such,

---

[157] ST. I-II. 59. 5. See also the other articles of this question for the relations between the moral virtues and passion.

[158] ST. I-II. 60. 1–4.

and within whose purview the other kinds could be collected and considered.[159] As a consequence, there are four moral virtues under which all other moral virtues can be collected as so many species of these four.[160] Accordingly, these four virtues (prudence, justice, fortitude, and temperance) are designated as *principal* or *cardinal*, those virtues that regard the good that needs to be instilled principally in man's practical reasoning, the operations of his willing, and the passions of his irascible and concupiscible appetites, respectively, especially as the latter militate against what reason and will command, either as his concupiscence incites him to something contrary to reason's command or as his irascibility bids him to flee from following reason's dictates. Thus, man must have the means whereby he can curb his concupiscence (temperance) or strengthen himself against the difficulties that face him (fortitude) if he is to pursue and attain to the good that is determined by reason.[161]

These cardinal virtues, the "hinges" so to speak from which the whole of man's moral life hangs, are not particular to Thomas but are part of the theological and philosophical traditions that he inherited, virtues spoken of by saints, theologians, and philosophers alike. And yet, as we have seen many times, these means whereby one's human activity is rightly ordered, means that are well within the agent's control, are sufficient only to the realization of man's imperfect happiness. Even as these four are brought to bear upon the whole of his life, and even upon things divine, they are not of a nature proportioned to the end for which man strives. It is necessary, then, to look for ways by which man and these naturally acquired virtues might be aided so as to aspire to his perfect happiness. This can only be effected through God's help, a help that manifests in the supernatural acquisition and perfection not only of the cardinal virtues, but most especially in the gifting to man of what are called the *theological virtues* of which there are three, namely *faith*, *hope*, and *charity*. These supernatural virtues

---

[159] ST. I-II. 61. 2 and ad3.

[160] See ST. I-II. 60. 5 for a list of 11 of these. See also I-II. 61. 3. Thomas goes into great detail concerning the many and diverse virtues subordinated to these four in the *secunda secundae*.

[161] ST. I-II. 61. 1–3.

are the ways by which man can participate in the Godhead, manifest more clearly and perfectly the image of God to which he has been fashioned, and be supplied with what nature lacks in his desire to attain his perfect happiness through whatever actions he can effect in the here and now as he anticipates the gift of his future glory.[162]

These virtues are called theological for three reasons, first, insofar as they have God as their object and, thus, are the means whereby man is directly rightly in his activities toward Him, secondly, as they are infused in man by God alone, and third, as man's knowledge of these virtues is obtained only insofar as they have been revealed to him by the Holy Scriptures.[163] They are distinct, then, from the intellectual and moral virtues insofar as their object is wholly beyond the grasp of human reason and will acting according to their natural principles. And yet, as virtues, they address the faculties of the human person, specifically those that distinguish man from the animals lacking reason and in which is found the image of God to which man is made and direct him to his perfect happiness in the same manner that the natural inclinations of his reason and will direct him to his end and good. Thus, just as man's speculative and practical reasoning is made possible by those principles foundational to all human reasoning as supplied by the habit of understanding (and then perfected by the virtue of the same name), so too in matters related to his supernatural end and happiness, the virtue of *faith* supplies man's intellect with those principles that direct him to this end, principles that become the foundation for the articles of faith. Again, just as his will intends something as it has been presented to it by reason under the aspect of good and as something that can be attained, so too does the virtue of *hope* regard as attainable that good which has been gifted to man through faith. Finally, just as the will rests only when the intended end has actually been attained, so too does the virtue of charity effect man's ultimate happiness and peace wherein his will rests in the end known through faith and intended through hope, having been united to and transformed into that very end and good for which man was made by these

[162] ST. I-II. 62. 1.
[163] Ibid.

virtues but especially in the experience of charity, a love and delight that begin now in this life and come to their perfection in the next.[164] Finally, just as there was an order of generation and perfection noted with respect to the passions, so too do we find this among the theological virtues. Thus, just as knowledge of the suitable gave rise to the binding of the appetite to this suitable good in love, a passion that impelled man in his desire to attain it, to overcome in hope any difficulties that its acquisition may present, and finally the resolution of his desire and hope in delight consequent upon his actual attainment of this good, so too does man through faith come into his initial possession of his most perfect end and good, which gives rise to his initial experience of charity as he understands that the object of his charity, God Himself, can actually be attained, something which fuels his hope, and, together with the doctrines of the faith, establish and deepen his charity over time, something which then redounds upon his faith and hope deepening them in like kind. Thus, insofar as charity "quickens" the seeds of one's faith and hope, charity becomes the "mother and root" of these and all other virtues.[165]

How we come to acquire the virtues depends upon whether one is considering the intellectual/moral virtues or the theological. The former, being habits, is developed in much the same fashion as was seen in the *Treatise on the Habits*; they have their natural "seed" or "germ," so to speak, in man by reason of his soul which establishes in each person "certain naturally known principles of both knowledge and action, which are the nurseries of intellectual and moral virtues, and in so far as there is in the will a natural appetite for good in accordance with reason."[166] Thomas also mentions, as before, that the virtues can be present naturally as an individual has a natural aptitude for one or the other of the intellectual and moral virtues by reason of the happy disposition of those sensitive powers or bodily condition that assist the powers of man in their proper activities. Nonetheless, the perfection of these virtues is not present in man naturally, but is only acquired through his activities as they

---

[164] ST. I-II. 62. 3.
[165] ST. I-II. 62. 4 and ad3.
[166] ST. I-II. 63. 1.

are directed to his good as determined by the order and rule of
his reason, as was discussed previously in the *Treatise on the
Habits*. The theological virtues, on the other hand, being pure
gift of God to man, are neither naturally present in man (as were
the other virtues in their inchoate and dispositive forms) nor
acquired by him through his activity. For these virtues are not
established according to the order and rule of man's reason, but,
rather, by God's acting upon man himself.[167] Having made this
distinction, however, Thomas then goes on to argue that even
the moral virtues must be infused in man by God. For "effects
must needs be proportionate to their causes and principles."[168]
In receiving the theological virtues, one is directed "sufficiently
to (one's) supernatural end, inchoatively: i.e., to God Himself
immediately. But the soul needs further to be perfected by
infused virtues in regard to other things, yet in relation to God."
Now, the intellectual and moral virtues that one may possess
are not of themselves proportioned to the work made necessary
consequent to the reception of the theological virtues. For the
intellectual and moral virtues are proportioned to man's life in
this world, and not to his life in the next. Thus, it is required
that man not only receives the theological virtues of faith, hope,
and charity in this life but also receives infused moral virtues
so that his everyday living might itself become transformed by
and strengthened in his faith, hope, and love of God, something
which he himself by his own activities could not effect. Thomas
illustrates this through the example of the consumption of food.
Through the virtue of temperance, the rule or order established
by man's reason regards the health of the body, regulating the
quality and quantity required for this, so that he might be free to
engage fully and properly in those activities that are definitively
human. Thus, while he intends his health, his health is intended
as a means to the greater end of that imperfect happiness which
is within his natural grasp. These are the heights to which this
virtue can aspire, as is demonstrated well by Aristotle's discussion of it in his *Nicomachean Ethics*.[169] However, in faith, hope,
and charity, there is now a transformation of one's life in light

---

[167] ST. I-II. 63. 1–2.
[168] ST. I-II. 63. 3.
[169] NE. III. 10–12.

of what has been revealed, accepted, and loved, something that impacts one's daily living, but which cannot be treated adequately by the virtues caused by one's own activities. There must now be an infused temperance that allows man to act in a way proportioned to the end that has now been revealed and to which he has bound himself through the theological virtues, namely that he order the consumption of his food in light of not just matters relating to his health, but also and primarily adopt the ascetical practices required of the Christian as revealed in Holy Scripture, something that can be done only through the aid that God gives. What appears, then, to be a heroic or a foolish exhibition of temperance to those outside the faith, is in fact, according to Thomas, a true, authentic display of virtue, that is to say a regulation and perfecting of activity undertaken in light of and for the sake of that most perfect of goods, something that defines the very character of virtue itself as they constitute the perfect qualification of the powers of one's person whereby one's activity can be rightly ordered to that attainment of this perfect good and end.[170]

The very heart of an act of virtue consists in the degree to which it conforms to the order or rule set forth by reason, specifically that it has disposed one's activity to such a degree that one can consistently do what is absolutely required and right in any given situation. To put this in more traditional terms, virtue allows one to determine and act in accordance with the mean that exists between the two extremes of excess and deficiency, that is to say, that one's activity embodies perfectly the good that has been determined by reason, neither exceeding this measure nor falling short of it. For example, one who possesses the virtue of temperance can, in any given situation, understand what would be an appropriate amount of food to consume, being readily inclined not only to the virtuous amount but also made able to act in this fashion. The mean is something difficult to discern, requiring an attention to the many and diverse issues discussed in the *Treatise on Human Activity*, specifically the varied ends involved, their order to one's ultimate end, and the circumstances that surround these. Nonetheless, a right way of acting exists in each situation, something that virtue allows one

---

[170] See ST. I-II. 63. 3–4, especially the replies to the objections of Article 3.

to discover and navigate well. The mean in the moral virtues that regard man's sensitive appetition is often something that reason determines with a view to the condition of the person, and specifically to how each one is situated in relation to his passions. Thus, a temperate taking of alcohol for one might be excessive to another who suffers from the vice of drunkenness, and thus whose temperance demands abstention. One person's temperate use of food might be deficient for another, either because the latter, for health reasons, requires more sustenance than is sufficient for the former, or because the former's health requires far less food than is normal for the average person. The moral virtue of justice, on the other hand, is concerned with those activities that take place between people as they seek to render to each other what is due to them. The determination of the mean here, then, is a true mean, rather than the prior which was determined in relation to the condition of the human person involved.[171] As for the speculative intellectual virtues, the mean is found in the mind's conformity with the things it knows, representing them for what they are, nor more and no less. Excess is found "if something false is affirmed, as though something were, which in reality is not," while deficiency arises "if something is falsely denied, and declared not to be, whereas in reality it is."[172] As for the virtue of prudence, since it must be in conformity with the things that it knows, and must determine and command what is to be done in light of that conformity, its mean lies in the rectification of reason as this power determines the mean in the moral realm. Finally, the mean in the theological virtues is not something that one can ever accomplish essentially. For one can never love God "as much as He ought to be loved, nor believe and hope in Him as much as (one) should," thus precluding the possibility of excess on one's part. Instead, the mean is accomplished accidentally, that is to say, in relation to man himself and not God. "For although we cannot be borne to God as much as we ought, yet we should approach to Him by believing, hoping and loving, according to the measure of our condition."[173] To illustrate what he means here, Thomas offers

---

[171] ST. I-II. 64. 1–2
[172] ST. I-II. 64. 3.
[173] ST. I-II. 64. 4.

the example of hope where the mean in relation to man exists between "presumption and despair . . . in so far as a man is said to be presumptuous through hoping to receive from God a good in excess of his condition; or to despair through failing to hope for that which according to his condition he might hope for."[174]

Just as there were intimate connections existing between the passions of man's sensitive appetition, so too do they exist among the virtues. From what has been said concerning prudence, it should come as no surprise that the moral virtues are all connected intimately, whether one considers their general properties or the matters with which they are concerned. With regard to the former, insofar as "discretion belongs to prudence, rectitude to justice, moderation to temperance and strength of mind to fortitude," it is hard to imagine how one could commend strength of mind in a virtuous act without it also being moderate, upright, or done with discretion. With regard to the latter, we have seen that the moral virtues cannot exist without prudence. However, it is also the case that prudence cannot exist without the other moral virtues. For prudence rectifies man's reasoning concerning those things to be done if his end is to be achieved, something that involves the rectification of his capacity to take counsel, to judge of what this produces, and to command what must be done, all of which are possible only insofar as he acts justly, courageously, and temperately, virtues which dispose him rightly to his end and good, dispositions that constitute the beginning of the considerations into which prudence enters in the discharge of its proper activities. And so, "just as we cannot have speculative science unless we have the understanding of principles, so neither can we have prudence without the moral virtues."[175]

Clearly, the moral virtues can exist without charity "insofar as they produce good works that are directed to an end not surpassing the natural power of man." However, if we consider those moral virtues that are infused and thus are proportioned to man's supernatural end, it is a different story. These virtues cannot exist without charity. For just as the natural moral virtues cannot exist without prudence, so too is it the case that the

[174] Ibid., ad3.
[175] ST. I-II. 65. 1.

infused moral virtues cannot exist without infused prudence, and that infused prudence itself cannot exist unless there be the right disposition of the agent to his ultimate end, something that is effected by charity itself. Therefore, charity is the root from which all the infused virtues grow and is infused together with them in man. For it is the nature of charity not only to direct man to his ultimate end but also to be "the principle of all the good works that are referable to his last end."[176] There are three consequences to this. First, that both charity and infused prudence guide the infused moral virtues, with charity discharging the function in the supernatural realm that natural prudence exerts in the natural. Second, if one were to lose the infused virtue of charity through the committing of a mortal sin, this would result in the loss of all other infused moral virtues. And third, that

> only the infused virtues are perfect, and deserve to be called virtues simply: since they direct man well to the ultimate end. But the other virtues, those, namely, that are acquired, are virtues in a restricted sense, but not simply: for they direct man well in respect of the last end in some particular genus of action, but not in respect of the last end simply.[177]

As for the relations that exist between faith, hope, and charity, Thomas reminds us that we call activity virtuous only insofar as it is both good and well done. Thus, one might perform a just act, but if the act is not done with prudence and all that this virtue implies, then the act will not be perfectly good, and the habit from which it arose will not have the perfect character of virtue. In the same way, then, faith and hope can exist without charity but only in an inchoate state and not as complete and perfect virtues. For it is only in charity that both faith and hope aspire to the good and the well in all their works and this insofar as through charity both faith and hope are rightly ordered, an order that could not be achieved in any other way.[178] In like manner, charity cannot exist without faith and hope. For it is

---

[176] ST. I-II. 65. 3.
[177] ST. I-II. 65. 2.
[178] ST. I-II. 65. 4.

the nature of charity that it includes within the love of God "a certain friendship with Him; which implies, besides love, a certain mutual return of love, together with a mutual communion." This fellowship that man enjoys with God, which consists in a certain dialogue with him,

> is begun here, in this life, by grace, but will be perfected in the future life, by glory; each of which things we hold by faith and hope. Wherefore just as friendship with a person would be impossible, if one disbelieved in, or despaired of, the possibility of their fellowship or dialogue; so too, friendship with God, which is charity, is impossible without faith, so as to believe in this fellowship and dialogue with God, and to hope to attain to this fellowship.[179]

In light of the preceding, one can see that prudence is foremost among the cardinal virtues as it directly addresses and rectifies reason in its practical counsel, judgment, and command of what is to be done. The other three cardinal virtues are ranked as they approach reason more or less depending upon the nature of their participation in the rational life. Justice ranks first among them as it is reason's appetite, and fortitude is greater than temperance as its object is more complex, thus requiring greater involvement of reason in its activities.[180] Among the intellectual virtues, wisdom is the greatest as its object (the supreme cause of all, namely God Himself) surpasses the objects with which the other intellectual virtues are concerned (those secondary causes consequent upon the first cause Himself). Prudence, as practical wisdom falls under speculative wisdom as prudence directs man to undertake all those things that are required for the beholding of wisdom itself.[181] Lastly, with respect to the theological virtues, since they all have God for their object, the judgment of which is greater is based upon which of these approach nearer to God than the others. Among these three, then, charity is foremost insofar as both faith and hope imply a certain distance in their meaning, "since faith is of what is

[179] ST. I-II. 65. 5.
[180] ST. I-II. 66. 1 and 4.
[181] ST. I-II. 66. 5. corpus, ad1 and 2.

not seen, and hope is of what is not possessed. But the love of charity is of that which is already possessed: since the beloved is, in a manner, in the lover, and again, the lover is drawn by desire to union with the beloved."[182] As to whether the virtues perdure into the next life, Thomas states that the moral virtues will continue in the blessed but in a perfected way insofar as their reason will no longer be subject to error, and their appetitive nature will be in perfect accord with reason, and no longer subject to the rebellion of man's fallen nature or troubled by the evils that afflicted him in this life.[183] The intellectual virtues remain in a perfected manner as well.[184] However, with respect to the theological virtues, neither faith nor hope remains. For at that time, their object will have been achieved.[185] Only charity remains as the possession of God that it implies and that what begins in this life is then perfectly attained and fulfilled in the next.[186]

The Gifts, The Beatitudes, and The Fruits of the Holy Spirit (Questions 68–70)

Although these three questions are part of the *Treatise on the Virtues*, nonetheless given their importance to the whole of the moral life of the Christian and to the very order of Thomas's moral theology as presented in the *Summa*, they deserve special attention.[187] The fact that they stand at the end of this treatise, that they comprise but 16 articles, and that the questions concerning the Beatitudes and the Gifts have been "too little read"[188] by theologians and scholars, should not cause one to pass them by, particularly in light of the lengthy considerations already expended upon the virtues, the habits, and the passions. For it is in these few articles that we find not only what is characteristic and essential to the Christian ethic, but also the very perfection of the internal principles necessary to

---

[182] ST. I-II. 66. 6.
[183] ST. I-II. 67. 1.
[184] ST. I-II. 67. 2.
[185] ST. I-II. 67. 3–5.
[186] ST. I-II. 67. 6.
[187] See Pinckaers (1993; 1995), pp. 134–167.
[188] Torrell (1996; 2003), p. 216.

the voluntary act, and a practical fleshing out, so to speak, of what, up until this point, has been decidedly general in scope.

With respect to the Gifts of the Holy Spirit, Thomas first distinguishes them from the virtues, and this in light of the way by which the Holy Scriptures express themselves (at Isaiah 11.2–3), an important decision given the varied approaches that theologians before him have taken concerning this question.[189] He notes that the word "gift" is not used at Isaiah 11 but rather "spirit," giving rise to his judgment that the seven are in man by way of "Divine inspiration," which inspiration denotes a "movement coming from outside" the human person, a movement that is not to be reduced to the material level, but rather indicates something that God effects within man that cannot be attributed to man's agency.[190] This external principle is distinguished from that principle of movement that is internal to man, namely his reason. Now, we have just seen in this treatise on virtue that as long as we consider the movements effected by reason, both with respect to itself and to the appetitive powers over which it holds sway, the moral and intellectual virtues are sufficient to their perfection and to that of man himself, "even as they were in many of the pagans."[191] However, in light of man's supernatural end and his incapacity to be oriented to and to strive after this by his own agency, another principle of movement, that one external to man, namely of God Himself, had to come into play if man were to achieve the perfection of his ultimate and true end. Man is effected or moved in this fashion only insofar as he is made in some way "proportionate" to his mover, namely to God Himself, and this to the point where he is so disposed to God that he becomes well or easily moved by Him, readily responsive to His promptings. Thus, a medical student can only readily respond to the learning offered by a master physician insofar as he has acquired a suitable disposition to this learning, something that would presumably include a certain maturation of his person, and the development of both his intellectual and moral virtues. Man, then, needs those perfections that are higher than the moral and intellectual virtues, perfections that

---

[189] As reviewed in the first part of his response in 68. 1.

[190] See note 21 on p. 208 of Torrell (1996; 2003).

[191] ST. I-II. 65. 2.

will dispose him to being moved by God, and it is these perfections that are referred to as the Gifts of the Holy Spirit, those
infusions that dispose him "to become amenable to the Divine
inspiration . . . to the promptings of God" and thus moved by a
principle that is higher than his own reason itself. Thus, a certain "instinct" is established in man whereby he is put into "a
position of perfect docility with respect to the action of the Holy
Spirit,"[192] something that allows man the opportunity to engage
in acts that are higher than the acts of virtue.

One might ask why these gifts are necessary in light of the
perfection that is gifted to man in the form of the theological
virtues. Thomas states that these perfections, unlike the natural
perfection that is afforded reason in its establishment as a power
and its operations, are not perfectly possessed and wielded by
man insofar as their object, God Himself, is known and loved
but imperfectly. Thus, just as the medical student previously
mentioned, having been admitted into the master physician's
class and become his apprentice, cannot conduct his discipline by himself, but only insofar as his master instructs him
and moves him to action, so too is it with man as he has been
imperfectly formed by the theological virtues. Although his reason has been perfected by them, much as the medical student's
mind has been perfected by his extensive training prior to and
as a condition of his apprenticeship with the master physician,
man's reason alone cannot move or prompt these perfections,
just as the knowledge acquired by the medical student is itself
insufficient to its right practical application. There must, then,
exist the promptings of the Holy Spirit if man is to engage in
acts that are higher than the acts of the natural virtues. This
point is sharpened by the fact that a mind, even perfected by the
virtues both natural and supernatural, is still prone to error as
it does not know all things. It is also subject to the whole of the
influence of man's passional and corporeal condition as these
directly impact the functioning of reason, as described in the
Treatise on Human Acts, not to mention all that man inherits
from his fallen condition.[193] The Gifts, then, are given to man so
that he might be guarded and kept safe from these things, hav-

---

[192] Torrell (1996; 2003), p. 208.
[193] Specifically, see Gregory's list in ST. I-II. 68. 2. obj. 3.

ing been made amenable to the promptings of the Holy Spirit.[194] Torrell explains this well when he emphasizes that the gifts do not take one beyond the theological virtues. Rather

> the gifts are granted "to help the virtues . . ." to attain their final goal, despite our timidities, lukewarmness, pettiness. Certainly nothing goes beyond faith or charity, but our reason, which hesitates and calculates, does not always allow them a free path. God then intervenes and takes us by the hand, so to speak, in order to make us advance more surely on his pathways.[195]

The gifts, then, address the human situation and allow man to surpass his imperfections "which are so many limits and shackles to the glorious liberty of the children of God."[196]

This liberty is very much in Thomas's mind in the third article where he considers whether these gifts are habits. For it seems in being moved in this fashion by the Holy Spirit that man might lose his status as a volitional agent and become more like an instrument or a tool in the Spirit's hands, thus making the notion of habit as descriptive of the gifts inappropriate.[197] Thomas replies that such would be the case if man were not capable of his own volitional activity but were solely passive to actions from outside of him. However, it is the case, as seen earlier, that there is both internal and external forces at work in man's activity, specifically that of reason and of God Himself, respectively. Consequently, the gifts as received by man must be described as habits in light of man's free will, that they constitute that disposition "whereby man is perfected to obey readily the Holy Spirit." Thomas draws a comparison with the situation where the moral virtues perfect man's sensitive appetite insofar as it partakes of the life of reason through them, making the appetite apt to follow reason's commands promptly. The same, then, is said with respect to the Gifts of the Holy Spirit, that just as the moral virtues, as good habits, make man's sensitive

---

[194] Ibid., ad3.
[195] Torrell (1996; 2003), p. 214.
[196] Ibid., p. 215.
[197] ST. I-II. 68. 3. obj. 2.

appetition prompt to obey his reason, so too do the Gifts, as habits, render man prompt to obey the Spirit's call.[198]

There are seven gifts that render the human person prompt to the call of the Holy Spirit, gifts that dispose his rational and appetitive powers, those that are directly necessary to his volitional act and that have been perfected by the theological virtues of faith, hope, and charity, to engage readily in their respective acts toward man's supernatural end: remember, the perfections of the theological virtues establish the union of man's mind with his supernatural object, but this imperfectly, requiring, therefore, the gifts themselves so that man might make use of the theological virtues, as he is incapable of doing this insofar as his reason and will are proportioned only to the natural virtues, as was described previously. His reason is addressed in both its speculative and practical aspects and this as they both apprehend or discover the truth, and as they make judgments concerning it. With respect to the former, the speculative intellect is perfected by the gift of *understanding*, the practical, by *counsel.* With respect to the latter, the speculative intellect is perfected by *wisdom*, the practical, by *knowledge.* As for the appetitive powers, these regard man's relations with others and in regard to himself. The former belongs to the will which is perfected by the gift of *piety.* The latter belongs to man's sensitive appetite under its irascible and concupiscible aspects. The former is perfected by *fortitude* with respect to his fear of danger, while the latter is perfected by *fear* with respect to his disordered desires for pleasure.[199]

In Question 69, Thomas turns from the Gifts to the Beatitudes as found in Matthew's Gospel. This turn is not original to Thomas, but travels the path blazed by the early Church Fathers, and especially St. Augustine, all of whom understood how important the Sermon on the Mount was as it provided one with a perfect model for Christian living in this world oriented to and anticipating life in the next. According to Pinckaers, Augustine's

---

[198] For a better and more extensive development of man's liberty in relation to the gifts of the Holy Spirit, consider Chapter IX of Torrell (1996; 2003).

[199] ST. I-II. 68. 4. corpus and ad3. The reader should consider the matters dealt with in Articles 5 through 8 of Question 68.

Commentary on the Sermon on the Mount is of central importance as it is that work to which most everyone in the Middle Ages appealed in their commentaries upon this Sermon.[200] For our purposes, Augustine's most original contribution in commenting upon the Sermon was to connect the Beatitudes to the Gifts of the Holy Spirit, wherein the stages that the Christian travelled in this life as manifested in the Beatitudes was only possible insofar as the Holy Spirit prompted and aided man, thus giving rise to the importance of the Gifts in this regard.[201] This is something that many medieval theologians followed in their commentaries, but especially Thomas for whom it became an integral component to the whole of the moral structure of the *Summa*.[202]

He begins in Article 1 with the distinction between the virtues and gifts on the one hand, and the beatitudes on the other. He situates his answer in the context of man's ultimate happiness, something for which man hopes, and because of this is said to possess already, albeit imperfectly, and to be moved thereto so as to approach and ultimately to possess it perfectly (as was seen, in a lesser way, in the *Treatise on the Passions*, where a love born from a knowledge of something as good imperfectly united the lover to the beloved, making the beloved at least intentionally present to the lover, which fueled both his desire and his hope to acquire that which he loves for the sake of his joy and rest in the beloved actually attained). The action implied by this is the work of virtue, "and above all by the works of the gifts, if we speak of eternal happiness, for which our reason is not sufficient, since we need to be moved by the Holy Spirit, and to be perfected with His gifts that we may obey and follow Him. Consequently, the beatitudes differ from the virtues and gifts, not as habit from habit, but as act from habit." To repeat, the beatitudes are identified with the activities that manifest following upon the habits of the theological virtues and the gifts of the Holy Spirit as these latter are infused in man, as described previously, so that he might engage in acts, these beatitudes, that are higher than those that flow from the natural moral and intellectual virtues.

[200] Pinckaers (1993; 1995), p. 140.
[201] Ibid., pp. 151–152.
[202] Ibid., pp. 154–155.

Thomas puts a finer point on this in Articles 3 and 4 where he considers whether the beatitudes have been suitably numbered, as well as their rewards. Appealing once again to man's happiness, he reminds the reader of the basic positions (discussed in the *Treatise on Happiness*) that people have taken concerning that in which they typically place their hope for their happiness, namely in the sensual, active, and contemplative lives. Clearly, the sensual life is an obstacle to man's future happiness, while the active life contributes to the disposition required of one to attain and enjoy it. The contemplative life belongs to the very essence of man's happiness, something that is imperfectly realized in the here and now, an anticipation or beginning of what will be perfected in the next life. It is fitting, then, that Christians be instructed by the Lord Jesus in his Sermon on the Mount concerning the ways that they should act in this life as they anticipate their happiness in the next in light of these three common approaches to happiness. In other words, the Beatitudes constitute those perfect acts whereby the Christian navigates this world, its goods, and its evils in the most truly virtuous way that is open to him, something that manifests itself as they willingly and freely seek for that good for which they could not aspire on their own, to which they are prompted by the Holy Spirit, a prompting made possible through the gifts they have received from Him, and all of this, consequent upon the union effected in them with God through the dispositions specific to the theological virtues. Consequently, three of the Beatitudes address and remove the obstacles presented by the sensual life, specifically with respect to the external goods (of honors and riches—"Blessed are the poor in spirit"), and those pleasures associated with the irascible and concupiscible passions ("Blessed are the meek" and "Blessed are they that mourn"), two perfect their relations with their neighbor (those to which one is duty bound, and those that manifest in a spontaneous giving to him—"Blessed are they that hunger and thirst after justice" and "Blessed are the merciful"), and two address the contemplative life ("Blessed are the clean of heart" and "Blessed are the peacemakers"). In keeping with what has been said above concerning the nature of the activity that each Beatitude represents, Thomas reminds the reader that there will be virtues and gifts associated with each Beatitude which incline man to the acts that they represent.[203] Thus, the Christian will not only moderate his desire for and use of riches and honor, he may even come to the point where he despises these insofar as they lose their allure to the degree that he becomes more and more desirous of God Himself;[204] he achieves not only a moderation of his appetites, but also may even be tranquil with respect to the irascible and utterly untroubled by the concupiscible; not only does he give to his neighbor what is due to him, he may also do this with such great desire; he is not only liberal with his wealth toward his family and friends, but he also may be this to such an extent that he considers only the need of those to whom he give, giving to all regardless of the ties of blood and affection; and his active life is such that the merits of his virtue and the gifts redounds upon himself, insofar as his heart is cleansed of all inordinate passion, and upon his relations with others, insofar as he and they enjoy the peace that comes with justice. As for the eighth Beatitude, Thomas states that it is "a confirmation and manifestation of all those which precede it." For by the very fact that one is confirmed in the acts represented by the Beatitudes, "no persecution can make him relinquish such goods. Hence, the eighth Beatitude pertains in a way to the other seven."[205]

The rewards that are promised to the Christian who seeks to embody in his life these actions, and by consequence who prays for their associated virtues and gifts, are presented, in Article 4, in such a fashion so as to speak to and overcome the core reasons why people generally seek after the sensual, active, and contemplative live for their happiness. The excellence and abundance of riches and honors pale in comparison to those to be obtained in heaven by the poor in spirit to whom is promised the kingdom of Heaven; the security that is sought cruelly and piteously by men through the destruction of others through aggression and war pales in comparison to the "secure and peaceful possession of the land of the living, whereby the solid reality of eternal

---

[203] On this point, I follow O'Connor's interpretation as noted in Volume 24 (1973) of his Blackfriars' translation of the *Summa Theologiae* (note "h" on p. 52).

[204] See Ibid., note "i," pp. 52–53.

[205] ST. I-II. 69. 3. ad5 (using O'Connor's translation in Blackfriars's edition).

goods" is promised to the meek; and to those who mourn over the burdens of this world, from which people seek relief in the sensual pleasures, is promised a consolation that is wholly satisfying and will not fade away as do those experienced in man's animality; to those who hunger for justice, something from which many withdraw for the sake of either preserving their own good or obtaining the goods of others, is promised complete satisfaction; to those who are merciful, something from which many withdraw so that they might not become involved in the misery of others, is promised God's mercy and so to "be delivered from all misery;" to those whose heart has been cleansed, is promised the very clarity of the vision of God Himself; and to those who make peace within themselves or with others is to imitate "the God of unity and peace. Hence, as a reward, he is promised the glory of the Divine sonship, consisting in perfect union with God through consummate wisdom."[206] Lastly, with respect to the eighth Beatitude, just as it is "a confirmation of all the beatitudes, so it deserves all the rewards of the beatitudes. Hence, it returns to the first, that we may understand all the other rewards to be attributed to it in consequence."[207]

The Fruits of the Holy Spirit (found in Galatians 5.22–3) are understood, first, in relation to our immediate and general understanding of "fruit" itself, namely that produce of a plant or tree that has come to its maturity, a produce that is sweet to the taste. It is related both to the tree that produces it and to the person who gathers it. Applying this to the spiritual realm, man's fruit can be understood in either way, namely as that which he produces or that which he gathers. The latter gathering applies only to the fruit of his last end, that which is sought only for itself and for no other reason, and as that in which he finds his true happiness and enjoyment. "For a man has both a field and a tree, and yet these are not called fruits; but that only which is last, to wit, that which man intends to derive from the field and from the tree." As for the fruits that man produces, these are understood in relation to his activities, both those that proceed from his reason (his moral and intellectual activity, perfected by the virtues he has acquired on his own), and those that

---

[206] ST. I-II. 69. 4.
[207] Ibid., ad2.

proceed from the Holy Spirit (that activity consequent to the infusions that he has received in the forms of the infused moral, intellectual, and theological virtues, and the Gifts that make them possible). Consequently, the Beatitudes and the Fruits of the Holy Spirit both refer to those activities of man that have sprouted from the Divine seed implanted in him.[208] And since these latter fruit are ordered to that ultimate fruit, that eternal life and happiness for which he strives as a Christian, these fruits are better understood as "flowers."[209] The question, however, arises: What is the difference, then, between the Beatitudes and the Fruits of the Holy Spirit, since both refer to a man's activity? Thomas states that the fruit is the more generic of the two, denoting something that is ultimate and delightful, while "Beatitude" denotes this but more specifically according to perfection and excellence. Thus, every Beatitude is a fruit, but only some fruits are Beatitudes. "For the fruits are any virtuous deeds in which one delights: whereas the Beatitudes are none but perfect works, and which, by reason of their perfection, are assigned to the gifts rather than to the virtues."[210]

The Fruits listed in Galatians, then, are distinguished from each other by reason of the different ways by which the Holy Spirit "produces 'sprouts' "[211] in man. This occurs in three ways, namely as his mind is set in order with regard to itself, to things that are near it, and to things that are below it. With respect to the first, the mind is well-disposed when it conducts itself well in both good and evil things. The mind's salutary disposition to good is found in love which constitutes that initial bond of the lover with the beloved, from which arises all the other emotions. In a higher way, we have the Holy Spirit given to man as this manifests in *charity*, the first of the fruits. From this unity of man with the Holy Spirit, there arises, secondly, *joy*, from which, third, a twofold *peace* results, the first as the Spirit's presence frees one from all disturbances from without, and secondly as the Spirit's presence calms the restless desires of man as it has now found its proper fulfillment. On the other hand,

[208] ST. I-II. 70. 1.
[209] Ibid., ad1.
[210] ST. I-II. 70. 2.
[211] Using Torrell's translation on p. 218 in (1996; 2003).

the mind's good disposition with respect to evil is found in two things, namely, as it is not disturbed when evil threatens, and when good things are delayed. To the former belongs *patience*, and to the latter, *long suffering*. With respect to those things that are near to man, he is well-disposed, first, to his neighbor in his will to do him good. This belongs to the fruit of *goodness*. This manifests, secondly, in *benignity*, wherein he carries out the good that he wills to his neighbor with a love that makes him fervent in this regard. In the event that his neighbor inflicts evil upon him, the gift of *meekness* curbs his anger, allowing him to suffer this evil with equanimity. The gift of *faith*, "which takes the form of fidelity toward men and the demotion of self in the submission of the mind to God,"[212] strengthens him in not doing harm to his neighbor either in anger or through fraud or deceit. Lastly, with respect to those things that are below him, a man's mind is well-disposed as his external actions and internal desires through the fruit of *modesty* in both word and deed, and *continency* and *chastity* with respect to his concupiscence.[213]

Conclusion to the treatise on the virtues
It is clear that Thomas has reached a high point in this treatise in his teachings concerning man's return to God. Beginning with his initial consideration and determination of man's true happiness at the beginning of the *prima secundae*, he sets the Christian's eye upon that very end for the sake of which man marshals all the means that are at his disposal. He examines the architecture of appetition as it is manifested in both the voluntary act and the passions, so that, together with the examination of the powers that was conducted in the *Treatise on Man*, the Christian might be fully aware not only of the necessity to habituate these cognitive and appetitive powers well through the virtues so that his own activity might aspire most effectively to his true end, but also of the extent to which God's grace must be operative in his life if he is to have any chance of acquiring that for which he was made. What results is not some syncretic approach to diverse materials both philosophical and theological, but rather an intelligent and articulate manifestation of the beauty and profundity

---

[212] Torrell (1996; 2003), p. 219.
[213] ST. I-II. 70. 3.

of the Christian understanding of reality, the response that is required of him, and the help that he receives, all of which will continue to manifest as Thomas takes up the external principles governing human voluntary activity, the details concerning the theological and cardinal virtues in what remains of the *secunda pars,* and finally and especially the life, death, and resurrection of Jesus and the sacraments that he established.

We have seen how important the virtues are. They perfect the powers of man and the activities that flow from them. They allow one to say that man acts well, and by extension, that the powers that give rise to this excellence in activity are good. Thus, a man thinks well, having a good mind, acts well, being of good will, and so on. More important, however, is the "good" and the "well" said of man himself, terms that are assigned not only because of the self-mastery that one achieves through the virtues, or the unity and the perfection that they effect in one's person, but rather because of the end to which the whole of a person's activities is directed by them, and which he seeks determinately, constantly, and perfectly through them. The good is always said in relation to the end, and the end of man does not consist in the external goods, the goods of his body, or those of his soul, as the *Treatise on Happiness* showed. The true good of man resides in his ultimate end, and by extension, his true virtue lies properly and only with those virtues that have for their object this ultimate end in a definite way, and thus constitute those means that are required to attain it. The primacy of the theological virtues, then, is made manifest in Thomas's thought, as well as the Gifts of the Holy Spirit which impel man to realize those acts that they and the theological virtues make possible, namely the Beatitudes and the Fruits of the Holy Spirit. The moral and theological virtues of the natural realm still retain their nature, allowing man to bring a certain perfection and direction to his acting, a certain realization of his humanity and happiness. But insofar as man understands that his good and his end consist not in any created thing, but rather in the Uncreated Himself, and, moreover, that in both mind and in act he is unable to encompass, be united to and possess the Uncreated (something that was amply shown in both the *Prima Pars* and the *Prima Secundae*), these natural virtues, that used to be the best to which man could aspire, now are seen to fail as the means to his end that they were once considered to be. They still function according to what they are, namely the means whereby man can realize his life in this world according to his own lights, namely as his rational powers have been ordered by whatever truth to which it has aspired, and in light of which he can effect order within his person, and with his neighbor, friend, family, and culture. But for the Christian, there needs to be not only virtues and gifts appropriate to this end and good that lies beyond his abilities, but also a re-orientation to the world itself, a way by which he might respond to everything that God is (as discussed in the *prima pars*) and has effected, in the present world as it is now directed to the next. Sokolowski puts it well when he says that the theological virtues are

> the dispositions for "acting" in the setting disclosed by Christian faith; they are the source of the "reaction" we are to have to the God who creates without any need for creation and who involves us in his own life through his Son. And strictly speaking we simply cannot act on our own in this new setting. Our natural place for acting, the scene we ourselves can manage to some extent through virtue, law, and reason, is the world of human affairs bounded by the impenetrable necessities of the cosmos. There we are on our own. But the beginning, the continuation, and the success of our life of responding to God are all a gift of grace.[214]

In this response, the Christian still lives his life in this world, but now in a qualitatively different way, as exhibited clearly by the Beatitudes and the Fruits of the Holy Spirit. What is natural can now, through the grace that God gives through His Holy Spirit, be infused in the Christian by His charity so that all that man thinks, makes, and does can be directed to his true ultimate end. But what is natural still remains as man finds himself in the world acting within it as directed to the next. He must still act prudently, justly, courageously, and temperately; must still act out of the freedom that is his; understand and guide the passions that are his; and take up the responsibility

---

[214] Sokolowski (1995), pp. 72–73. One should, at the very least, read chapters 5 and 6 ("Natural Virtue" and "Theological Virtue") of this work.

that goes with all of this, but most especially as he is made to the image of God. The natural, then, is now compenetrated by the supernatural insofar as the Christian responds in this world to that which has opened up to him in faith, hope, and love, namely a world that is now seen

> as existing through generosity and God is appreciated as the one who could be all that there is, with no diminution of goodness or greatness. The theological virtues are what enable us to "act" in this Christian setting, in the light of a generosity that has no measure in the virtues and excellences of natural behavior.[215]

This is something that is well and practically brought out by his treatment of the Beatitudes and Fruits wherein the uniqueness of the Christian life is displayed, something that is applicable to the lives of all Christians, offering a "portrait of the spiritual man,"[216] and is not something that is restricted to a select few.[217]

Treatise on Vice and Sin (Questions 71–89)

Having considered the virtues and the perfections that they effect in man's voluntary activity toward his ultimate end, Thomas now considers the means whereby man's growth in virtue and his happiness can be frustrated, namely through vice and sin. This treatise has six concerns. The first (Question 71) addresses both vice and sin in themselves, followed by the distinctions that can be made among them (72), the comparisons that can be made between them (73) and where in the person

---

[215] Ibid., p. 77.

[216] Torrell (1996; 2003), p. 216, note 48, quoting a work by R. Bernard. See the whole of Torrell's commentary upon this section, as well as the larger context within which he develops this (pp. 200–224). One might also wish to consider the Edward O'Connor's introduction and appendices to his translation of Questions 68 through 70 (Blackfriars, Volume 24). Lastly, one might also consider Pinckaers (1993; 1995), pp. 134–167 for his judgments concerning how this material, sourced in Augustine's commentary on the Sermon on the Mount might be applied profitably to a renewal of Christian ethics (see especially pp. 160–163).

[217] For this point, see what Pinckaers refers to as the "Catholic" interpretation of the "Sermon on the Mount" in (1993; 1995), pp. 136–137.

they principally reside (74). Questions 75 through 84 consider the causes of sin, those internal (76 through 78), external (79 through 83, with 81 through 83 dedicated to original sin), and of sin itself, insofar as one sin is the cause of another (84). Lastly, the effects of sin are examined (85 through 89). I will limit this exposition to the more salient points of this treatise, leaving readers to explore the details on their own, something that should be possible given our concentration upon the overall nature of Thomas's moral teaching in light of which the privations that undercut it will be more readily and easily understood.

While the subject matter of this treatise is important, it does not occupy Thomas's energies in the way or to the extent that it has for moralists and theologians since his day. Thomas's moral theology, as stated previously, is centered upon man's happiness and the means whereby this might be attained. Consequently, matters, such as duty, obligation, freedom, conscience, law, vice, and sin, have their place within his thought but, nevertheless, do not rise to the point where they determine the context within which his ultimate end is articulated, and the internal and external principles of its attainment are investigated. This is especially true of the treatise concerning vice and sin. The privative reality that it describes exists only insofar as human activity, in its proper and common manifestations as directed to the attainment of man's end, is deformed, disordered or contrary to reason, nature, and man's end. One, then, should view this treatise as the principles that underlie a teratology, if you will, of man's voluntary activities (the abnormalities of which will be offered in great detail in the *secunda secundae*) as he seeks that which is less than his perfect end and good, or seeks his perfect end in ways that are disordered and inappropriate, a discussion that is important but which takes places and makes sense only in light of the manifestation of the full being of man's moral activity. In short, the concern in Thomas's ethics is that man's good be possessed, and this to the fullest extent of which he is capable. This occurs best when his activities are founded upon that love that unites him most perfectly to his end both now and to come, in light of which all other matters take their place and are manifested and experienced properly. A moral vision centered upon its defects or faults, and the fear that naturally attends this, does not serve as the most effective ordering principle whereby a man's activity can be rectified.[218]

As virtue was broadened and deepened within the Christian understanding of reality, so too is vice.[219] Unlike the pre-Christian thinkers who considered the viciousness of man to be a part of his natural state and thus something in need of culture, learning, virtue, and law, the Christian understood that man's malevolence was not natural to him since he had been created by a Being who is infinitely good and incapable of effecting such evil in His creation, as was discussed earlier in the *prima pars*. Man's viciousness, then, does not enter the world by God's creative activity, but through the actions effected by man himself. In light, then, of a doctrine of creation and the goodness of God Himself, "bad people do not merely act against what they are, against their human nature . . . (they) act against their creator: they do not merely act badly and unlawfully; they also sin."[220] Sin, then, is something specific to the Christian understanding of reality, one which denotes "a word, deed, or desire that is contrary to the eternal law," that is to say, an act that is voluntary in nature and is so disordered that it is incommensurate with God's reason and thus constitutes a violation of His eternal law.[221] Vice also indicates a dereliction of order and a violation of reason, but centers upon that order established by man (an order that gives rise to the natural virtues), and refers primarily to those habits or dispositions that are discordant with his nature and reason. Sin, on the other hand, refers primarily to the inordinate acts that violate God's eternal law and the order that is established by it.[222] The Christian attends to both orders, seeking the natural virtues as an effective way to fight against the fallen condition in which he finds himself in

---

[218] For a detailed treatment of this and many other associated points, consider "Part Two: A Brief History of Moral Theology" in Pinckaers (1993; 1995), pp. 191–326. One should also consider Sokolowski's (1995), pp. 62–67 diagnosis of the modern approach to morality and the serious faults to which it is heir.

[219] In what follows in this paragraph, I draw heavily upon Sokolowski (1995), pp. 70–72.

[220] Sokolowski (1995), p. 71.

[221] ST. I-II. 71. 6.

[222] ST. I-II. 71. 1–5.

this world, but always in light of his passage to the next, which requires the infused virtues and the gifts of the Holy Spirit. In his hope, he is bolstered not only through the grace he receives from God, but also by the real possibility that he will be released from this condition and have victory over it, a hope to which the pre-Christian person could not aspire, especially as this victory over sin and death is effected through the redemptive act of Jesus Christ, as will be discussed in the *tertia pars.*

Sins can be distinguished in varied ways. "Every sin," Thomas states, "consists in the desire for some mutable good, for which man has an inordinate desire, and the possession of which gives him inordinate pleasure." Thomas divides sin accordingly into those that are spiritual and those that are carnal, the former as one's pleasure is "consummated in the mere apprehension" of the thing desired, such as seeking the praise of others, and the latter as one's pleasure is "realized in bodily touch," such as seeking the goods of the table, the bottle and the bed.[223] If one were to concentrate, however, on the description of sin as an inordinate act, one can divide sins according to which of the three orders that govern man is violated by sin, namely those orders established by the rule, first, of his own reason over his own actions and passions, secondly, of God over man through His Divine law, and lastly, of the community over man who in his nature requires the society of others.[224] Sins can be distinguished also according to the extent to which they violate these three orders. A sin is called *mortal* if it destroys the very principle or principles upon which these orders are established, specifically as one turns away from one's true end. However, if one's actions do not destroy the principles upon which an order is established, but introduce an inordinateness in the things that follow upon this principle or principles, one does not turn from one's true end but introduces something unbecoming to the order to this end. Such sins are called *venial.*[225] As for the comparisons that can be

---

[223] ST. I-II. 72. 2.

[224] Thus, we have sins against one's own person, God and one's neighbor. See ST. I-II. 72. 4.

[225] ST. I-II. 72. 5. See also ST. I-II. 88–89. Examples are dangerous to offer without a full examination of the other factors that go into the assessment of irreparable or reparable damage, something treated by the remaining articles of Question 72.

made among the sins, this can be suggested generally by attending to the intention that the agent has in sinning as opposed to that when he is engaged in virtuous acts. In the latter situation, there is great harmony in all that one does as one follows the rule of reason in the three orders that govern him in his pursuit of the goods these orders promise. In the former, however, there is chaos in what he does insofar as the measure of reason and the goods to which this measure aspires are disrupted and replaced by the subjective rule of one's individual appetite, the good and the rule being determined by whatever one happens to find appetible. "For sin does not consist in passing from the many to the one, as is the case with virtues, which are connected, but rather in forsaking the one for the many."[226] Thus, the unity of the virtuous life, which consists in the directing of all that one thinks, speaks and does to one's ultimate end and good, and in light of which one acts well in relation to those lesser ends and goods that are ordered to this ultimate end and good, all of this is cast off to the degree that one directs one's life in accordance with one's desires for the varied mutable and thus lesser goods of one's experience.[227]

Questions 75 through 84 consider the causal factors directly relevant to sin. Generally speaking, the situation is clear: "the will lacking the direction of the rule of reason and of the Divine law, and intent on some mutable good, causes the act of sin directly, and the inordinateness of the act, indirectly and beside the intention; for the lack of order in the act results from the lack of direction in the will."[228] Although the will causes sin as it fails to apply the rule of reason or the Divine law to its activities, nevertheless there are other factors that contribute to man's voluntary activity, specifically the role that reason plays,

---

[226] ST. I-II. 73. 1.

[227] This chaos is detailed explicitly in the remaining articles of Question 73. Question 74 speaks of sin's seat, so to speak, within man, that it is primarily within the will as the sinful act is an intended voluntary violation of the orders spoken of above, and is secondarily in the sensitive appetites insofar as they are naturally inclined to be moved by the will. The reason is also subject to sin insofar as its errors in thought and its lack of rectitude in its command of the powers over which it has responsibility are culpable.

[228] ST. I-II. 75. 1.

and less proximately, the contributions and influences that may be exerted upon both reason and will by the sensitive cognitive and appetitive powers, specifically, the imaginative, concupiscible, and irascible powers, as detailed in the *Treatise on Human Activity*. All of these contribute to the genesis of man's sin as they play their respective roles in man's seeking after mutable or transient goods in an inordinate way, that is to say, contrary to the rule of reason or the Divine law. To be precise, the seeking after these mutable or transient goods belongs to man's sensitive powers but especially to his sensitive appetite, the lack of an appropriate rule "appertains to the reason, whose nature it is to consider this rule," and finally, "the completeness of the voluntary sinful act appertains to the will." These constitute what Thomas calls the interior causes of sin.[229] As for the sin's external causes, these are considered as such only insofar as they move the interior causes to sin. However, since the will, reason, and the appetites of themselves cannot be moved directly and necessarily by any external force (save God who cannot be a cause of sin, as discussed previously), all external influences move one to sin only insofar as the will assents to these influences and the enticements that they offer.[230] Lastly, one sin may be the cause of another indirectly, as it removes an impediment to further and often more serious sin; directly, by disposing one to sinful acting, making one more inclined to act in such ways; materially, by preparing the situation caused by one sin to be ripe for another, and lastly as one sin is committed for the sake of another as that in which the sinner's end consists.[231]

Thomas takes each of these factors and determines their operations in detail. The intrinsic causes are covered by Questions 76 through 78, where each question specifies a particular factor essential to the failure of reason, sensitive appetition, and will to act in a rectified fashion. Reason's failure in a sinful act consists in an ignorance that could have been eliminated but was not.[232] The sensitive appetite's failure consists in the indirect

[229] ST. I-II. 75. 2.
[230] ST. I-II. 75. 3.
[231] ST. I-II. 75. 4.
[232] See ST. I-II. 76. One might also consider the discussion on this found in the *Treatise on Human Activity*.

influence it can exert upon the will through the passions, and this in two ways. First, insofar as the passions act as a kind of distraction by reason of their force, centering one's attention upon the things with which they are concerned, or upon the actions that they urge, and this to the determinant of the will's (and reason's) proper activity, and secondly, insofar as the will (and reason) are unduly influenced in their determinations and judgments by the force of one's passions as these latter have been affected by that which gives rise to them, namely through the "vehement and inordinate apprehension of the imagination and judgment of the estimative power."[233] Lastly, the failure of will in a sinful act is found in what Thomas calls its malice. The disorder from which the will suffers in any sinful act is that in loving the lesser mutable good to which it has inordinately turned, putting aside the order of reason or the Divine law, it is willing to suffer the loss of a spiritual good so that it might obtain the temporal good that it so desires. This posture of denying a spiritual good for the sake of a temporal good, of choosing purposely the privation or relative evil in its limited goodness over the proper fullness that a participated good has both in itself and as it leads to absolute goodness, is called malice.[234] The failures on the part of both reason and sensitive appetition, while leading to sin, do not constitute malice so described. For in malice "the will is moved to evil on its own accord."[235] This occurs either as the agent has a corrupt disposition inclining him to evil and thus to this decided choice or as the will has been released from whatever prevented it from choosing in this way. Thomas mentions the loss of one's hope of eternal life through despair, or the loss of one's fear of hell through presumption as examples of the latter. However, one's malice is brought about, it is assuredly a more grievous cause of sin than that malice that attaches to those sins committed through passion insofar as the movement of the will to the lesser

---

[233] ST. I-II. 77. 1. See Article 2 for details concerning how reason specifically is influenced by the passions. The issues of culpability are covered in Articles 3, 6, and 7, while Article 4 addresses the root of sin in one's disordered self love, and Article 5 considers the three kinds of sin that arise from failure in the sensitive appetitive power.

[234] ST. I-II. 78. 1.

[235] ST. I-II. 78. 3.

good is its own entirely, that this movement is not transitory but one which abides in the will having a certain permanent quality about it, as the love of such a one has been centered upon the lesser with all the strength and capacity that is available to this higher and more self-possessed of the appetitive powers.

The external causes of sin are treated in Questions 79 through 83, beginning with God (79), then the Devil (80), and ending with man, particularly the first parents, which occasions an examination of original sin as it is transmitted to the entirety of the human race (81 through 83). God cannot be the cause of sin insofar as sin denotes a departure from the order that God establishes in His creative act, an order which directs all things to Him as that in which they find their ultimate end and perfect good. For God to will that something depart from this order is impossible insofar as this would involve Him in willing something that He had created to seek its end and good in something other than Himself, a direct contradiction to the teachings of the *Treatise on Happiness* and the *Summa* itself.[236] Rather, the cause of man's falling away from His created order lies in his free will,[237] in light of which the Biblical passages concerning the spiritual blindness and hardness of heart that come upon man from God are to be interpreted, namely as the withdrawal of God's grace from man as he has placed before God an obstacle to the giving of His gifts.[238] It is in this way that the gifts of the Holy Spirit and the infused virtues are lost. The devil's influence is limited by the fact that the will of man is within man's direct control and in no other's. Consequently, the influence of the devil is restricted to the effect that he can have upon those other powers of man that can influence his willing, namely his sensitive appetite and his reason. Thus, the devil can incite man to sin through presenting something appetible to his senses and thus provoke his passions, or through the persuasion that he can effect upon man's reason, and this specifically through his imagination. The decision to sin, however, is entirely man's own.[239]

---

[236] ST. I-II. 79. 1.
[237] ST. I-II. 79. 2.
[238] ST. I-II. 79. 3.
[239] ST. I-II. 80. 1–4.

As for the original sin of man's first parents, this is transmitted to their descendants through the common nature that all receive from the first parents, a nature that is disordered insofar as the original justice that characterized man's condition was lost consequent upon this first sin, a grace that was then denied to all subsequent generations, placing them in need of the redemption that Christ effected.[240] This disorder manifests not only in the lack of submission of man's will to God, but also in the effect that this has upon the will's control over the other powers of man's soul and of his body, and of the length of life that was his under original justice, as was discussed previously in the *Treatise on Man*.[241]

The last cause of sin that is considered before its effects (in Questions 85 through 89) is that of one sin with respect to another sin (Question 84). Following upon the corruption of human nature in the loss of original justice, Thomas, as led by Scriptures, identifies covetousness as the root of all sin, and pride as their beginning. Covetousness refers to that "inclination of a corrupt nature to desire corruptible goods inordinately," something that man satisfies most effectively through the power and opportunity that money affords him in the commission of any and all manner of sin, thus standing as the root from which all sin derives.[242] Pride denotes an inclination of a corrupt nature to be contemptuous toward God Himself, that one not be subject to His order and His command. In this turning from God is found the beginning of all manner of evil, particularly as this is manifested in turning toward goods that are corruptible so that in their acquisition man might satisfy the desire to excel all others and attain to the perfection and excellence that come with such riches, and the power and position that they afford.[243] Pride is said to be the "queen" of all sins,[244] a universal vice which stands at the head of what Thomas, following St. Gregory the Great, calls the seven capital or deadly sins, those sins that are

[240] ST. I-II. 81. 1–3.
[241] Consider Velde (2005), pp. 143–166 for a fuller treatment of these matters.
[242] ST. I-II. 84. 1.
[243] ST. I-II. 84. 2.
[244] ST. I-II. 84. 4. ad4.

most dangerous to the Christian's life insofar as they are the principles and directors of all other sins as these seven are the latter's final cause, that for the sake of which all manner of sin is undertaken. Four of them regard the goods of the soul, the body and those external to the human person, while the other three address the avoidance of good on account of some evil that attends them. *Vainglory* regards the first insofar as it is that sin whereby man inordinately desires honor and praise from others, a good that is enjoyed merely through such things being apprehended. *Gluttony* and *lust* describe those inordinate desires for the goods of the body, those that regard the preservation of the individual and that of species, respectively. Lastly, as stated previously, *covetousness* regards that disordered desire for riches. As for the other three, *sloth* avoids spiritual goods that are one's own but that require an effort on one's part that is deemed excessive. *Envy* and *anger* regard another person's good, the former as being a sadness that one experiences at another's good fortune, specifically as it is "a hindrance to one's own excellence," and the latter as this adds to envy the desire for vengeance.[245]

The last issue that Thomas considers in this treatise is the effect of sin. He begins in Question 85 with the degree to which the good of human nature has been corrupted by sin. This good is threefold, namely the principles that constitute man's nature and the powers that flow from these, secondly, those natural inclinations to virtue that were examined in the *Treatise on Virtue*, and lastly the gift of original justice. The latter of these was wholly destroyed, as we have already noted. The first of these remains untouched, as we saw in the *Treatise on Man*. The natural inclination to virtue, however, while not destroyed by sin, is nonetheless diminished by it, insofar as man, through his engagement in disordered activity, effectively weakens these natural inclinations to virtue by strengthening those habits and vices opposed to them.[246] These vices do not destroy these natural inclinations (since they are rooted in man's very nature, something that is not destroyed or diminished by sin), but instead serve to place obstacles to their full and proper

---

[245] ST. I-II. 84. 3–4.
[246] ST. I-II. 85. 1.

realization.[247] The result of this, as we saw earlier in relation to original sin, was the disruption of all that was effected through original justice, namely that man lost that order proper to him and enjoyed before the fall, both within his own person (of reason perfectly over all that was beneath it) and to God Himself (of reason perfected in its subjection to Him). Being diminished in his natural inclination to virtue, man suffers what Thomas calls the "wounding of his nature" which manifests in four ways, namely the wound of *ignorance* as man's mind is no longer ordered fully to the true, the wound of *malice* as man's will is no longer ordered to the good, the wound of *weakness* as his irascible aspect is no longer ordered properly to the arduous, and lastly, the wound of *concupiscence* as his concupiscible aspect is no longer ordered rightly to its proper object by reason. Such wounds attend the original sin of man's first parents, and are further strengthened in their hold upon each individual person as he or she engages in sinful activity.[248] Death and other bodily defects are indirectly caused by the first sin insofar as the withdrawal of original justice effectively disrupted the body's subjection to and harmony with the soul, something that one would expect given both the kind of disruption that occurred at the psychic level, and that the material nature of man in the original state, as now, is subject to the principles of generation and corruption, something that in the prelapsarian state was checked, so to speak, by God's gift of original justice.[249]

The Treatise on Law (Questions 90–108)

Having completed his investigation concerning the intrinsic principles of man's voluntary activity, Thomas now turns in the last two treatises of the *prima secundae* to those principles that are extrinsic. We have seen that although man's happiness consists in his union with God, nonetheless his efforts to

---

[247] ST. I-II. 85. 2.

[248] ST. I-II. 85. 3.

[249] ST. I-II. 85. 5–6. See, also, the discussion in the *Treatise on Man.* The remaining questions of this treatise (86–89) deal with the mark or "stain" that sin leaves upon the soul, and the debt that sin incurs (with a discussion concerning the distinction that is to be made between venial and mortal with an eye to the specific debt they incur). I leave these to the reader to consider on his own.

achieve this are insufficient: as noted earlier, his activity is not proportioned to the end for which he was created. He must be raised up, so to speak, in his desires and activities so that he might attain to and be united with his ultimate good and end. When the intrinsic means whereby man aspires to his happiness were discussed, it was necessary, in light of this principle, to include the Gifts of the Holy Spirit and the infused virtues as the means whereby this insufficiency on man's part could be addressed. This, however, is not the full extent of the help that man receives from God. In his movement to his ultimate end and happiness, external forces make a direct contribution, and this insofar as man is not a solitary animal, and is thus not sufficient unto himself for all his needs, but requires the society of others and all this affords him if he is to flourish in his humanity. In this regard, God aids man in two ways, namely through the guidance that He can effect through His law, and the aid that He can offer through His grace. The former divides into two parts: the first dealing with law in general terms (90–92), and the second examining its various parts or kinds (93–108).[250] Torrell divides this treatise into three parts. The first, extending from Questions 90 through 97, reconciles man's freedom with the law that permeates the whole of creation with which man participates in the forming of his own laws, and thus makes his own particular contribution to the common good and the good of creation. "But God has reserved himself the right to intervene in salvation history. Thus, he promulgated two kinds of law: the *Old Law*, which Thomas examines in minute detail (98–105), and the *New Law*, which Thomas identifies with the grace of the Holy Spirit (106–8)."[251]

On one's first encounter with a treatise on law, one might expect it to be entirely proscriptive in nature. This, however, is not the case. Instead, this treatise reflects the tenor of all that has preceded as it seeks to develop the means, now external, whereby man might aspire not only to the maturation of his nature, but also to the beginnings of a retrieval of his original

---

[250] ST. I-II. 90. Prologue.
[251] Torrell (2005), p. 34. The Blackfriars' translation of the *Summa* follows this division (Volumes 28–30: 1966, 1969, 1971).

posture before God and of his happiness. Question 90 is centered upon the presentation and defense of the definition of law, namely as "an ordinance of reason for the common good, made by him who has care of the community, and promulgated." From the start, one should note with Torrell[252] that this definition of law is not centered first upon obligation, but rather upon the "common good" as that for the sake of which a law exists. The punitive understanding that many consider essential to law is not mentioned in this context, nor does Thomas's definition utilize the notion of the limiting of one's freedom that often marks many people's approach to law. Rather, the law is presented in this treatise as it has an "educative value," specifically in establishing solid guidance and the practical means to the acquisition and practice of the virtues, with the hope of developing not only a virtuous character within those people who are subject to the law, but also that they might aspire to the point where the law becomes so internalized that it becomes second nature to them, and, consequently, something that is, as it were, transcended, the law's task having been completed.[253] One can see, then, that if law is to function in this manner, it must be formulated and effected not only by reason itself, but also by a reason that intends primarily not the good of any one individual, but rather the good of the society of which the individual is a member. This is most effectively realized by the one, the few, or the many within that culture who have been charged specifically with the responsibility of forming those laws that will govern it, something which they openly declare and publish, and to which each member of the society voluntarily binds himself or herself, seeing the law as that which will measure or rule his or her activity for the sake of taking advantage of the help that it can effect in the realization not only of the good of the culture, but also ultimately in the attainment of each individual's ultimate end and good. Thus, to return to an image that Thomas used earlier in the *Treatise on Man*, just as the sensitive appetite is governed by reason through a politic rule,

---

[252] Torrell (1996; 2003), pp. 282–283, n. 26.

[253] Torrell (2005), p. 34. See especially Chapter 4: Natural Virtue in Sokolowski (1995) for how it is that the virtuous and the "godlike" person transcend the law as its educative purpose has been fulfilled.

and is perfected in its activities through its participation in the life of reason which manifests perfectly in the acquisition of the virtues of temperance and fortitude, so too are the people of a society governed by the law, and perfected in their respective activities through their participation in that for which the law is established, namely that they, in their nature as rational animals requiring the community of others for the realization of what is potential to their humanity, might work together most effectively to acquire their happiness, or at least to realize the conditions wherein one might seek for this effectively.[254]

The general nature of this account gives rise immediately to two questions. First, since there are many different kinds of communities to which man belongs, is there correspondingly different kinds of laws that govern them? Secondly, the rectification of reason in its governance of the powers and activities of the individual is effected through its conformation to the greatest of truths, and its appetite united to and intending the highest of goods. In light, then, of the analogy in the prior paragraph, what serves to rectify the reason or reasons of a society's authority so that the laws promulgated by them do indeed retain their nature as laws, and do not descend into forms of violence as Thomas refers to laws that have lost this character?[255] Question 91 deals with the former question, and in the course of its exposition suggests an answer to the second which anticipates its fuller development in the course of the more detailed examination of the particular kinds of law that follows (in Questions 93 through 108).

Thomas distinguishes four general kinds of law, namely, the eternal, natural, human, and the revealed divine law, the last of which comprises the Old and New Laws of Holy Scripture. The eternal law refers to that governance that God's reason exerts over the "community" of the universe itself. This was referred to earlier in the *prima pars* in the discussion concerning God's providence over the whole of creation wherein all things have their being, nature, and ends, and on account of which the whole of reality is ordered well with respect to itself, and to that from

---

[254] ST. I-II. 90. See also Question 92 where Thomas discusses the effects of law.

[255] ST. I-II. 93. 3. ad2.

which it derives and in which it finds its completion. The eternal law, then, is the first of all laws and the foundation for all the rest.[256] The natural law constitutes the particular and especial way by which the rational creature participates in the eternal law. This participation is marked by the fact that the rational being "is subject to Divine providence in the most excellent way in so far as it partakes of a share of providence, by being provident both for itself and for others."[257] Through his intellectual nature, man has a natural proclivity to his end and can effect his own activity in pursuit of this end, both individually and in the communities to which he belongs. He can thus partake, in varying ways and to varying degrees, in the governance that God effects over reality, where "the light of natural reason, whereby we discern what is good and what is evil, which is the function of the natural law, is nothing else than an imprint on us of the Divine light."[258] It is in this participation of the eternal law that the rational creature, in Torrell's words, "is called upon freely to take up the inclination toward its end, thus becoming a kind of providence of its own for itself and others."[259] This providence is manifested in the third kind of law, the human, wherein man establishes laws which constitute further specifications of those most basic inclinations that are imprinted in man by reason of his participation in the eternal law, namely to do good and to avoid evil, so that he might order well and rightly his voluntary activities in this world in accordance with what is good and true for the sake of his end and happiness.[260] Lastly, Thomas argues that a fourth law, the Divine, is required to direct man's voluntary activities, and this for four reasons. First, that man might be guided effectively in his activity toward his true end and good, something that the natural and human laws cannot effect since they are not proportioned to man's revealed end, as was discussed previously. Second, that man might be delivered from the uncertainty and error that often follow upon the difficulty in making his own practical judgments concerning how he

---

[256] ST. I-II. 91. 1.
[257] ST. I-II. 91. 2.
[258] Ibid.
[259] Torrell (1996; 2003), p. 283.
[260] ST. I-II. 91. 3.

is to act in this world with a view to the next, something, again, that the natural and human laws cannot effect. Third, that man might be directed well even in the laws that he establishes so as to govern the interior activities of himself and others, something which by its very nature escapes the reach of the human law, such being competent to guide only man's transitive activities. Lastly, that man might be instructed concerning those good and evil deeds to which the reach of the human law does not extend, again, by its very nature, deeds that are required of man in light of his ultimate end and good.[261] This divine law, as stated above, is distinguished into the Old and the New, as the imperfect is distinguished from the perfect respectively. The former directs man well with respect to the sensible and earthly goods, while the latter directs man well with respect to intelligible and heavenly goods. Again, the former addresses man's transitive acts, while the latter also addresses his intransitive acts. Finally, the former rules through fear of punishment, while the latter rules through love.

In what follows, Thomas considers these four laws in greater detail, the eternal in 93, the natural in 94, the human in 95 through 97, and the divine in 98 through to 108, with the Old Law receiving a great deal of attention (98 through 105, covering the Old Law in general, and its moral, ceremonial, and judicial precepts in particular), and the last three questions dedicated to the New Law, the Law of the Gospel.

In light of the foundational and supreme nature of the eternal law described above, one might wonder to what extent this law is known to man. Since this law manifests the very wisdom of God as it measures and directs all things, this law, in itself, is something known only to God and to the blessed who are united to Him and behold His essence. The knowledge of the eternal law, then, is understood in its effects and the likeness to the cause that is discerned therein, a principle we have met before in the *prima pars* when discussing the existence of God, what we could know of His essence, and how we could name this appropriately. Thus, for rational creatures, the eternal law is known at least in his grasping of the elemental truths or common principles of the natural law, that manifestation of the eternal law consequent

---

[261] ST. I-II. 91. 4.

upon the rational being's participation within the eternal law itself.[262] The natural law, then, becomes an issue of importance as man discerns his place within God's providence, particularly as he develops his own law and thus become a kind of providence for himself and others, as stated previously.

Its foundational precept, *that good is to be pursued, and evil is to be avoided*, is known habitually and self-evidently by the practical reason, in much the same fashion as the foundational principles of thought are by the speculative reason. And just as every intellectual discipline depends essentially upon foundational principles of speculative thinking, so too does every precept of the natural law depend upon this first and foundational precept. As we have seen many times before, the human person has a natural inclination to that which is perfective and completive of him, that is to say, to that which is apprehended by him as good. Thomas takes the order of man's natural inclination to good as offering guidance with respect to the order of the precepts of the natural law that flow from its first and foundational precept. For the difficulty in formulating the precepts of the natural law consist not so much in identifying what for many is incontestable, namely to seek good and avoid evil, but rather to identify what constitutes true goods and evils. Thomas appeals, first, to that natural inclination that each thing has toward the preservation of its own being. Thus, with respect to man, whatever conduces to the preserving of his life, and deflecting those things that endanger it, belongs to the natural law. He appeals, secondly, to those natural inclinations that man enjoys consequent upon his animal nature, specifically, to the begetting and rearing of offspring. Lastly, he appeals to those natural inclinations specific to man's rational nature, namely to know the truth in all of its manifestations, to seek the good that is in accord with his rectified reason, to live in community with others for the sake of his happiness, and other such matters proper and basic to his humanity, and to avoid whatever harms the integrity and growth of these. All such matters belong to the natural law and constitute the most basic specifying of its first and foundational principle.[263] In addition

[262] ST. I-II. 93. 2.
[263] ST. I-II. 94. 1–2.

to these, all acts of virtue belong to the natural law insofar as human beings have a natural inclination to act in accordance with reason, that is to say, to act virtuously. Certain specific acts of virtue, however, do not belong to the natural law as some virtuous activity does not directly derive from the natural inclination of man's nature, but are only undertaken in light of the determinations of reason itself.[264] One might wonder to what extent the precepts of the natural law are present in each person, and that if variations do appear, whether this weakens Thomas's position concerning the natural and seemingly self-evident nature of these precepts and thus of their binding character. Thomas states that unlike the necessary things with which the speculative reason is concerned in its operations, the practical reason deals with the contingent and the singular as it is that power which deliberates specifically concerning what and what not to do, as we have seen in the *Treatise on Human Acts*. Thus, although all will know and act in accord with the practical reason's fundamental principles, the problems arise when one begins to apply these principles to the particulars with which one's voluntary activity is concerned. Inevitably, given the details involved, the difficulties presented by practical reasoning, and the condition of the agent himself (perhaps he is deficient in those powers whereby he can reason practically, or has been reared in an evil fashion and thus accepts as right what is against the natural law, or is confused by the play of his passions, all of which will impact adversely the functioning of his practical reasoning), there will be differences among people concerning their understanding of the precepts of the natural law, and the application of them to their activities.[265] Nonetheless, Thomas states that this does not affect one's natural grasp of the fundamental precepts of the natural law, those which can never "be blotted out from men's hearts,"[266] although one may be hindered in their application in particular circumstances by the aforementioned difficulties. With respect to those precepts of the natural law that are further removed from these fundamental ones, being secondary to them, Thomas

---

[264] ST. I-II. 94. 3.
[265] ST. I-II. 94. 4.
[266] ST. I-II. 94. 6.

states that these can indeed be blotted out from a person's heart by evil persuasions and any vicious customs, corrupt habits and the like that afflict one, perverting one's understanding and pursuit of the good in much the same way that one who has fallen into error concerning one's reasoning to conclusions is in a sense removed from the necessary propositions that form the foundation of one's thinking.[267]

Given that man reads, so to speak, the eternal law as it manifests in the natural inclinations with which the natural law is concerned (something that results in the general nature of this law as well as the difficulties that attend its translation into the particulars of everyday voluntary activity), it is prudent for man to form his own laws so that he might both guide himself and others in his and their desire for full human flourishing and ultimately for his and their happiness. Man's desire to engage in virtuous activity, and to pursue all the other goods to which he is inclined by his nature, cannot be effected by any one person acting alone, but rather requires a community acting for the sake of its common good by means of which the individuals who are its members will have the greatest opportunity to achieve their end and good. This training in virtue is effected through paternal correction for those well inclined. But for those who are not, fear and force must be brought to bear upon them, something that is effected through the laws that a community enacts, laws that effect not only a training in virtue upon those least disposed to it, but also a peace for those who are and who wish to advance without the hindrances presented by those who would do evil.[268] The integrity, then, of the human law depends directly upon the degree to which it follows upon and embodies the natural law itself. As was stated earlier, those human laws that stray from this rectitude are no laws at all, but are simply forms of violence.[269]

The majority of people for whom the human law is fashioned are those who are imperfect in their virtue and thus require

---

[267] Ibid.

[268] ST. I-II. 95. 1. See also ST. I-II. 96. 1.

[269] ST. I-II. 95. 2. One should also consider Articles 3 and 4, which consider the qualities that human law should possess and the various divisions that can be made within it.

the guidance and force that the law can provide. Thomas thus argues that since the law is formulated with this kind of person in mind (seeking to bring them to the point where they might engage more fully in the life of virtue), it would be prudent that the burdens that are carried and enjoyed by those more perfect in virtue not be imposed upon those who aspire to this kind of virtue. To this end, then, laws are to be enacted that prohibit

> only the more grievous vices, from which it is possible for the majority to abstain; and chiefly those that are to the hurt of others, without the prohibition of which human society could not be maintained: thus human law prohibits murder, theft and such like.[270]

In this approach, the majority are led to virtue

> not suddenly, but gradually. Wherefore (the law) does not lay upon the multitude of imperfect men the burdens of those who are already virtuous, namely that they should abstain from all evil. Otherwise these imperfect ones, being unable to bear such precepts, would break out into yet greater evils.[271]

The same principle is applied to the prescription of virtuous acts through law: only those that

> are ordainable to the common good—either immediately, as when certain things are done directly for the common good,— or mediately, as when a lawgiver prescribes certain things pertaining to good order, whereby the citizens are directed in the upholding of the common good of justice and peace[272]

are so prescribed.

Human laws that are just, that is, as they derive in some fashion from the natural and eternal laws, bind the consciences of those to whom these laws are addressed. Care, however, must be taken on the part of the authority who forms and

---

[270] ST. I-II. 96. 2.
[271] ST. I-II. 96. 2. ad2.
[272] ST. I-II. 96. 3.

promulgates these laws that they not be oppressive or burdensome to those imperfect in virtue as just described. The laws formulated by man must seek the common good but not to the extent that they ignore the condition of those upon whom they are imposed, or that they do not address all in the community in an equal or equitable fashion, or that they are not realistically proportioned to the people's capacities in their growth in the virtues. In cases where the laws made by man do not regard these conditions, such do not bind one's conscience, "except perhaps in order to avoid scandal or disturbance, for which cause a man should even yield his right." However, if a law is enacted that is contrary to the Divine law, then such a law must not be observed under any circumstance.[273] Thus, although one may find oneself subject to the authority that has the care of the common good of a community of which one is member, nonetheless given the conditions under which the authority's law is a law in the first place, one finds oneself subject to this superior law, and, all things being equal, to this superior law through the lesser human law in whose light the latter should be fashioned.[274] The imperfect law, then, should not be despised for the sake of the perfect, but recognized for the good that it is and the role that it plays not only with respect to the common good of the society itself, but also with respect to the common good, so to speak, of the eternal and divine laws themselves. Thus, even the authority that frames the laws of a community comes under the human law's directive force, those laws that they themselves have fashioned, fulfilling them of their own free will and not out of the constraint that is imposed upon the majority of those imperfect in virtue, choosing rather to act in this way as an example to their people and to avoid the Lord's reproach at Matthew 23. 3, 4.[275] Lastly, human law must allow for dispensation in those circumstances under which adherence to a particular law would in fact be counter to its intent, that is, for the sake of the common good. This is accomplished insofar as the authority makes laws that apply for the most part, allowing for prudential decisions on

[273] ST. I-II. 96. 4.
[274] ST. I-II. 96. 5.
[275] ST. I-II. 96. 5. ad3.

the part of the citizens concerning its applicability when faced with these sorts of circumstances.[276] The authority should also have an eye to whether a law needs to be changed. This must be done with good reason. For any change in human law is "of itself prejudicial to the common good" insofar as it weakens the law's binding force through the change that it effects upon the customs to which a people are adapted under law. Custom plays an important role in the people's observance of the law, and every change in custom will weaken or even undermine the degree to which people will observe the law. One must judge carefully, then, whether the good gained through a change in law will compensate for the harm that is done in this respect.[277]

This brings Thomas to the consideration of the divine law. He turns, first, to the Old Law, that law given to the Jewish people as recounted in the Old Testament of the Holy Scriptures. The questions concerning the Old Law that would probably arise among the people whom the Dominicans served in their pastoral ministries would be the Old Law's nature, relation to the New Law of Christ, and worth in light of the Gospel since the latter had fulfilled the Old Law, and thus seemed to render it of little or no worth to the Christian.[278] Thomas begins with an affirmation of the goodness of the Old Law, first, insofar as it has, at the very least, the character of law as described previously, namely as it accords with and follows upon right reason and prohibits the human person from engaging in activities that are contrary to reason's order. In this, it shares much with the goodness found in the human law. However, they differ

---

[276] ST. I-II. 96. 6. See the body of the article for the conditions allowing for the dispensation from a just human law.

[277] ST. I-II. 97. 1–2. See Article 2 for the conditions under which this may be done.

[278] One might even consider the ancient heresy of Marcion that may have lingered in the minds of people. This heresy considered the Old Law to be wholly opposed to the New, thought that the God of the Old was the antithesis of New, and argued that He was "the instigator of Christ's own passion and death." (David Bourke, Volume 29 of the Blackfriars' translation (1969), p. xiv). Bourke sees in Thomas's initial exposition of the nature of the Old Law an implicit refutation of this heresy "most directly hostile to the Old Law as such."

in their respective goodnesses as the human law is concerned with the common good, while the Old Law concerns the ultimate end to which the human person is called and the means whereby he might be made fit to partake of it. However, the Old Law is imperfect as it could not confer this ultimate end upon man, something that was reserved only to Christ and the New Law itself. The Old Law, then, was established by God as propaedeutic to the New, specifically as it bore witness to the person of Christ, and as it prepared people for His advent, and this by withdrawing them from their disordered way of living consequent upon their own sins and that of the race itself, and disposing them to the perfect means of their salvation.[279]

Having the character of law, the Old Law addressed a specific community, namely the Jewish people, those chosen by God to receive this blessing and from whom would arise the very means of their salvation, namely Christ Himself.[280] This Law was promulgated through God's ministers, the angels, by whose ministry the people chosen by God were readied for the New Law, a law to be promulgated not by any angel but by God Incarnate Himself.[281] The Old Law was well suited to the people chosen by God, acting perfectly in this introductory fashion as it combined both that which was familiar to them, namely those precepts that could be discerned through reason as described earlier in the natural law, and those that were not, namely those precepts that conduced specifically to what was required of them so that they might attain to their supernatural end. Thomas, following the patristic and subsequent commentary tradition,[282] divided the precepts of the Old Law into three categories, namely those that addressed the moral, ceremonial, and juridical practices governing the Jewish people. The moral precepts form an important part of the Old Law insofar as through them, there is effected the main intent of the Divine Law, namely that man become fit for friendship with God, something

---

[279] ST. I-II. 98. 2. See also Article 4 where Thomas describes the effect the Old Law had upon the pride of man with respect to his knowledge and power, deflating both so that he might more readily understand and be accepting of the salvation of which he stood in such great need.

[280] ST. I-II. 98. 4.

[281] ST. I-II. 98. 3.

[282] See Volume 29 (1969) of the Blackfriars' translation, p. xix.

that can occur only as man is made good through acts of virtue which the moral precepts of the Old Law intend.[283] In addition to the rectification of man's character through the virtues, there also needs to be an ordering of the many and varied activities whereby he "makes profession of his subjection to God," something that is effected through Divine worship and is the subject matter of the ceremonial precepts of the Old Law.[284] Lastly, the juridical precepts of the Old Law established the specific ways by which justice was to be effected among the members of this special community but now in light of that ultimate end and good to which the Old Law now oriented them.[285]

In order that the moral precepts of the Old Law might make man fit for friendship with God and prepare him for the gifts to be bestowed in the New Law, there is incorporated within the Old Law all that is specific to the natural law, namely those precepts that are easily derived from the foundational principle of practical reasoning, and those that follow upon the deliberations of the wise, those from whom the people of the Old Law are urged to learn those precepts of the natural law that are less than obvious. These, together with those matters that require Divine instruction,[286] constitute a law that attains to a higher perfection than that of which the human law, remaining faithful to what is implicit in the natural law, is capable of achieving. For the community to which the human law is addressed requires that its moral precepts govern acts of justice only, detailing the duties that man has within the civic community and regulating the activities among them so that they might live in peace. The community governed by the Divine Law, however, "is that of men in relation to God, either in this life or in the life to come. And therefore the Divine Law proposes precepts about all those matters whereby men are well ordered in their relations to God," which includes not only acts of justice, but also of all the other virtues whereby man effects, insofar as he can, that right order of all that he thinks, says, feels, and does, as discussed throughout the *prima secundae*,

---

[283] ST. I-II. 99. 2.
[284] ST. I-II. 99. 3.
[285] ST. I-II. 99. 4.
[286] ST. I-II. 100. 1.

and especially in the treatise on the habits and virtues.[287] Capital among these moral precepts are those contained in the Decalogue or Ten Commandments. They comprise those precepts that are either easily deducible from the foundational principles of practical reasoning or those that "become known to man immediately through divinely infused faith."[288] They relate to all that is found within the moral precepts of the Old Law, establishing the primary relations that must exist in this community between man and God, and man with his neighbor under God. The first three commandments regard man's relation with God, to Whom he owes three things, namely fidelity, reverence, and service, each of which is assured through his observance of the prohibitions specific to these three commandments, and which "together epitomize right action on the part of man to God."[289] The other seven commandments assure that man understands and acts upon those debts that he has to his parents, by honoring them, and to all within his community, by not harming them through word, thought, or deed.[290] The order of the Ten Commandments is important, for man finds himself in right relation with his neighbor only to the extent that his relations with God are rectified, that justice among the people of this special community will only be attained properly and fully in their fidelity to, and reverence and service of, God. For it is only in one's right order to the ultimate end, that the order of the parts to the whole, the very structure of the community striving toward its good and end, can properly be understood and acted upon, an order that is effected by and culminates in charity.[291] Consequently, given the importance of the Decalogue both to man and to the community to which it is promulgated and the fact that these precepts are given by God Himself and express His intention for His people, nothing of the Decalogue is dispensable.[292]

Just as the natural law had to be specified by the human law, so too must the moral precepts of the Old Law be further specified

---

[287] ST. I-II. 100. 2.
[288] ST. I-II. 100. 3.
[289] See Volume 29 (1969) of the Blackfriars' translation, p. xxiv.
[290] ST. I-II. 100. 4–5.
[291] ST. I-II. 100. 6. See also ST. I-II. 99. 1. ad2. and 100. 10.
[292] ST. I-II. 100. 8.

through the ceremonial and juridical precepts (Questions 101–3 and 104–5, respectively). Thomas completes his examination of the Old Law with extended treatments of these two precepts, the details of which cannot be accommodated properly by this present work. In brief, let it suffice to say that the ceremonial precepts are promulgated so that the members of this community might understand how God is rightly worshipped which

> consists essentially in worship of him alone, a worship based on faith and love (the first principles), its basic constituents being fidelity, reverence and service (the first three precepts of the Decalogue), and a worship which is articulated and expressed in the form of the sacrifices, sacred things, sacraments and observances of the ceremonial precepts.[293]

The juridical precepts detail the manner in which the Decalogue might be realized practically within this community under God, specifically as these determine those relations that exist between the ruler and his subjects, those enjoyed among all subjects of this community, those that exist between the community and the foreigner, and lastly those between father and son, husband and wife, and master and servant.[294]

Having dealt with the Old Law, Thomas now considers its completion in the New Law or the Law of the Gospel, the New Testament. As the perfection of the Divine Law, it is to be expected that it will have not only its own particular character, but also essential relations with all other forms of law that have preceded, something that fittingly explains its place at the completion of the *Treatise on Law*. We have seen that the eternal law constitutes the very fabric of reality, realizing the existence, essence, order, and relatedness of all things, and that the natural law is the rational being's unique participation in the eternal law, and from which the human person in

---

[293] See Volume 29 (1969) of the Blackfriars' translation, p. xxv. See also the general description of this very detailed set of questions on p. xxiv, as well as some comments that are made concerning this detail on pp. xxvi–xxvii.

[294] See Volume 29 (1969) of the Blackfriars' translation, p. xxv. One would be well advised to read Bourke's excellent introduction to this section of the *Summa*.

particular develops the positive or human law so that he might govern himself rightly in his social nature and in his desire not only for the common good of his community but also for his very happiness. However, we have seen many times before that man's own efforts (and now we include also man's communal efforts) are insufficient to the attainment of his true end and good. Thus, the Divine law, among other things, becomes a necessity as that which is gifted to man and is so proportioned to the end for which he is made that man has now the hope whereby he might attain to his happiness. The Old Law is propaedeutic to the New, and, as we have seen, includes not only a reference to the natural law in its moral precepts (and by extension to the human law rightly based upon the natural), but also anticipates, foreshadows, announces, prepares, figures, and promises all that is to come in the New. The first difference noted between the Old and the New Law, as well as the first declaration of the latter's perfection, is found in the answer to the very question that begins Thomas's treatment of the New Law, namely whether this law is a written law. He draws one's attention immediately to the heights and nobility of this law, namely that primarily and essentially this New Law "is the grace itself of the Holy Spirit which is given to those who believe in Christ . . . a law that is inscribed on our hearts"[295] and not, as Augustine states, "on tables of stone" as were the 10 Commandments of the Old Law. The meaning here is clear, namely that although there are "the teachings of faith and those commandments which direct human affections and human actions,"[296] which constitute its written aspect, these are secondary to what is the essence of the New Law, namely "the inward presence of the healing grace of faith"[297] which is nothing other than that unique "presence of God's Holy Spirit" consequent upon the salvific act of Jesus Christ. It is to this presence and inward healing that the written aspect of the New Law disposes and, when received, guides one with respect to this grace's use.[298] It is this grace of the Holy Spirit bestowed

[295] ST. I-II. 106. 1.
[296] ST. I-II. 106. 2.
[297] ST. I-II. 106. 2.
[298] ST. I-II. 106. 1, ad1 and ad2.

inwardly that constitutes the essence of the New Law and saves and justifies man in a way that the Old Law promised but itself could not effect.[299] This might beg the question why the New Law was not given immediately upon the fall of man. Thomas offers three reasons for this. First, as with any infused grace, sin acts as an obstacle to the inward reception and presence of the Holy Spirit which the New Law constitutes. Only the redemptive act of Christ could eliminate this barrier to the outpouring of the Holy Spirit, and this was something, secondly, that could not be effected at once, but required "an orderly succession of time" whereby the perfect is preceded by the imperfect, where that which is imperfect prepares one for the advent and full realization that the perfect promises. Part of this preparation, thirdly, required that man acknowledge his condition, his weakness, his inability to raise himself up out of this state, and thus his need for God's grace, something that was accomplished as he was "left to himself under the state of the Old Law."[300] The outpouring of this grace not only constitutes the perfection of the Divine Law gifted to man, the fulfillment of what was promised under the Old Law, but it also establishes the present state of the world as that which *can* approach most nearly to man's ultimate end as the grace of the Holy Spirit that the New Law pours out is now most perfectly effected, something to which the human person stands in varying ways according to his disposition to the Holy Spirit. Thus, while many might wish to be conformed more closely to the graces of the Holy Spirit conferred by the New Law,

> nevertheless we are not to look forward to a state wherein man is to possess the grace of the Holy Spirit more perfectly than he has possessed it hitherto, especially the apostles who *received the firstfruits of the Spirit*, i.e., *sooner and more*

---

[299] See also ST. I-II. 100. 12 where justification properly denotes the causing of justice, and improperly a sign of justice or a disposition to it. The Old Law did not justify in the proper sense (only the New Law could do this), but it could justify improperly insofar as it "disposed men to the justifying grace of Christ" and as it signified Him insofar as "the life of that people foretold and foreshadowed Christ."

[300] ST. I-II. 106. 3. See also 98. 6 for an explanation in relation to the timing in the giving of the Old Law, which mirrors much of what is said here.

abundantly than others, as a gloss expounds on Romans 8.23.[301]

As for the comparison of the New Law with the Old, Thomas affirms that there is indeed a difference between the two. The difference, however, is not one of kind, as if the two were distinct from each other as one species is from another, which is not the case since both laws intend the same end, and subject man to the one God of both the Old and the New Testaments. Instead, the Old Law is compared to the New as the imperfect is to the perfect, where "the Old Law is like a pedagogue of children . . . whereas the New Law is the law of perfection, since it is the law of charity."[302] More specifically, the Old Law addresses those who do not act out of virtuous habits but who require the discipline and coercion of the law (and thus the fear of punishment and the desire for rewards) to act virtuously. This "law of fear" is superseded by the "law of love" as the inward graces that constitute the New Law make man possessed of virtuous habits wherein they "are inclined to do virtuous deeds through love of virtue, not on account of some extrinsic punishment or reward."[303] We have already mentioned that the New Law fulfills the Old "by supplying that which was lacking in the Old Law," namely the means whereby man might be justified and made virtuous, something that was foreshadowed in the Old Law, but could only be effected in the

---

[301] ST. I-II. 106. 4. Presumably, this would also speak to the state of a saint in the present time. Also see ad1 of this article where Thomas speaks further about man's state under the New Law as he awaits his beatific state to come in the next life. All of this seems to imply that the fullness of the Holy Spirit has been given, but that the obstacle that remains is on man's part in his conformation to this inward grace under the conditions that remain to him having been saved and justified.

[302] ST. I-II. 107. 1.

[303] Ibid., ad2. See also how Thomas qualifies this in relation to those under the Old Law who had the charity and graces of the Holy Spirit, and thus belong to the New, and those under the New who have not attained to its perfection and must be led by the fear of punishment proper to the Old Law. "But although the Old Law contained precepts of charity, nevertheless it did not confer the Holy Spirit by whom *charity . . . is spread abroad in our hearts* (Romans 5.5)"

New "through the power of Christ's passion."[304] In addition to this, Thomas states that the New Law in contained in the Old Law as the mature oak tree is contained in the acorn, or the man is contained in the boy, thus drawing out what is implicit in the relation of the perfect to the imperfect.[305] Lastly, the Old Law is more burdensome than the New only with respect to the external works that it demanded, being far more numerous than those commanded by the New Law, particularly with respect to the ceremonial precepts of the Old. However, with respect to man's interior acts, the situation is reversed, particularly as the New Law requires "a virtuous deed to be done with promptitude and pleasure," something that would be easy for one who is virtuous, but not so for one who is without virtue or imperfect in it.[306]

This leads, then, to a definite determination of what is contained within the New Law itself. First, with respect to external actions, Thomas states that it is quite fitting that the grace that is the New Law manifest in certain external works, specifically through the sacraments established by Christ as means whereby grace is conferred. The reasoning for this lies in the fact that this grace of the New Law was given to man by God made Incarnate, who through his passion, death, and resurrection sanctified and justified man, making him capable not only of receiving the Holy Spirit into his person, but also of effecting works of faith having been inspired by the Spirit. Thus, one would expect the faithful, so filled by the Spirit, to engage in works prompted by this presence, this love, and all that follows upon these. Prompted by grace, these acts manifest in those that are necessary to a faith inspired by such a love, acts which are proscribed by the New Law. Thomas mentions the confession of one's faith as an example. More interestingly, however,

---

[304] ST. I-II. 107. 2. Thomas also states that Christ fulfilled the precepts of the Old Law in both his works and his doctrines, the former in coming under them during his earthly ministry, and the latter in three ways, namely by "explaining the true sense of the law . . . by prescribing the safest way of complying with the statutes of the Old Law . . . (and) by adding some counsels of perfection," the last of which we will shall speak in greater detail shortly.

[305] ST. I-II. 107. 3.

[306] ST. I-II. 107. 4.

are those acts that are not necessarily opposed to or in keeping with this faith animated by love. These are left to the discretion of each person and are not proscribed or prohibited by the New Law. The very fact that such matters are not set down in, and thus determined by, a written law (as was the case for the Old Law), shows that not only the New Law is indeed the perfection of the Old, but also the degree to which the person animated by this grace has been healed and justified by the presence of the Spirit within him, freeing him, so to speak, from those things that made him moral before, namely fear of punishment and desire for reward, and establishing within him the mature stance of one who is truly virtuous, acting from a love for that which is truly good, fearing only that he might not manifest this love in ways befitting its source and desired end.[307] The maturity of this position is not wholly unexpected. For we see here the fulfillment of the notion of law, that is to say, that law, as a means to happiness, is something that draws one who is animated by its perfection to the point where the law itself is transcended, if you will, having become part and parcel of one's very being. The law for such a one is "left behind" insofar as one now aspires most assuredly to and is on the threshold of the ultimate good to which the whole of the law is oriented. The New Law, consequently, is called the "law of liberty" which enables man to act freely, that is to act on his own accord, not becoming a law unto himself, but has been liberated from a fallen notion of freedom (where he is free *from* all that would bind him, allowing him to become his own law) and has come into the fullness for which he was intended (where he is now free *for* that which he was created). For having received this grace of the New Law, there is infused in man the virtues spoken about earlier that incline him "to act aright," to "do freely those things that are becoming to grace, and shun what is opposed to it."[308] Some, however, might say that the external acts determined by the New Law were insufficiently set forth, particularly in light of the extent to which these were determined by the Old Law, making the New Law appear somewhat

---

[307] Thus, even one's fear becomes mature under the New Law. See ST. II-II. 19 for example.

[308] ST. I-II. 108. 1. ad2.

bare in comparison.[309] In his response, he reiterates the position that he detailed above, namely that only those things that are related essentially to "the reception or right use" of the graces bestowed by the New Law come under specific prescriptions or prohibitions. For the reception of grace under the New Law, we have the seven sacraments established by Christ himself. As for the right use of the New Law's grace, this is effected by works animated by charity. "These, insofar as they are essential to virtue, pertain to the moral precepts, which also formed part of the Old Law. Hence, in this respect, the New Law had nothing to add as regards external actions." As for the determination of these with respect to the ceremonial and judicial precepts, these are left to man's discretion under the New Law, since these two categories of precepts "are not in themselves necessarily connected with inward grace wherein the Law consists." They become the responsibility of those who are charged specifically with their care, ranging from the determinations appropriate to the individual himself, up to and including those appropriate to temporal and spiritual governing bodies, namely the state and the Church. Thus, Thomas takes seriously James's pronouncement (at 1.25) that the New Law is *the law of perfect liberty*, one which proscribes or forbids only in connection with sacramental matters and moral precepts that have a necessary connection with virtue.[310]

The most specific determinations of what is contained in the New Law are found in the last two articles of this question. The first of these asks whether the New Law sufficiently directs man in those intransitive activities that are central to his character, the virtuous life, and in general to the manifestation of what his life should look like as a Christian. The answer harkens back to the completion of the *Treatise on Virtue*, namely that the Christian's interior life is ordered most perfectly under the New Law by everything that is contained in the Sermon on the Mount. This Sermon is not only "replete with all the precepts whereby a Christian's life is formed," it also details, "the whole process of forming the life of a Christian."[311] What

---

[309] See the objections to ST. I-II. 108. 2.

[310] ST. I-II. 108. 2.

[311] ST. I-II. 108. 3. sed contra and corpus.

follows in Thomas's response is a very brief but extremely rich commentary on the entirety of the Sermon (and not just on the Beatitudes discussed previously), whereby he explains the specific way by which the interior life of the Christian is ordered, beginning with an understanding of what his ultimate end is, establishing the authority by which this doctrine is promulgated, and then ordering his intransitive activity in relation first to himself, and then as it touches upon his neighbor. Accordingly, the Sermon tells the Christian how to rectify his volition of what is to be done, and his intention of the end, the former through prescribing that man should refrain from all evil works and their occasions, both external and internal, and the latter by seeking not earthly riches but those in heaven in all that he does. As for his neighbor, the Sermon forbids rash, unjust, and presumptuous judgment of him, as well as entrusting his neighbor "too readily with sacred things, if he be unworthy." Lastly,

> He teaches us how to fulfil the teaching of the Gospel, namely, by imploring the help of God; by striving to enter by the narrow door of perfect virtue; and by being wary lest we be led astray by evil influences. Moreover, He declares that we must observe His commandments, and that it is not enough to make profession of faith, or to work miracles, or merely to hear His words.[312]

In the final article, Thomas determines the place of what are called the evangelical counsels of poverty, chastity, and obedience in the manifestation of the Christian life. He makes, first, a distinction between a commandment and a counsel, the former implying an obligation to fulfill it, while the latter "is left to the option of the one to whom it is given." In relation to the New Law, commandments are determined according to what is necessary for one to do so as to attain to one's happiness, while counsels are offered to make "the gaining of this end more assured and expeditious." Thus, in the Sermon on the Mount, man is commanded to seek his happiness not in the goods of this world, but rather in those of the next, to seek not

[312] ST. I-II. 108. 3.

temporal riches, but spiritual ones. Thomas then points out that man is not prohibited from the goods of this world. Rather, he is simply commanded not to allow them to become first in his love. He can, thus, use these goods so long as they do not take first place in his affections, that place reserved for God alone. Nevertheless, if man wishes to aspire to his ultimate end and good with all that is at his disposal, then he is counseled under the New Law to give up entirely the goods of this world, something that he does most effectively by heeding the counsels to poverty, chastity, and obedience, which regard respectively the external goods of riches, carnal pleasures, and the honors that he might seek from other men. Since those in religious orders seek to dedicate their lives wholly to Christ and to the New Law, these three counsels are indispensable, while for the rank and file, these counsels do not rise to the level of vows but rather are taken up when and if the situation allows, thus, in keeping with the principle stated earlier, namely of not imposing excessive burdens upon those who are young in the faith, but always encouraging them to grow in the life of virtue, and eventually to take up those practices that are counseled by the New Law.

This exceedingly brief treatment of the New Law should not prejudice one against its importance. For we have here not only that which fulfills and perfects the Old Law, but also what Thomas considers to be the definition of the truly virtuous person, one who acts lovingly and freely out of the habits that he himself can effect but especially through the Gifts that the Holy Spirit has infused within him, which manifest both in the activities characteristic of the Christian life, as indicated in the Sermon on the Mount and especially in the Beatitudes, and in the fruits specific to these, as described earlier. In its perfection, law is not something external to the human person, but is something that is so internalized that Thomas, following Scriptures and the patristic authors, describes as written upon one's heart, the interior action of the Holy Spirit present through faith and operating through charity. This, together with the whole of the natural law, "inscribed in the conscience of every person and formulated by the Decalogue in the setting of the Old Covenant,"[313] not only constitutes the "interior

---

[313] Pinckaers (2005), p. 368.

foundation" of Thomas's moral theology, but also sets the stage for both the *Treatise on Grace*, and the whole of the *secunda secundae* wherein the New Law and Grace itself are brought to bear upon the very descriptions of the virtues both theological and moral, offering a very detailed description of what the virtuous Christian life looks like and very clear guidance with respect to its attainment for the sake of man's happiness, something, however, that can only be completed in light of the material with which the *tertia pars* deals.[314]

Treatise on Grace (Questions 109–114)

Thomas divides his considerations on grace into three parts: the first dealing with its necessity, essence, and varied kinds (Questions 109–111 respectively), the second with its cause (Question 112), and the third with its effects (specifically justification and merit, Questions 113–114). Since this treatise (along with the prior one on law) considers the external principles that come to bear importantly upon man's voluntary activity, the necessity of grace is first addressed. In light of those powers that are essential to man's voluntary activity, he asks directly whether man could know any truth, wish for any good, or effect any good deed without grace. With respect to man's grasp of truth, he restates what was developed in the *prima pars*, namely that man's reasoning is possible only insofar as God has established providentially this power to act as it does, wherein by its own "intellectual light" it can know all that falls under its purview in man's experience of the material world, and this without further intervention on God's part.[315] Anything else that extends beyond what is within the reach of man's natural powers (things

---

[314] Consider Pinckaers' description of Augustine's account of the process of the Christian life in light of the Beatitudes, the Gifts, and Fruits (1993; 1995), pp. 152–155, and (2005), Essays 7, 10, 18, 19, and 20. Also, see Torrell (1996; 2003) who speaks beautifully of this indwelling of the Holy Spirit on pp. 200–224.

[315] This argument recognizes that the very thought processes in which man engages are attributable remotely to God as man is determined in his nature and existence by God, but that part of God's providential governance of creation allows for the reality of secondary causality, that man, so established, can now attain here to truth on his own, that is, with respect to that which falls within his purview.

with which faith and prophecy are concerned) require the "light of grace" through which the human intellect is strengthened in its approach to and understanding of these higher things. Something similar is said with regard to man's desire of good and the effecting of the good in his activities, something that has already been detailed in the discussions concerning the infused virtues, the gifts of the Holy Spirit, and the Beatitudes. Through God's providence, man is so established in his nature to desire and seek after what is good. In the prelapsarian state, it was well within man's natural capacity to both desire and effect the good that was proportionate to his nature, satisfying all that was required for this and was found wanting only with respect to those goods that surpassed the reach of his nature, such as the infused virtues. Postlapsarian man, however, cannot supply himself with all those goods proportioned to his nature, although he can on his own effect good works of a singular nature, such as building, farming, and other such matters. Consequently, he requires grace to carry out works of supernatural or infused virtue, as well as to heal his nature that has been disordered by the sin of the first parents. The necessity of grace, then, is clear with respect to the operations involved in man's voluntary activity insofar as he is ordered to an end that exceeds the capacity of his powers, requiring, therefore, assistance with respect to that knowledge and desire that are integral to his activity ordered to the attainment of his ultimate beatitude but which exceed the proportions of their respective strengths.[316]

The implication here for man in the prelapsarian state is that he was naturally able to refer all his loves and desires properly to God as to their (and his) ultimate end and good. Thus, he required no grace from God over and above that which moved him to this rightly ordered love in the first place, unlike fallen man who requires the healing of his will's disordered desire for goods other than God even before he can be moved by God to love Him above all other things. What is affirmed here is what we have seen many times before, namely that from man's creation, he was made for God, finding his ultimate happiness only in union with Him.[317] This is natural to him, even though

[316] ST. I-II. 109. 1 and 2.
[317] ST. I-II. 109. 3.

it is beyond the reach or proportions of his powers, even in the prelapsarian state, something which, according to Pinckaers, testifies to "a basic harmony between human nature, which is at the source of our human freedom and personality—whence proceeds our action—and the gratuitous gift of supernatural life," a fact that indicates that Thomas did not suffer from the divide between the natural and the supernatural, or between nature and grace that has troubled so many since him.[318] Again, in his pre-fallen state, man could fulfill all the commandments of the law by his own power, requiring only the gift of charity whereby he is moved by God to act in this manner. Not so for fallen man who requires not only this gift of charity but also the healing of his nature as previously indicated.[319] In this, and the prior three articles, we see that the human person in his fallen state stands in need of a twofold grace, namely one which both heals his nature and elevates him to the supernatural status that he had enjoyed before the fall, and a grace which helps him to actualize this restored state in both his transitive and intransitive activities, an actualization that he himself cannot effect (for to do so would be for him to act beyond the nature of his own capacities, as we have already seen with respect to the infused virtues and the graces that accompany them). This healing and elevation, then, are only realized in man's voluntary activity, in both its natural and supernatural modes, through the continuous help that man receives from God in the form of this grace.[320]

Clearly from what has been said, the human person cannot merit everlasting life naturally through his own efforts; his merit extends only to that which falls within his own power.[321] Even the preparation involved so that he might receive habitual grace for the first time in his conversion is something that is effected by God Himself, in moving "the soul inwardly" or inspiring man's "good wish" through a gratuitous gift of grace

---

[318] To begin to get a sense of the controversies that this discussion has occasioned, consider Kerr (2002), pp. 134–148, and Pinckaers (2005), pp. 359–368.

[319] ST. I-II. 109. 4.

[320] See Joseph Wawrykow (2005), pp. 194–195 for an excellent description of these two graces.

[321] ST. I-II. 109. 5.

prior to his turn to God. We have seen in the *prima pars* that God not only establishes the whole of creation but also moves it to seek Him as its good and completion. We have also seen that man wills all that he wills under the aspect of goodness, which constitutes the initial determination of his will to its proper object, something experienced by man, however, as a determination to goodness generally speaking; everyone desires to be happy, but are not sure about that in which his happiness consists, as we have seen in the *Treatise on Happiness.* In his desire, then, to seek out that which perfects him, the human person takes up the pursuit of wisdom and of virtue, as recounted especially in Aristotle's *Nicomachean Ethics.* However, as we have seen in the first two articles of this question, and more specifically in the first question of the *prima pars*, man's reach far exceeds his grasp; as Aristotle states in Book X of *The Nicomachean Ethics*, man knows that he is like the gods and can imitate their activity, but is, nonetheless, not defined entirely as one of them, but must manifest his happiness in the here and now according to what he is in light of which he manifests the best of the intellectual and moral life in the context of the culture or city in which he lives. This is the extent of his natural grasp, the height to which man's natural happiness can extend. We have seen, however, that in light of God's revelation, understood here as a grace illuminating, elevating, healing, and strengthening both man's intellect and will, man is gifted gratuitously, over and above the initial determination of his will, with the grace whereby he is helped in his desire to be happy in a most specific and determinate way, namely to seek union with God, something which now, in light of this helping grace, becomes a distinct possibility that he willingly accepts and pursues. This tills the ground, so to speak, of his being, disposing him suitably to the reception of habitual grace whereby he is converted or turned to God, thereby specifying the generality of his will's natural desire for goodness, elevating him so that he might cross, so to speak, the gap that exists between the created and the Creator, and healing him so that he might be released from the effects of sin, both his own and those inherited from the race's first parents. In this state, he is found pleasing to God, is ordered anew both in the powers of his person and in his relation to God, and, in light of what we have seen before, readily and willingly inclined to perform acts of supernatural virtue, but still standing in need of this helping grace to actualize this readiness and willingness to do good.[322] Grace, then, abounds, first, in the eternal law in the establishment and order of creation, but in a special way in man who participates, as rational and volitional—as made to the image of God—in the eternal law through the natural law itself. Man is thus established in his nature toward his perfection and strives with all that is at his disposal toward this, both in his intellectual pursuits and his moral endeavors, particularly with respect to the states or cities that he forms and the human laws he establishes to govern them and hopefully bring them to their end. But he is frustrated in his attempts, as recounted at the start of the *Summa*.[323] God, then, intervenes in time and gifts His people with the Old Law, preparing them for the reception of the New Law, that grace which effectively will satisfy the very desire for goodness that was written into the very fabric of the human person in his creation, and all of this, at each step of the way, respecting and working with the nature of man's person, specifically in light of his freedom, as has been recounted often throughout this work.

The human person stands in need of all of this, not only because he cannot on his own grasp his ultimate happiness, but also because he cannot even raise himself up from the sin in which he finds himself both personally committed and inherited from his kind. Only God can restore the luster of man's original nature stained by sin, draw him back to the order that he once enjoyed, and forgive the debt that he has incurred.[324] But even this restoration is not effected perfectly until man comes to the end of his journey in the next life, and especially with the general resurrection of the dead at the end of time. The grace that God bestows in this life heals man's nature to the extent that although his mind is made well, his corporeal aspect and the powers related to it, particularly his carnal appetites, are not

---

[322] ST. I-II. 109. 6 and ad1 and ad3. See also Wawrykow (2005), pp. 195–197.

[323] ST. I. 1. 1. See this point beautifully exhibited in the first eight chapters of Book One of the *Summa Contra Gentiles*.

[324] ST. I-II. 109. 7.

fully restored to the obedience that they exhibited with respect to reason in the prelapsarian state, as discussed in the *Treatise on Man*. Thus, while it is possible for man to abstain from mortal sin, he still experiences those venial sins that find their genesis in the disorder that still reigns within his sensitive and vegetative nature. Realistically, however, mortal sin will still abound, given that human reason is not perfectly subjected to God in this life, not to mention the myriad of other external forces at work in the life of man as these come to bear upon his intellectual, moral, and social development.[325] Most especially does man require helping grace continuously not only to activate the potential to supernatural acts that come with the gift of habitual grace, but also to do this throughout his entire life, particularly in the face of what remains unrepaired in his nature and in the evil that comes his way from those who are unredeemed. This is the grace of perseverance in good to the end, an important aspect of the virtues of both hope and fortitude.[326]

From the preceding, the essence of grace is clearly something that is gratuitously bestowed upon man through God's love. Specifically, it is that by which God "draws the rational creature above the condition of its nature to a participation of the Divine good."[327] This participation effects all that has been discussed above, qualifying man's soul in such a way that he finds himself moved "sweetly and promptly to acquire his eternal good," a description that highlights the voluntary nature of man's participation in the Divine goodness which grace constitutes.[328] It is important to note that grace is not identical with virtue. The virtues all have a dispositive effect upon the varied powers of one's person to act well, both in themselves, but especially in relation to the nature in which they are found and the end that this nature pursues. The acquired virtues dispose man well with respect to this nature, and in a limited way, to his end (as just discussed, namely the contributions that they would make to the realization of man's imperfect happiness), while the infused virtues dispose man to a higher nature, that is to say "in relation to

[325] ST. I-II. 109. 8.
[326] ST. I-II. 109. 9–10.
[327] ST. I-II. 110. 1.
[328] ST. I-II. 110. 2 and ad2.

a participation of the Divine nature" which, in being received, makes the human person to become "born again sons of God." The virtues, then, both acquired and infused, are derived from and ordained to these respective natures, the acquired virtues from the light of reason and to its natural end, and the infused virtues from the light of grace and to its supernatural end. By these virtues, the human person is able to act well, particularly as the infused virtues "enable man to walk as befits the light of grace."[329] Consequently, grace, being prior to virtue, has its very seat, so to speak, in that which is prior to and gives rise to the powers of one's person, those powers that are properly addressed and perfected by the virtues themselves. This seat is the very essence of the soul itself, which, so graced, participates "in the Divine nature after the manner of a likeness through a certain regeneration or recreation."[330]

Before examining the causes and effects of grace, Thomas considers its various divisions, and this as he draws heavily upon the patristic sources. First, there is *sanctifying* and *gratuitous* grace, the former "whereby man is united to God," and the latter whereby he "cooperates with another in leading him to God."[331] The second division distinguishes *operating* from *cooperating* grace, a division that applies importantly to both habitual and helping grace that were discussed above. Operating grace is that which is effected by God alone, that grace wherein He is the only mover, so to speak, of man who is passive in regard to it. Cooperating grace, on the other hand, is that which is effected by God but in which man can cooperate, where man is both moved and mover and not wholly passive in regards to this grace. Thus, we can distinguish operative and cooperative habitual and helping graces. Referring back to the earlier discussion of Question 109, Article 6, wherein one's conversion from a nongraced state to a graced one was described, we can discern the work of an operative helping grace that prepares man's soul for its conversion effected by habitual grace. In its operative form, habitual grace effects the elevation and healing of man's soul, qualifying it so that man, through that cooperative form of habitual

---

[329] ST. I-II. 110. 3.
[330] ST. I-II. 110. 4.
[331] ST. I. 111. 1.

grace, is now made capable of performing supernatural acts of virtue. That he acts in a way befitting his new status as a son of God, a partaker of the Divine nature, is a consequence of further helping graces under both descriptions. In their operative manifestation, these helping graces

> keep the person on the path to God and make possible perseverance in grace; they do so by overcoming temptation and by providing correct intention to the person in the willing of the end of all of the acts that person will go on to do when in the state of grace.[332]

In their cooperative manifestation, these helping graces "contribute to the merit of the person, allowing that person to contribute in a meaningful way to the achievement of eternal life."[333]

In Question 112, Thomas brings greater precision to what he has implied so far concerning the cause of grace. Since grace is "nothing short of a partaking of the Divine nature," something which the human person is incapable of effecting, it must be the case that "just as it is impossible for anything to set fire but fire, so it has to be God alone to divinize, by sharing communion in the divine nature by means of the participation of a sort of assimilation."[334] The notion of deification employed here signals the patristic influence upon Thomas's thought, as they both have 2 Peter 1.4 in mind.[335] It reflects what is involved in the elevation of human nature by grace, namely that man has progressed, so to speak, from what he found himself naturally to be into the realization of that to which he was initially made through the gift of God's grace, namely the realization of what it is to be made to God's image and of all that becomes possible

---

[332] Wawrykow (2005), p. 198.

[333] Ibid., pp. 198–199. See the whole of Wawrykow's discussion of these distinctions on pp. 197–199. The reader should also consider the other distinctions that Thomas offers concerning grace in Articles 3 and 4 of this question, namely that of prevenient and subsequent grace, and the gratuitous graces offered by St. Paul at I Corinthians 12. 8, 9, and 10.

[334] ST. I-II. 112. 1. The translation is taken from Kerr (2002), p. 149.

[335] Torrell (1996; 2003), pp. 126–127. See also Kerr (2002), pp. 145–147 and pp. 149–161.

to him in the grace that he has and continues to receive, something that is made possible by the Incarnation and Christ's
salvific act, opening the way to a life that is pleasing to God,
and to its completion in His gift of beatitude in the next life.
This grace is not something for which one can prepare; the
reception of operative habitual grace by which man is healed
and elevated presupposes the gift of operative helping grace,
both of which are effected by God alone. Even with respect to
the desire of the will for that in which its perfect good is found
and the freely chosen acts in which man engages to achieve this,
are both of them brought about by God, as was detailed in the
discussion above concerning Article 2 of Question 111. Thus,
man prepares himself for grace, but this only insofar as he has
been prepared by God and guided in his steps by God toward
this.[336] This preparation on man's part does not necessitate that
habitual grace be given; this gift is purely gratuitous on God's
part. However, if God has dispensed helping grace in preparation for the gifting of habitual grace, then the latter will follow
assuredly insofar as this is "ordained by God" whose "intention
cannot fail."[337] This, then, accounts for the fact that habitual
grace is greater in some than in others, as God has so prepared
and gifted people freely according to His wisdom. Thomas
recalls a point that was developed earlier in the *prima pars* in
explanation of these differences, namely that "the beauty and
perfection of the Church may result from these various degrees;
even as He instituted the various conditions of things that the
universe might be perfect."[338] As for man's knowledge that he
enjoys God's grace, this can be accomplished by either a direct
communication to man by God, something experienced by a
very few, or indirectly, as man imperfectly deduces this gift by
the effects that he experiences, specifically "when he is conscious of delighting in God, and of despising worldly things,
and inasmuch as a man is not conscious of any mortal sin," as
well as the sweetness experienced by those who enjoy grace, and

[336] ST. I-II. 112. 2.

[337] ST. I-II. 112. 3.

[338] ST. I-II. 112. 4. See Wawrykow (2005), pp. 206–209 for a comparison of
Thomas's treatment of grace in the ST to that of a much earlier work, his
Commentary on the Sentences of Peter Lombard, which helps one under-
stand more deeply the issues discussed here.

not by those who do not. This knowledge, however, is conjectural at best since certitude concerning such matters is reserved to the knowledge enjoyed by God alone.[339]

Lastly, Thomas considers the effects of grace. Several of these can be discerned in the material that has preceded (specifically, as stated in Article 3 of Question 111, the healing of the soul, the desire for good, carrying into effect the good that has been proposed, perseverance in good, and the attainment of glory), all of which he discusses under the headings of justification (113) and merit (114). The former is said of those who were previously nonbelievers. It denotes that movement of their soul from its sinful state to that of justice, specifically a movement which rectifies the order of their internal disposition with respect to God Himself, and of their lower powers to their reason.[340] This remission of sin that is justification is effected only by an infusion of God's grace, something that occurs in conjunction with their freely seeking and accepting this grace, both of which movements are effected by God's grace, as already discussed above.[341] This movement of their mind by God wherein they are converted is something that is effected through faith, something that implies, among other things, a turning from their former life, and a despising of their sins.[342] And although God's work of creation, the drawing forth of all things from nothing, is His greatest work with regard to the modality of the activity of which He is capable, nonetheless, with respect to what is effected through His activity, this justification, wherein those so graced are both healed and elevated and which "terminates at the eternal good of a share in the Godhead, is greater than the creation of heaven and earth which terminates at the good of mutable nature,"[343] an incredible thing when one considers that Thomas does not consider this justification to be miraculous insofar as the soul "having been made to the likeness of God . . . is fit to receive God by grace."[344] Thus, man's justification is not something worked in him contrary to his nature, but

[339] ST. I-II. 112. 5.
[340] ST. I-II. 113. 1 and 6.
[341] ST. I-II. 113. 2 and 3.
[342] ST. I-II. 113. 4 and 5.
[343] ST. I-II. 113. 9.
[344] ST. I-II. 113. 10.

rather in concert with it, restoring it partly to the perfection that it once enjoyed before the fall, and anticipating its full restoration in the life and the resurrection to come.

As for the question of merit, Thomas states that although, simply speaking, man merits no reward from God for the deeds that he does (given the lack of equality existing between the created and the Creator), nonetheless as God has ordained that good acts performed by those in grace merit the reward of eternal life, He thus makes it possible for man's efforts to have some value toward his salvation.[345] Those, then, who have been healed, elevated, and aided by God's grace enjoy a certain status that they did not enjoy previously wherein, animated and impelled by the grace of the Holy Spirit, they are made capable of actually performing acts of such a kind that merit everlasting life. In this situation, "the worth of the work depends on the dignity of the grace whereby a man, being made a partaker of the Divine nature, is adopted as a son of God, to whom the inheritance is due by right of adoption."[346] It is, then, out of this deification, that the human person, having been reconciled to God through the forgiveness of his sins, and impelled by the gifts of the Holy Spirit, can partake of activities befitting this new status, activities that of their very nature merit eternal life. However, one cannot merit this first grace whereby he is justified, healed, and elevated. This is purely a gift from God.[347] The same can be said of one's restoration to grace having lost it through some transgression (God's mercy is wholly operative in this situation),[348] and one's perseverance in grace while a "wayfarer" upon this earth.[349]

Conclusion to the Prima Secundae

At the very least, it should be evident to one who has read through to the end of the *prima secundae* that Thomas's moral theology draws heavily upon the matters with which the *prima*

---

[345] ST. I-II. 114. 1.

[346] ST. I-II. 114. 3.

[347] ST. I-II. 114. 5. However, if God so wills it, one may merit this grace for another. See Article 6.

[348] ST. I-II. 114. 7.

[349] ST. I-II. 114. 9.

pars deals. Repeatedly throughout the *prima secundae* appeals were made to God's providence and governance of creation, to the psychological principles governing the nature and operations of the human soul, to the manner and nature of man's access to and knowledge of God's nature, to the very order of creation itself and man's place and role within it, to a description of man's pre-fallen state, and the history and result of his fall, to the Trinitarian life itself and its presence in all of creation, and many other matters. The prefacing of Thomas's moral theology by matters proper to fundamental theology and the metaphysics, epistemology, and psychology upon which this area of theology draws serves not only to contextualize the discipline of moral theology within the wider field of theology as a whole, laying the ground for its completion in the Christological, sacramental, and eschatological theology with which the *tertia pars* deals, but also demonstrates the richness and the catholicity of the moral life, specifically that it is something that is not to be distinguished in a hard and fast manner from the other areas of theology, let alone from the natural arts and sciences, and especially philosophy itself. The contributions that are made by the speculative disciplines to the right ordering and thus the rectification of the practical activity that flows from all that is required of man's voluntary activity are essential even to the most cursory of readings of Thomas's moral doctrine. To put this in different terms, although the primary agent in the *secunda pars* is man himself, one cannot describe sufficiently man's end and the means that he employs in its achievement without an important appeal first to the speculative and practical disciplines that directly support the realization of his voluntary activity, and secondly to the work of God as it is now, in this context, focused upon the limitations natural to man's voluntary activity and how these can be overcome in man's desire for his true end and good, something that will only be completed in light of the *tertia pars*. The whole of Thomas's moral theology, then, is dominating by the question concerning man's happiness. The whole of the *secunda pars* deals with it, determining either what it is (in the *Treatise on Happiness* that stands at the head of this part of the *Summa* and of Thomas's moral doctrine) or the means whereby it might be attained (both generally considered—all the remaining treatises of the *prima secundae* that deal with the principles of human voluntary activity, both internal and external to man—and specifically—the close examination of the theological and cardinal virtues in the *secunda secundae*). The material of the *secunda pars* is focused upon the conditions of man's *reditus* to God, and this in light of and in dependence upon all that must be known with respect to the *exitus* so that his return to that first principle from which all being, intelligibility and goodness arose might be successful, something that can only be effected through the agency of Christ himself in the *tertia pars*. Before Christ is considered, however, Thomas details the specific means whereby the general principles of morality might be brought to bear upon the entirety of man's voluntary activity toward his end, good, and happiness. It is to this that Thomas turns in the *secunda secundae* and his treatment of the theological and cardinal virtues.

Secunda Secundae

This part of the *Summa* is the largest, extending over 189 questions. Its *prologue* (the longest of all the prologues found in this work) is instructive not only for the divisions of the material of which the *secunda secundae* will treat, but also for the rationale that Thomas provides concerning its structure. As was done previously in the first chapter of this book, let the prologue be quoted in full with some commentary:[350]

> Having set out the general theory on vices, virtues and other topics related to morals, we must turn now to specific details about each. Generalities about morals have a limited value because actions are so individual. There are two ways available for dealing with any specific point about morality: the one is to look at the moral topics themselves, examining, for example, one or another particular virtue or vice; the second is to look at people in their respective callings, for example, to subjects and superiors, those pursuing the contemplative and those pursuing the active life, or to other differences among people. Accordingly our own specific consideration

[350] The translation of this prologue is taken from Volume 31 (1974) of the Blackfriars' translation of the *Summa*.

will concern, first, themes relating to all stations in life; secondly, details related to particular callings.

Two brief comments. First, Thomas divides his considerations in
the *secunda secundae* into two, specifying the particular details of
the general moral theory developed in the *prima secundae* as they
are applicable, first, to all people regardless of their positions
within human society, and second to those who have particular vocations important to the community, particularly to that
of the Church. The treatment of the first occupies the greater
part of the *secunda secundae*, extending from Questions 1 to 170,
while the second extends from Questions 171 to 189. Secondly,
Thomas understands that while moral discourse requires careful attention to its general principles (as was the case in the *prima
secundae*), nevertheless it cannot remain at this level if it is to be of
value to those who seek their end, good, and happiness. For this
is something that is attained through their practical activities,
those that deal directly with particularities and not generalities.
In short, moral theology and the doctrines that are developed by
it are directed ultimately toward the good that can be manifested
in one's life through one's practical, voluntary activity. Thus,
although it is important to know the nature of passion, virtue,
vice, law, and grace, in short, to know the internal and external
principles governing man's voluntary activity, the goal of moral
theology is for one to become good, virtuous, and lacking in
vice, to have a proper order to and control over one's passions, to
be subject to the law, and desirous of grace, in short, to act well
in relation to and pursuit of one's ultimate end.

With respect to the distinction of the material into these two
sections, he continues:

> As to the first of these two headings, observe that to resolve
> problems about virtues, Gifts, vices and precepts one after
> the other would mean repetition on some points. For exam-
> ple, to treat adequately of the commandment, *Thou shalt
> not commit adultery*, would entail going into the meaning of
> adultery, a specific sin, knowledge about which depends on a
> knowledge of the virtue it opposes. The method will be more
> concise and pointed if within the same treatise the discussion
> includes together with a virtue the corresponding Gift, the

opposite vices, and the applicable precepts, affirmative or negative. Such a method is suited, moreover, to the specific meaning of the various vices; we have already shown that vices and sins are differentiated in kind on the basis of their matter or objective, not on the basis of other variations, e.g., sins of thought, word or deed, sins of weakness, ignorance or malice, and so on; it is the same matter about which virtues do right and vices opposite go wrong.

Thomas repeats the concern that he had stated in the prologue to the *Summa* itself but now with respect to the matter at hand. He states that those who have treated of the virtues previously had not ordered their material properly with the consequence that their accounts were needlessly repetitive, hindering the neophyte's progress in his knowledge of moral matters and their application to the particulars of his life. To avoid this, he frames the material with which the *secunda secundae* deals in light of the virtues themselves so that each treatise will consider (i) a particular virtue, (ii) a Gift of the Holy Spirit that corresponds directly to that virtue, (iii) the vices that are opposed to this virtue, and (iv) those precepts that are directly related to this virtue. The reader will recognize this order as that which guided Thomas in the *prima secundae* where he treated of the virtues, followed by the Gifts, vice, and sin, and finally the law itself. Thomas then concludes with the specific distinctions that will determine the treatises of the *secunda secundae*, and the order of treatment:

> The entire subject matter of morals being thus condensed under a discussion of virtues, these, in turn are to be reduced to seven. Three are theological, and they must be the first topic; the other four are cardinal, and will be the second. As to the intellectual virtues, prudence is one of them and is included and listed among the cardinal virtues. Since, as already shown, art is a right conception about things of our making, it does not come under moral science, the concern of which is actions of our doing. The other three virtues of the mind, namely, wisdom, understanding and knowledge, share a common name with certain Gifts of the Holy Spirit, and so we will examine them in conjunction with the discussion

of Gifts corresponding to certain of the virtues. A point made earlier is that all other moral virtues are in some way reducible to the cardinal virtues; consequently, as part of the treatment of each cardinal virtue, we will include all other virtues annexed to it in any way, along with the opposed vices. In this way, we will pass over nothing of significance to morals.

The order of treatment, then, is laid out as follows: the theological virtues of faith, hope, and charity are considered first (Questions 1 through 46: faith, in Questions 1 through 16, hope in 17 through 22 and charity in 23 through 46), followed by the cardinal virtues of prudence, justice, fortitude, and temperance (Questions 47 through 170: prudence in Questions 47 through 56, justice in 57 through 122, fortitude in 123 through 140, and temperance in 141 through 170). This order is determined by what is required for man's happiness. Since this consists in man's union with God, those means whereby man's activity is most perfectly ordered to the attainment of this union are primary. Thus, while the cardinal virtues are important to man's voluntary activity, they do not conduce to the attainment of his true end in the same way or as directly as the theological virtues do. The theological virtues have as their primary object God Himself, while the cardinal virtues are directed to man's life in this world and the rectification of his activity in relation to it as their object.[351]

---

[351] Reflecting upon Thomas's decision to organize all moral matters dealt with in the *secunda secundae* within the scope of virtue, Torrell states:

> If the fact of placing happiness at the beginning already marks all of moral reflection with a focus towards the Good in itself, it is clear that an account of all that favors the pursuit of this Good will be first. The concrete obstacles that may be encountered in this pursuit . . . will never be the primary focus of Thomas's discourse. Thomas Aquinas's morality of virtues, governed by beatitude, gives rise to a Christian life that is resolutely oriented toward the positive." (Torrell (2005), pp. 39–40)

This point highlights, yet again, the character of Thomas's moral doctrine as distinguished from a morality centered upon conscience, duty, law, etc., as discussed earlier in the *prima secundae*.

That Thomas collects all of the moral virtues within the four cardinal virtues should not be a surprise, given that he argued for this earlier in the *prima secundae*.[352] Likewise, it should be no surprise that Thomas accords a central place to the Gifts of the Holy Spirit in his descriptions of these seven virtues.[353] For, as we have seen in the *prima secundae*, although the human person naturally desires that in which his happiness consists, the attainment of such is something to which his natural powers and activities are not proportioned. The human person thus requires supernatural aid if he is to attain to his true end. The Christian life of activity is defined essentially by the ultimate good and end to which it is oriented, and the kinds of activities that are required of man so that he might aspire to this end and be found ready for the gift of God Himself. One, then, can appreciate the decision to order the particularities of moral theology within the virtues and the supernatural means whereby the human person is strengthened so that he might act beyond that which is proportioned to his nature. One can also understand the subordinate position of vice, sin, and the varied precepts to that of the virtues and gifts. For these matters do not constitute the essence of Thomas's moral theology but serve secondary roles, as vice and sin detail the common errors into which people fall in the discharge of their voluntary activity, and as the precepts, both positive and negative, warn against these so that man might progress more assuredly in the virtuous life and achieve his happiness. In addition to these things, care must be taken in the wider application of the order of exposition to that of its realization in one's moral activity. Previously, we have seen a definite order in the presentation of the varied "stages" of the voluntary act, and also in the arousal, continuance, and termination of the varied passions that make up one's sensitive appetition. One, however, was warned not to identify the order required for proper exposition with that required for its realization in one's life, as if every voluntary act

[352] at ST. I-II. 61. 3.

[353] To faith corresponds the Gifts of intelligence and knowledge; to hope, the Gift of fear; to charity, wisdom; to prudence, counsel; to justice, the Gift of piety and the virtue of religion; to fortitude, the Gift of courage; to temperance, chastity and the gift of fear. See Pinckaers (1991; 2003), pp. 28–29.

demanded a strict adherence to the chronology of the 12 steps described, or that every particular passion experienced in one's life began immediately and proximately with love in the concupiscible, manifested in the irascible, and resolved into either joy or sorrow. The same is to be observed here in the order that Thomas employs in his exposition of the particulars involved in the virtuous life. As Pinckaers states

> the virtues form a living, structured organism ... [they] always work together in concrete action, each contributing its part, just as the members of our bodies interact as we move about. When we act justly, for example, in the context of our professional work, prudential judgment plays a directive role; we need courage to make certain decisions and implement them, and a certain moderation to temper our desires. Charity, too, intervenes, according to our commitment to higher values. In this context, it would be ridiculous to attempt to acquire one virtue after another, following the listing in the *secunda secundae*. The virtues are all of a piece; they are interrelated, and they progress as a harmonious whole.[354]

The scope and the detail of the *secunda secundae* is clearly vast. It includes a treatment of 53 virtues within the discussion of the three theological and four cardinal virtues. It develops descriptions of numerous vices that undermine these virtues in varying ways. It details the many precepts that are promulgated to aid man in his acquisition of these virtues and to avoid their opposed vices, as well as the order that must be effected among all the virtues in man's voluntary activity as he seeks his happiness, something that necessitates the Gifts of the Holy Spirit effecting that order of which man himself is incapable due to his fallen condition. The nature of this book does not allow for a detailed coverage of the material contained in the *secunda secundae*, a pity given that one of the reasons that the *Summa* was composed was for the clarification of moral matters that it could offer his readers, namely young ordinary Dominicans as they sought guidance in the proper discharge of their pastoral duties. For these, as well as for the modern reader, the *secunda*

---

[354] Pinckaers (1993; 1995), p. 227.

secundae presents a detailed portrayal of Christian life in the world, a playing out, so to speak, in man's voluntary activity of the Gifts of the Holy Spirit, and the graces that are given to him, especially in the form of the Old and New Law culminating in the Sermon on the Mount and the Beatitudes themselves.[355] Nevertheless, in keeping with the introductory nature of this guide to a sustained reading of St. Thomas's *Summa*, attention has been directed primarily to the themes and the general principles important to this work as a whole, and, in this particular instance, upon which this study of the virtues depends, with the hope that the reader will be able to engage those parts of the *Summa* beyond the scope of this book in a profitable way. Having dealt, then, with these seven virtues in a general fashion in the *prima secundae*, I would like to highlight one of them, namely temperance, so that the reader might have an example for his own reading of the other six virtues.

The Treatise on Temperance (Questions 141–170)[356]

The virtue of temperance is not well understood today. Many consider it to be little more than the moderating of the pleasures involved in eating, drinking, and sexual relations. Some consider this virtue to be akin to a medicine that one takes when excesses in these areas erupt, and thus to be a temporary asceticism to regain one's control over these pleasures. Others consider the importance of temperance to lie in its prophylactic function, as that discipline whereby one prevents problems from arising in these areas in the first place, as the means whereby one does not become a slave, so to speak, to these pleasures. Temperance, so described then, is little more than

---

[355] As Pinckaers states,

> The study of virtues provided in the *secunda secundae* was one of the major models of its kind and certainly the most complete in Christian tradition. Consequently, this monumental analysis has dominated Christian theology. In the Middle Ages it was read and utilized more than any other part of the *Summa*. (Pinckaers (1993; 1995), p. 228).

[356] Some of the material presented here appeared earlier in my article "Thomas Aquinas and the Importance of Fasting to the Christian Life," published in *Pro Ecclesia* 17 (2008): 343–361. It is used here by permission.

a bitter remedy or an austerity that is self-imposed, depriving one of the common bodily pleasures. It is hard to imagine this virtue, so described, as being anything other than a misery, one that promises better, more sober days to come. At best, it would be a frustration that one must bear, given the demands of one's life and the things that must be accomplished, something that marks the mature individual as he attends to the important tasks involved in the pursuit of his happiness.

Thomas's account of temperance is in marked distinction from this crude and rather reductionistic account. It does not deal just with matters of quantity but is described as that cardinal virtue that applies to the whole of man's concupiscible appetition, guiding it to its own perfection, and incorporating it into the whole of his virtuous life as it is directed to his happiness in union with God. Thus, at the very least, the essence of Thomas's approach to temperance will not be found in its restrictive or repressive practices, but rather in the harmony that can be established in one's person through this virtue, wherein one marshals all that one is so that all of this might be brought to bear most effectively upon those things in which one's true happiness and peace are found.

Thomas orders his treatment after the manner described in the prologue to the *secunda secundae*, namely by considering the virtue of temperance and the Gift of the Holy Spirit associated with it (Question 141), the vices opposed to temperance (Question 142), the parts of temperance (generally, in Question 143, and then specifically in Questions 144 through 169, with attention devoted also to those particular vices opposed to these parts), and the precepts that govern temperance (Question 170). The quantity of this material is in marked distinction from that which constitutes Aristotle's treatment of temperance in his *Nicomachean Ethics*, where it is discussed in three short chapters (10 through 12 of Book III, 1117b23–1119b18). In his account, Aristotle focuses upon those pleasures specific to the sense of touch, leaving aside the other pleasures that attend every human activity as they are not directly relevant to the virtue that he has in sight. His attention is limited to the most powerful of these pleasures, those involving sexual contact and the consumption of food and drink, as these require moderation if one is to engage in the tasks specific to one's humanity and required for one's happiness. Thomas, on the other hand, casts his net more widely. He too considers those animal or bodily pleasures associated with touch. However, given his articulation of the end to which the human person is oriented in all that he does, there is both a widening of the consideration of those virtues that pertain to temperance, as well as a deepening of the descriptions of those matters commonly associated with temperance and with which Aristotle particularly deals under the same heading.

Thomas begins, in Question 141, with the description of temperance as a virtue, namely as it is that which moderates the influence that the animal pleasures to which man is naturally inclined exert upon his voluntary activities. The concern is that these pleasures be experienced not only in a moral fashion, that is, in accordance with reason, but that they not interfere with all that is required on the part of reason and will in a fully voluntary act. The seductions of the pleasures connected with the sense of touch are well known, particularly as they powerfully draw reason away from those things that look not only to the greater good of man (which sensitive appetition by its nature cannot regard), but particularly to the Divine good to which man is called as he seeks his happiness. Augustine is quoted as stating well the fact that temperance preserves "one's integrity and freedom from corruption for God's sake," and that it seeks that "tranquillity of soul" that can only result from the right ordering of one's desires in light of their specific contribution to the attainment of man's true end. So great is this integrity, freedom and tranquillity in the life of the temperate person, that Thomas describes such a person as properly beautiful, as he who in his temperance displays all that is fitting and proportioned to his humanity in thought, word, and deed, as one who is wholly lacking in those vices that destroy the harmony of his person and disorder his affectivity, which effectively disrupts the entirety of his virtuous activity, and not just that connected to his temperance.[357]

As noted earlier, temperance addresses properly the concupiscible aspect of man's sensitive appetite. In this, it is that

---

[357] ST. II-II. 141. 1 and 2, especially the objections and responses to both articles.

virtue that perfects the passions involved in the pursuit of sensible particular goods, and the avoidance of their opposed evils, namely of love, desire, and joy on the one hand, and of hatred, aversion, and sorrow on the other; its moderating effects extend specifically to these, but also to the other passions of his irascibility that arise from the concupiscible and eventually terminate therein.[358] Nonetheless, as man's concupiscible appetition is rooted in his love for that which he considers to be good, which then manifests in all the other passions but particularly in his desire for that which he loves and the pleasure that he takes therein, temperance is then said to address specifically man's desire for and pleasure in sensible goods, especially those associated with the sense of touch, those in which he takes greatest delight and which consequently can exert the most deleterious effects upon his volitional activity. The idea, then, is not simply to exert control over the most powerful pleasures experienced by man, namely the pleasure he takes in food, drink, and sex. Instead, there is an attention to the recognition of the nature of these pleasures as they are concomitant and essential to those activities that are directed to the preservation of one's individual nature and the nature of the species itself, a recognition that, in light of man's true end and good, can allow then for the right integration of these activities into the life of man as he seeks to realize his happiness. If man can successfully integrate these activities and their concomitant pleasures into the whole of his moral life, then all the more will he be able to attend to the moderation that he needs to bring to the lesser pleasures that accompany all other activities in which he engages, activities that do not directly concern the preservation of nature but which nonetheless can be used for the sake of his true end and good.[359]

It is clear, then, that temperance looks to the establishment of an internal order wherein man will desire and enjoy rightly the particular material goods of this life. He seeks a tranquillity or serenity of soul from which this right desire will flow, something that is effected only insofar as he turns from a particular attention upon those goods to which his nature so powerfully

[358] ST. II-II. 141. 3. ad1.
[359] ST. II-II. 141. 4. corpus, ad1 and ad3, and Articles 5 and 6.

calls, and attends to them, instead, under the perspective and rule of the highest good to which he is called. This latter turn, as Pieper so well describes, is one that is selfless, one that addresses the very individual in such a way that he effects the right order and tranquillity of a nature directed to that which is truly good, as opposed to that one which is directed to his own particular and limited good, one that denotes a selfishness rather than a selflessness. As he states:

> genuine self-preservation is the turning of man toward himself, with the essential stipulation, however, that in this movement he does not become fixed upon himself . . . Temperance is selfless self-preservation. Intemperance is self-destruction through the selfish degradation of the powers which aim at self-preservation.[360]

The discipline of temperance, then, finds its power not in the discipline itself but rather in that to which it is directed; as great as every virtue is, each finds its ultimate description and value in its relation to the acquisition of the end and good of man. Specifically, temperance seeks that inner order and tranquillity whereby man might attend most powerfully and effectively to those actions that involve goods that extend beyond his own self, those that demand attention to the goods of others, specifically those involved in fortitude, justice, and prudence, not to mention the theological and intellectual virtues. As Pieper states, temperance:

> in its strict and ultimate sense is not "realization" of the good. Discipline, moderation, chastity, do not in themselves constitute the perfection of man. By preserving and defending order in man himself, *temperantia* creates the indispensable prerequisite for both the realization of actual good and the actual movement of man toward his goal. Without it, the stream of the innermost human will-to-be would overflow destructively beyond all bounds, it would lose its direction and never reach the sea of perfection. Yet *temperantia* is not itself the stream. But it is the shore, the banks, from whose

[360] Pieper (1954; 1966), p. 148.

solidity the stream receives the gift of straight unhindered course, of force, descent, and velocity.[361]

In light of this description, it becomes a matter of some urgency to understand the varied parts of temperance as well as the vices that are destructive of it. As is common to all virtues, the virtue of temperance constitutes a mean between the two extremes of excess and deficiency, thus giving rise to the two vices of *intemperance* and *insensibility*, respectively. The latter is rarely encountered given the nature and power of the pleasures with which temperance deals, those associated with the preservation of the individual and his species. And so, those who act in such a way that they develop a habitual disposition that endangers a right engagement in proper nutrition and propagation of the species act against nature and thus act viciously. Again, the point of temperance is not to destroy the pleasures associated with touch, but rather to integrate them properly into the life of reason oriented to the attainment of one's happiness. It is within this context that a proper regulation of these pleasures can be achieved, and even, in some cases, strictly limited, as in fasting, or even put aside, as in the practice of virginity. These, however, are not to be equated with insensibility, but constitute, rather, abstentions that are praiseworthy only insofar as they are for the sake of a higher end. Since these abstentions are in accord with right reason (and do not constitute some deeper malaise wherein one does not find anything pleasurable or does not prefer one thing to another), they are considered to be exhibitions of temperance.[362] The extreme of excess is far more common and traditionally is looked upon badly as it, first, destroys the beauty associated with temperance (thus intemperance is described as disgraceful), second, devastates its selfless character (the intemperate become imprisoned by the strength of their own lusts, so restricting their access to the true and the good that they become stubborn and selfish, seeing only what the force of their concupiscence allows them to behold), and third, requires brute force to be applied to one so constrained if he is to be released from the grip of his intemperance. The tradition thus considers

[361] Ibid., p. 175.
[362] ST. II-II. 142. 1.

intemperance to be a sin unworthy of the maturity of a man and is akin rather to the condition of a child who exhibits little control in his desires, is centered primarily upon his own person, and requires strict discipline in both mind and morals for his development.[363] It is judged accordingly as the most disgraceful of sins as it involves man inordinately with those pleasures that are most repugnant to his excellence insofar as they cloud the clarity of his mind to behold what is real and true, corrupt the purity of his intention for the good, and devastate the beauty that arises in the pursuit of such things.[364]

Thomas determines the parts of temperance in Question 143, and thereby sets forth the remainder of this treatise's considerations. He divides them into three kinds, namely those that are integral, subjective, and potential. The first of these describes those parts of temperance that are "the conditions the concurrence of which are necessary" for the realization of the virtue in question.[365] In comparison to a house, the integral parts designate such things as the walls, roof, and foundation.[366] Thomas identifies two integral parts to temperance, namely *shamefacedness* (Question 144) and *honesty* (Question 145). Secondly, the subjective parts of temperance designate the varied species collected within it. These species are four, two of which regard the pleasures of touch involved in nourishment (the virtue of *abstinence* for food—Question 146, with *fasting* being the act specific to the regulation of the consumption of food, and *gluttony* being the opposed vice, Questions 147 and 148 respectively—and *sobriety* for drink—Question 149, with *drunkenness*, the opposed vice, discussed in Question 150), while the other two regard those pleasures associated with procreation (*chastity* with regard to the act itself—Question 151—and its perfection in *virginity*, discussed in Question 152; the vice opposed to chastity, *lust*, is discussed in Questions 153 through 154). Lastly, the potential parts of temperance are those that are secondary to it, that is, as they observe that mode which is proper to temperance (the moderating of the pleasures of touch) but in other areas. These

[363] ST. II-II. 142. 2.
[364] ST. II-II. 142. 4.
[365] ST. II-II. 143. 1.
[366] ST. II-II. 48. 1.

potential parts regard matters, then, that are not as difficult to moderate since they deal with the restraint of one's appetite concerning inclinations other than to those of food, drink, and sex. These virtues are annexed to temperance by way of a likeness to what is principal in temperance. They are directed to "secondary acts or matters not having, as it were, the whole power of the principal virtue."[367] Thomas indicates a great number of these which are divided into three categories, namely those that regard movements of the soul toward things that require a particular moderation, those that are applied to the decorous manifestation of the movements of the body, and lastly those that pertain to things external to one's person. The first of these covers the general moderation that must be exerted upon the will as it is affected by the play of the passions (through the virtue of *continence*— Question 155, and its opposed vice of *incontinence*, discussed in Question 156), and upon two specific passions, namely anger as it seeks revenge (something moderated through the virtue of *clemency* and *meekness*—Question 157, with the vices of *anger* and *cruelty* opposed to these two in Questions 158 and 159) and hope as it issues into daring (something moderated through the virtue of *humility*, that virtue which he considers under modesty, in Question 161, with a good bit of attention dedicated to the vice opposed to it, namely *pride* in Question 162, which then leads to a consideration of the first parent's sin in Question 163, the punishment allotted in 164, and their respective temptations in 165). The movements of the body are perfected by the virtue of *modesty* (Question 160) which is divided into many parts, but which in his order of treatment are reduced to four, namely humility, *studiousness* (in Question 166, with its opposed vice of *curiosity* in Question 167), *modesty in the outward movements of the body* (Question 168) and *modesty in outward apparel* (Question 169). Lastly, the moderation that is exerted upon things external to one's person include the virtues of *lowliness, contentment, moderation,* and *simplicity,* virtues that Thomas includes under his treatment of modesty in its four forms.[368]

The detail that Thomas presents here is extensive and serves to construct an effective vision of what was left necessarily gen-

---

[367] ST. II-II. 48. 1.
[368] See his explanation for this at ST. II-II. 160. 2.

eral in the *prima secundae*, namely of the temperate person as he works toward his true end and good, aided by the infused virtues and particularly the Gift of the Holy Spirit specific to temperance, namely that of the fear of the Lord, "whereby man is withheld from the pleasures of the flesh."[369] The broadening and deepening of the description of temperance, certainly beyond that which is articulated by Aristotle, is attributable directly to the very nature of the goal to which man is oriented. For we have seen that the value of virtue does not consist primarily in itself, but rather as it is integral to the achievement of man's end. As man's understanding of his true end and good develops, so too does his understanding of the nature of the activity in which he must engage if he is to realize this end, and the extent to which it must be perfected by virtue. In the case of temperance, then, the Christian vision of it still involves the very things with which Aristotle was concerned, namely with the moderating of the pleasures of touch in relation to food, drink, and sex. But it now includes anything else that touches upon the moderating of one's activity toward the object of his happiness, namely God Himself. If this reorientation of the Christian's focus is understood, one could then account not only for the complexity of temperance, but also for what many consider to be some of its seemingly extreme and even "unnatural" ascetical practices. When so approached, these practices not only reveal their responsibility, but also constitute a powerful statement of being Christian in this world, something that is expected from all who love God with the entirety of their person. All of these points are nicely suggested in the Gift of fear that aids man's progress in the virtue of temperance. We have seen that all Gifts of the Holy Spirit have as their principal object God Himself, and that they constitute the supernatural means whereby man can aspire to those acts that exceed the natural capacity of his humanity, but which are still required of him if he is to aspire to his true end and good. The Gift of fear is such that it represents not a servile fear of God, but rather fear's mature form, that is to say, a reverence or respect born out of one's love for God that directly intends that no offense be offered to Him in much the same way that one would fear to

[369] ST. II-II. 141. 1. ad3.

offend a much loved and respected parent. This fear, then, is to be distinguished from one that considers the punishment that might be received rather than the offense that might be given. In this mature stance, the Christian shuns whatever might keep him from God, particularly with respect to those matters above with which temperance is concerned, things that can wreck such great destruction in all that is essential to man's activity toward his Creator. To exhibit these points more effectively and to offer a guide to the reading of the other parts of temperance, allow me to examine two things, first, the integral parts of temperance, and then one of its subjective parts, namely, the virtue of abstinence, and this specifically in relation to the practice of fasting, and the vice opposed to it in gluttony.

Shamefacedness and honesty: the integral parts of temperance (Questions 144 and 145)

The first of those conditions the concurrence of which are necessary for the perfect realization of temperance, *shamefacedness*,[370] denotes the natural fear that one has for anything that is base and thus disgraceful. Such a thing is especially pertinent to temperance as it moderates those passions which, if left to their own devices, would lead the human person into the most base and disgraceful kinds of activities. Temperance, then, as it derives from a rightly ordered love, carries with it this healthy and sound fear of all that is opposed to the temperate life. Together with that fear which constitutes the Gift of the Holy Spirit specific to the virtue of temperance, shamefacedness powerfully denotes the affective experience of the temperate person who, in the face of the base and disgraceful, is revulsed by it in the entirety of his person,[371] specifically as he considers the reproach that would be visited upon him if he were to engage in such actions and the ignominy that would result, both of which are most keenly felt by him in the face of his own sin as this most powerfully testifies to the defects of his character in his desire to honor God as He deserves insofar as this is within his capacity.[372] *Honesty* is a literal translation of *honestas* which intends to signify that

---

[370] which translates the Latin *verecundia*.
[371] ST. II-II. 144. 1.
[372] ST. II-II. 144. 2–4.

decorousness, politeness, and decency that is associated with the morally good person, but especially with the temperate person who exhibits a beauty particular to temperance. That temperance is associated with beauty arises from the view that beauty results from "the concurrence of clarity and due proportion" of the parts of some whole to which one's attention is turned.[373] Thus, with respect to one's body or visage, such a view would consider beauty to be predicable of these insofar as they exhibit an excellent proportion among the many parts of which they are composed, and a certain glow, radiance, bloom, splendor, or freshness that is exuded by the totality itself. *Honesty* is defined in this light, namely as a "spiritual beauty (that) consists in a man's conduct or actions being well proportioned in respect of the spiritual clarity of reason."[374] Nothing could be more opposed to the base and the disgraceful than that which is honest in this sense. For this reason, then, the honest is an integral part of temperance as the excellence of one's nature is displayed in all of its freshness for all to see as this is revealed in one's perfected activity toward one's true end, good, and happiness. Such a one is desired in a properly and definitively human way by reason of one's excellence, an excellence that radiates the perfection of one's nature as one strives for one's happiness in a fully rectified way, something that deserves not only the honor that is often accorded to such a person, but also the praise for and love of wisdom itself.[375]

Abstinence (Question 146)

Turning to the first of the subjective parts of temperance, Thomas defines abstinence as that virtue which governs one's enjoyment of the basic pleasures connected with food. The objection, however, is raised that many would consider this governance or regulation as something proper not to the moral life, but instead to the medical or health sciences. For implicit in the very notion of regulation is that one seeks the right quantity and quality of food, that is to say, a healthy diet, something

[373] ST. II-II. 145 .2.
[374] Ibid.
[375] ST. II-II. 145. 2–4, and especially 2. ad2 for the latter point concerning the praise of wisdom.

best determined by the health sciences as they reflect upon the bodily condition and needs of the individual in question. This, on the face of it, would seem to disqualify abstinence from being a moral virtue.[376] In response to this common objection, Thomas agrees that it does in fact belong to the medical arts that they determine what constitutes a healthy diet. Granted, a simple withdrawal or denial of food would seem to define the practice of fasting and thus constitute a practice incommensurate with the goals proper to the health professions. This, however, does not essentially define the practice of fasting as Thomas understands it. The theologian is not concerned with some "micromanaging," if you will, of what is indeed proper to the medical arts. Rather, he is concerned with the moral component that is essential to the practice of fasting, something that arises as it is undertaken for the sake of attaining a definite purpose over and above that which is proper to the medical sciences but which cannot be so extreme as not to have "due regard for those among whom one lives, for one's own person, and for the requirements of health."[377] The theologian, then, is concerned with the pleasures associated with the table as they can powerfully draw the human person away from the good determined and commanded by reason, a difficulty compounded by the fact that these pleasures are so intimately connected with man's most basic desire, namely to preserve his life for which food is an absolute necessity.[378]

Fasting (Question 147)

Fasting, then, is designated as that activity which the virtue of abstinence manifests as it determines the mean in the consumption of food. This activity has a threefold purpose. The first is that it acts as a powerful means whereby the varied movements of man's concupiscence might be regulated, restraining them from seeking their own particular goods at the expense of the true goods of one's humanity. As noted previously, temperance,

---

[376] See the initial objections to ST. 146. 1 and 2, and 147. 1.

[377] ST. II-II. 146. 1. c. and ad2. Thomas not only quotes Augustine here, but also Peter who encourages all Christians to "join . . . abstinence with knowledge" (2 Peter 1.5–6).

[378] ST. II-II. 146. 2.

and thus fasting by extension, addresses the concupiscible passions of man's sensitive appetition, but especially the pleasures associated with the sense of touch. In this connection, it is important to note that although the pleasures of the bed and of drink are intense and require the regulation of temperance most especially, nevertheless, these pleasures and the things with which they are concerned do not speak to the body's preservation in the same way that food does. In this regard, there is a particular urgency with respect to the proper regulation of one's food, specifically as it strengthens what Thomas, following St. Paul, calls the body's opposition to the spirit and thus impedes its efforts to bring the body and one's sensitive passions under the rule of right reason, something that is far more subtle than the obvious effects of excessive drink and inappropriate sexual activity but every bit as deleterious to the moral and spiritual life of man. This will be made very clear when we examine the vice of gluttony, and in particular those vices that this vice engenders. Thomas stresses especially that the practice of fasting is undertaken to protect a person's chastity, since excessive indulgence in the pleasures of the table has the effect of turning the human person to desire strongly and inordinately the other pleasures of the flesh. The second purpose in fasting is found in the sobering effect it has upon one's person, making one fit to contemplate the higher or heavenly things better, or, at the very least, to pursue one's intellectual studies more freely. Lastly, fasting is an effective way to make reparation for one's sins. Clearly, then, this practice is not something prescribed by the physician who cares for the body. Instead, it is properly prescribed by the physicians of the soul, if you will, by those who are responsible directly for the spiritual care and perfection of one's person. And just as the doctor or the dietician set down a strict regime to be followed so that one's health may be attained and preserved, so too do ecclesial authorities have the responsibility to make determinations concerning the character of this practice, obliging Christians to take it up so that the very integrity of their person, their purity of sight, and the establishment of a right comportment with God may be attained and preserved.[379]

[379] ST. II-II. 147. 1–3.

There is, then, an obligation to fast on the part of the Christian, something that must be prudently required of him by the ecclesial authority under which he has placed himself. This prudence requires not only an eye to the needs of the body, but also the determination of the fast's time, place, and manner not be penal in character. Given the great good to which this ascetical practice is oriented, it must be presented and understood as something fitting and suitable. The ecclesial authorities, then, have a responsibility to educate their people as to the purposes and benefits of fasting so that the people might thus be encouraged and strengthened in its practice. For it is only in light of the spirit and purpose of the fast that they will be willing to forego goods and pleasures of a licit nature. Moreover, the precept to fast should be understood as having the status of a general obligation so that, given a reasonable excuse or set of circumstances, the Christian may be exempt from the keeping of the fast without incurring sin; again, the fast must be commanded for the sake of the Christian's spiritual well-being and integrity, and not primarily as something onerous and penal.[380] Therefore, common impediments to fasting must be discerned and considered in determining whether a particular person should be bound to the fast or not. These include the age of the participants (both the young and the aged are exempt, the former because of their developmental needs which extend into their 20s, the latter for the maintenance of their health in their twilight years[381]); the health of the individual (the sick are exempt, as are those who are under a doctor's order not to fast); one's profession (they are exempt who perform hard work, or work that must be done during the fast whose success would be impeded by the demands of fasting); those who find themselves on pilgrimage (they are exempt whose journey requires that it be done during the fast, or whose journey is so arduous that fasting would endanger its success[382]). Economic conditions also exempt one from the fast, but only in those cases where one does not know where and when one's next meal will come. Thus, beggars are exempt, but not the poor, that

---

[380] ST. II-II. 147. 3.

[381] The only exception to this rule is in times of great need or peril when all, even animals, are called to fast.

[382] See *IV Sent.*, d. 15, q. 3, a. 2 for these and other reasons.

is, those who have a reasonable assurance of regular meals and a ready supply of food enough to preserve them in their existence, and who can thus profit from the practice of fasting.[383]

The times for fasting are set with an eye to those seasons within a church's liturgical year where its members are called to raise their sight to heavenly things and to seek forgiveness for their sins. Thus, before the celebration of major liturgical feasts, Christians are called to a devout preparation which importantly includes fasting; again, the mind is set most sharply to consider these most high things, the appetite is drawn away from other goods and set upon the highest good, and the comportment of the person before God is addressed properly through fasting. Thomas notes that the season of Lent is an especially important time to fast. He also includes fasting in the preparations one makes before receiving the sacraments, particularly baptism, the Eucharist, and ordination, where, with respect to the latter, both the priest-to-be and the people whom he will serve are called to fast so that they will be ready to receive and enjoy most fully and appropriately this great gift.[384]

Lastly, the severity of the fast must balance both the spiritual and the bodily goods of the individuals who take it up. The ecclesial authorities then must urge their charges to seek control over their desires, to turn their eyes to God, to seek forgiveness for their sins, but not at the expense of endangering their bodily health. The principle, then, is to give to nature what it requires and to withdraw from it what is enjoyed over and above this so that the fruits promised by the practice of fasting might be attained. According to Thomas, this amounts to one meal per day during a fast. However, Christians must not abstain from water during their fast since it sustains life and is required for digestion and bodily refreshment. Medicines and digestives are allowed when ordered by a doctor. Care, however, must be taken in the consumption that is allowed during a fast. For one might eat the allowed meal in an intemperate fashion, or drink water to the point where one's hunger is alleviated, or take medicines and digestives fraudulently, that is, as if they were food. Such actions not only rob the Christian of the benefits of the fast,

---

[383] ST. II-II. 147. 4 and responses.
[384] ST. II-II. 147. 5–6.

but also lead him to sin anew, as these actions show contempt for the ecclesial authorities under whom he has placed himself voluntarily, and to whom he looks for guidance and comfort in the spiritual life.[385] Even the one meal allowed during the fast is put off from the time that the people normally eat the main meal of the day. So, instead of noon, Thomas suggests that three in the afternoon would be an appropriate time to eat during a fast. This delay helps to break one from one's custom, to make one's fast more prominent in one's daily routine, and to keep in mind the reasons for the fast in the first place, as well as being disposed to the fruits that derive from it. One does not harm one's nature by this small delay, and there is also the benefit of eating at that time when Christ's Passion had concluded, which also helps the one fasting to link his own suffering to that endured by Christ. Again, only those capable of delaying their main meal are bound by the precept.[386] As for the meal itself, the focus is upon those foods that will best serve one's body, but at the same time allow one to benefit most fully from the fast. And so, excessively tasty and luxurious foods are discouraged. Wine, fish, and vegetables are permitted, but meat is not. Eggs and cheese, being derived from animals whose meat is not permitted, are discouraged, particularly during the most important fasts. The principle guiding these choices is one that is based partly upon the medical knowledge of the day (certain foods encourage a predominance of certain humors which incline the human person to actions and thoughts not in keeping with the purpose of the fast), and presumably on their own experiences (that certain foods require more of the body's energy for their assimilation than others, that some foods more directly impede the success of the fast than others, with meat being that which most strongly draws one's energies away from contemplation, and centers it upon the pleasures of the flesh).[387]

Gluttony (Question 148)
If one fails to heed the directives established by one's ecclesial community concerning fasting and goes on to establish

[385] ST. II-II. 147. 6.
[386] ST. II-II. 147. 7.
[387] ST. II-II. 147. 8

practices contrary to them, one begins to develop the vice of gluttony. This vice is not to be confused with any physiological condition leading to practices that are materially akin to gluttony. For Thomas defines it as an inordinate desire that one has developed by decidedly abandoning what reason and the medical arts have determined to be a mean in consumption, and allowing one's appetite to run riot, consuming food with no care for the requirements of one's spiritual and bodily health. In this particular disordering of one's love and consequent desire, there is established the proclivity to repeat this defective state and activity in other areas, turning one effectively from the higher goods of one's humanity, contemplation, sorrow for one's sins, and the very control that needs to be exerted over the entirety of one's person if one is to seek effectively for one's happiness. In short, in the abdication of reason's right rule with respect to one's nourishment, one lives and chooses as if one's belly were one's god. Such a person is ready to do whatever it takes to enjoy these pleasures, even despise God and disobey His commandments, specifically the third where the human person is directed to take his rest on the Sabbath, that is, to rest in God for a time, and not in the things and pleasures of this world.[388]

Gluttony takes on many forms. It can be seen in relation to the *food* that one eats or to the *eating* of this food. With respect to the former, a person can manifest a disordered desire for food in three ways, namely in seeking costly or luxurious foods, second, that they be prepared with excessive effort, and finally to consume food in excessive amounts (thus eating *sumptuously*, *fastidiously*, and *hastily*, respectively). As for the eating itself, gluttony can be manifested in two ways, namely in the mode of one's eating (in eating too quickly, at the wrong times, when one in not hungry, being impatient to eat while awaiting its preparation—thus eating *ravenously*) and in the manner of one's eating (that is, without observing due propriety and restraint in one's consumption—thus eating *excessively*).[389] The dissipation that constitutes gluttony is detailed in what Thomas calls its "offspring"[390] of which there are five. First,

---

[388] ST. II-II. 148. 1–2.
[389] ST. II-II. 148. 4.
[390] This translates *filiae,* which is often rendered as "daughters."

gluttony gives rise to a *dullness of sense surrounding the operations of the intelligence.* For if the bodily aspects upon which one's thinking relies are impaired by all that accompanies disordered consumption, one's ability to think will be radically compromised (not to mention one's capacity to contemplate the highest things necessary for one's reclamation and happiness). Secondly, gluttony spawns what Thomas calls an *unseemly joy.* In the impairment of the higher rational faculties, the sensitive appetites of the human person, all of which are directed to their consummation in either joy or sorrow, are allowed to indulge in either. He makes appeal to Aristotle who states in his *Nicomachean Ethics* that excessive wine has the effect of making one confident and joyful without due cause. One could also make appeal to the latter books of Plato's *Republic* wherein we see the decline of the human person's character in the tyrant as he throws off the right ordering of his nature, allowing his appetites to exercise a rule which reason ought to exert. In any event, the principle noted previously is at work here, namely that when the virtue of temperance is missing, people's affective nature, no longer integrated into the whole of their humanity, begins to manifest itself in deformed ways. Third, gluttony engenders a *loquaciousness* not befitting the temperate person. Again, with reason impaired by one's gluttony, one risks losing whatever measure one had in one's speech, erring often on the side of excess. Finally, there is *scurrility*, a lack of due measure in one's actions. In speech, this scurrility becomes inappropriate joking. On the part of the body, Thomas notes that gluttony often produces a general *uncleanness*, which manifests itself in inordinate bodily secretions, a probable reference to the glutton's typical lack of concern for his appearance and hygiene, or, more literally, to the fact that the glutton is more physiologically disposed to excessive sweating and unpleasant bodily odors because of his excessive weight and poor health.[391]

Conclusion

From this consideration of abstinence, fasting, and gluttony, one can see the degree to which their descriptions are broadened and deepened by the end to which the Christian is

[391] ST. II-II. 148. 6.

oriented. One also senses the pressing need for the aid that one receives from God (in the infused virtues and the gifts of the Holy Spirit) to engage in these newly described virtues, an aid that gives one hope that one might go beyond the natural fast that is within one's power and aspire to a discipline and virtue that lie beyond. For without this supernatural end and the gifts whereby it is attained, abstinence and fasting could consider nothing more than the health of the body and this, perhaps, so that the higher activities potential to man in the world might be undertaken more profitably, particularly his intellectual endeavors both speculative and practical. Within the context established not only by the *Treatise on Happiness* but also by the ordering principles at the heart of the *Summa* itself, abstinence, fasting, and gluttony (as well as the other acts that define temperance and its opposed vices) denote not only what is appropriate to their natural manifestations, but these as they now are manifested in the rectified activity that characterizes the Christian as he realizes his happiness in this world, anticipating its completion in the next. An indication of this is found in a striking phrase employed by Thomas to describe fasting's subjective effect upon the Christian who practices it, namely, that such a one exhibits a *hilaritas mentis*,[392] a cheerfulness of both heart and mind. He does not refer to that lightheartedness which might accrue from the health benefits that accompany the practice of fasting. Rather, he points to the fact that fasting, as it is one of the subjective parts of temperance, is an important way by which the unity, integrity, and peace of one's entire person, both body and soul, are achieved and maintained, something that radically and effectively centers one's mind and desire in a most powerful way, allowing for the other aspects of the Christian life to be pursued with greater vigor.

The unity, integrity, and peace that are intrinsic to temperance are particularly important in light of the fallen nature of man and the difficulties of his rectification that follow upon the disorder that predominates in his person. One can understand, then, why Thomas considers the practice of fasting to be something that the ecclesial authorities should require of its people, as it is a powerful way whereby their charges can be

---

[392] See ST. II-II. 146. 1. ad4, noted by Pieper (1954; 1966), p. 181.

encouraged to undertake a practice so seemingly contrary to both nature and habit, and yet so necessary to the fulfillment of their desire for their true end and good. One can also understand why Thomas insists that this command have the character of a general obligation, and that it always have an eye to prudential application, specifically in light of the needs of the body and the duties of life. Over and above this, however, there is the understanding on the part of an ecclesial community that the practice of fasting is to be commanded as it offers Christians a unique opportunity to reflect upon things that they normally do not entertain, that is, without the discomfort and suffering that naturally accompany the voluntary withdrawal from food. To put this in different terms, just as an appropriate amount of fear has a clarifying effect upon both mind and will, but too much renders them ineffectual,[393] so too do the sufferings and discomforts experienced in the practice of fasting have the effect of turning one's mind and heart to those things that one would not normally consider. The hope is that in the suffering of fasting, one might find the opportunity to reflect upon one's life and to rectify one's mind and will so that one might comport oneself better before God and live the Christian life more fully. In this respect, fasting, so undertaken, can become an expression of a rational being's free and deliberate decision to place himself in a situation wherein he might consider and embrace those things that are painful and difficult, but, nonetheless, vital to his very health as a Christian. This point might be better understood in comparison with the lesser but very common experience of the passions impelling people to great and important activity. In the experience of great pressure exerted by others or a particular situation, many find that they respond well and, in fact, do their best work under such circumstances. The demands made upon them, the fear they experience, and other such things, sharpen their minds, clarify what needs to be done, and order their actions so that they might accomplish the goal effectively. Sorrow, regret, and shame with respect to one's actions have a similar effect.[394] While these things are good, how much more fully does a person act from his humanity when he does not wait

---

[393] For this point, see ST. I-II. 45. 2.
[394] See ST. I-II. 37. 1 and 39. 1.

for life to impact upon him in these ways so that he might do his best, but rather that he, through his own rational deliberation and prayerful choice, brings these situations about so that he might humanly (rather than animally and reactively) behold what is hard to behold, embrace what is hard to embrace, and act accordingly? Fasting, then, becomes one opportunity wherein one can act in the fullness of one's humanity, bringing all that one is, consciously and deliberately, into the contemplation of and submission to the things of God.

The practice of fasting, then, undertaken apart from this context, appears as little more than the voluntary imposition of pain and suffering for the sake of one's health, one's appearance, or at most one's studies. When viewed, however, within a Christian context, fasting becomes an implicit recognition and a personal declaration to oneself and to the world of the fact that one has been made to the image and likeness of God, and that one has a choice of comporting oneself either to the world below or to the one above, of resting either in the pleasures of this world or in those found in God Himself. The Christian understanding of abstinence, fasting, and gluttony (and by extension every other part that constitutes the description of temperance and its opposed vices) becomes meaningful, then, in light of the human person's very nature and destiny as articulated and understood within the Christian world view. Fasting, together with the other subjective parts of temperance, places one at the defining moment of one's humanity and exhibits to the world the decision that one has made concerning which way one stands in the determination of what constitutes one's true end, good, and happiness, something that is repeated in varying ways and to varying degrees in every other virtue described in the *secunda secundae*. However, in light of the infused virtues and the gifts of the Holy Spirit that make this practice and all others definitive of temperance possible, the Christian practice of temperance especially becomes a witness to the grace and love of God acting in the life of man, allowing him to comport himself to the source of his being and completion, a comportment that results in a profound gratitude, appreciation, and joy on the part of the Christian for God's many and great gifts, and an opportunity to express, in the practices of abstinence and fasting, the lengths to which he will go to seek out the means whereby he might be healed as he realizes his salvation in his present condition, hoping always for the joy and peace to come in the heavenly condition, which he anticipates by these and the other practices of temperance in the here and now. Implicit in these considerations is Thomas's understanding of what constitutes perfect virtue and why virtue apart from the Christian context can be described only as imperfect.

If a Christian does not fast, he encourages by his neglect, the varied vices associated with gluttony to take hold of his person. His intemperance dulls his heart and mind to the fullness of his nature and destiny, preventing the recognition of the graces that are offered continually to him. This robs him of the lightness of character that is his in faith, hope, and love, and inflicts unnecessary hardships upon him whose sight is riveted upon the changing realities of this world, blinding him to the nobility of his nature and the heights of his destiny. Through fasting, the Christian steels his mind and heart to what must be done and declares in this very discipline a hope in that which lies beyond the everyday natural desires of this world. The danger, of course, is to lose sight of the purposes of fasting and the reasonableness attached to the details of its practice. In addition, then, to the guidance that the Christian receives from both the medical and ecclesial communities, and the graces afforded by the Holy Spirit, Thomas completes his understanding of fasting in light of the teachings and example offered by Christ during his earthly ministry, something found in the *tertia pars*.[395]

Briefly stated, Thomas notes that in teaching people how to pray, Christ describes the demeanor that one must take in order to fast well, and thus to avoid its hypocritical display, something that empties it of all its value. In this posture, one must always have one's sight upon fasting's spiritual purpose, in the absence of which one's practice would easily fall prey to "self-admiration, vanity, self-importance, (and) impatient arrogance."[396] Thomas observes that Christ himself took up the practice of fasting not as if he required it, but rather to provide a model for all Christians to imitate. Christ's fast, he notes, was

---

[395] For this material concerning Christ and fasting, see ST. III. 40. 2, and 41. 3.

[396] Pieper (1954; 1966), p. 185.

not all encompassing, but instead was something he took up to show Christians how to pray and engage rightly in contemplation so that they might be prepared to undertake the important duties of their lives. And so, before he teaches, Christ retires to the desert where he fasts and prays. In this, he offers a way by which Christian preachers and teachers, for example, can conform their minds effectively to the highest of things and order their persons so that they might best serve their flock and their students. Again, before he takes up his public ministry, Christ fasts in the desert for forty days. This austerity, which does not go beyond what was exhibited by Moses and Elijah, serves to instruct all those who undertake any kind of ministry that they need to engage in great prayer and fasting as a means whereby they might put their house in order and speak rightly and effectively from the fullness of God's revelation. In bringing order to their persons and a control over their concupiscence, such people are made strong so that when temptation does arise, they will be prepared to resist and even expel it from their lives and the lives of others. In Pieper's view, then, Christ calls these and all Christians to undertake the rigor of the fast, so that by it they might make progress in achieving and maintaining the "selfless self-preservation" that is at the heart of temperance. This, together with the advancement in temperance's other subjective parts, is integral in becoming truly beautiful, where "the glow of the true and the good" shine forth from the well-ordered person that one becomes in temperance.[397]

The points that have been made here concerning Thomas's understanding of temperance, its integral parts of shamefacedness and honesty, the subjective part of abstinence, the practice of fasting, and the vice of gluttony, can be applied in like manner to the remaining parts of temperance, which, when taken together, offer a detailed picture of the Christian understanding and manifestation of temperance in this world as directed toward and anticipating the next.[398] The reading offered here can also serve as the general manner in which one might then

---

[397] Pieper (1954; 1966), p. 203.

[398] For an excellent presentation of the Christian life as described in the entirety of the *secunda secundae,* consider the collection of essays by Pieper in (1986; 1997) and (1954; 1966) on each of the 7 virtues.

approach the other cardinal virtues, as well as the theological virtues. Naturally, a great deal of extremely interesting material has been set aside by the nature of this reader's guide. Nonetheless, a careful reading of the *prima secundae*, particularly the treatises concerning the habits, virtues, beatitudes, gifts, vices, and grace, will supply one with the principles necessary to a productive reading of the materials found in the *secunda secundae*. One should note especially the treatise on the virtues, the general descriptions that are offered there of each virtue, the explicit relations that Thomas establishes among them, the centrality of the theological virtues and especially that of charity, and lastly the status of prudence as it is the "queen" of the cardinal virtues. Among the many striking things said about charity, one should note ST. II-II. 23. 1 where Thomas describes charity as that fellowship or friendship that exists between God and man, "a reciprocity of love . . . founded on God's self-communication when, by grace, he makes man a participant in his own happiness."[399] Again, we have here not only a testimony to the degree to which Thomas's theology is inspired by the very text of Scripture itself (in this case, John 15.15), but also the degree to which he uses Aristotle's understanding of friendship (as found in Books 8 and 9 of his *Nicomachean Ethics*) in his exposition of this most excellent of the virtues, that virtue which, together with the other theological virtues, provides those means by which one attains God himself and enjoys communion with and rest in Him as one's ultimate end and good.[400] No true and perfect virtue is possible without charity as it is that virtue which most perfectly orders all that a man thinks and does in his efforts to be happy. Charity, then, becomes the very form of virtue itself as it directs most perfectly the acts proper to all the other virtues to the ultimate end itself, thus rectifying their own activities most perfectly in light of that which is highest and best.[401] As for prudence, its importance has been described already; it is that virtue which allows the human person to act and live well in this life insofar as this requires that he take counsel, judge, and command rightly in

[399] Torrell (2005), p. 43.
[400] See ST. II-II. 23. 6.
[401] See ST. II-II. 23. 7 and 8.

every moral action he undertakes, something that constitutes the business of prudence, making it a requirement, then, for all the other cardinal virtues, specifically as it belongs to prudence "to decide in what manner and by what means man shall obtain the mean of reason in his deeds."[402] However, as important as prudence is to the other moral virtues, it is still the case that it and they be informed by charity if they are to be true examples of perfect virtue, that is, virtues ordered and informed by the most perfect love that man can manifest in his life as he acts for the sake of his true happiness.[403]

The Treatises Concerning the Gratuitous Graces (Questions 171–178), the Active and Contemplative Life (179–182), and the States of Life (183–189)

A word or two must be said concerning the last section of the *secunda secundae* wherein Thomas considers a number of things that do not pertain to all Christians but only to a few. The latter are distinguished in three ways, first, through the gratuitous graces that some receive, specifically in the form of prophecy (171–4), rapture (175), the gift of tongues (176), the gift of the word of wisdom and knowledge (177), and of miracles (178); second, through the leading of the contemplative life as distinguished from the active one (179 through 182); and lastly by the various duties and states of life (183) and the state of perfection in general (184), which latter gives rise to the perfections of the episcopal state (185) and those of the religious (186 through 189). The concerns of this section of the *Summa* are decidedly ecclesial with an emphasis placed upon Thomas's mature thought on the nature of religious orders and particularly his own, something for which he fought most energetically throughout his life. Once again we see in these treatises Thomas's dedication to the Scriptures as he draws heavily upon the discussions concerning charisms and ministries found in St. Paul's letters to the Corinthians and Ephesians, respectively.[404] Whether we speak of these gratuitous gifts, or the specific states of life that Thomas considers here, all "were ordered to the good of the

---

[402] See ST. II-II. 47. 7.
[403] See Torrell (2005), pp. 45–46.
[404] Pinckaers (1993; 1995), p. 229.

whole Church, and their diversity should remain at the service of its unity, under the inspiration of charity."[405]

Among the many questions that comprise these treatises, I would like to linger briefly upon two that address the state of perfection, a state to which every Christian is called and yet, given the varied duties of one's life and the gifts that each receives, admits of progress and thus of degrees. Thomas defines a "state" generally as a position wherein one is disposed in some way in accordance with one's nature, and this with a certain permanence. What he has in mind is that which results from an obligation that one has freely taken upon oneself in light of which one is subject either to the rule of another or to his own, the former indicating a state of servitude, the latter, a state of liberty.[406] These both can manifest in a twofold fashion when they concern spiritual affairs. Servitude can be either to sin or to justice, while liberty denotes freedom from the same. True servitude, he states, is realized in that situation where one is bound to sin habitually and is free from any restraint imposed by justice to do whatever evil act one so desires. True liberty, on the other hand, characterizes that one who is free from sin and is in service to that which is just, thereby inclining him to seek the good in all that he does.[407] Perfection is found in the latter, specifically as one attains to the proper end of true liberty, namely union with God himself. Since it is charity that unites the Christian to God, Thomas maintains that the perfection of the Christian life "consists radically in charity."[408] This perfection can be spoken of in three ways, two of which pertain to man. The first is that perfection which is appropriate to God alone wherein he loves himself "as much as he is lovable." The second is that which is enjoyed by the blessed in heaven, those whose entire affectivity is directed to God as much as it possibly can be. The third describes the present life wherein one struggles to remove those obstacles that hinder one's movement in love toward God. For most Christians, this manifests in the life

---

[405] Ibid.
[406] ST. II-II. 183. 1. These states characterize both civil and spiritual communities. See Articles 2 and 3 for their diversification specifically in relation to the Church.
[407] ST. II-II. 183. 4.
[408] ST. II-II. 184. 1.

of virtue, as described in the first section of the *secunda secundae*, where each person, in faith, hope, and love, in prudence, justice, fortitude, and temperance removes from his loves and affections all that is contrary directly to charity, that is to say, to conduct one's life in such a fashion that one avoids all mortal and venial sin. However, there are a select few within the Christian community who not only avoid illicit things and practices, but also those of a licit nature as they might in some way act as hinderances in their desire to tend wholly to God Himself. It is with the latter that we find the maturity of the perfection that is possible to the Christian while he lives in the world, a perfection that manifests not only in the avoidance of sin, but also in a total gifting of himself to God by denying even those things that are moral and good but which might hinder his own personal advance toward God. To those who avoid mortal and venial sin and who engage in a right and proper use of the things of this world, the perfection of charity belongs, albeit in its initial form and up to and including a certain proficiency in it.[409]

The question then becomes what rule most effectively gives rise to this perfection? Does it consist in the observance of the precepts or commandments found in Holy Scripture, or rather in the evangelical counsels themselves?[410] Thomas's response is nuanced. He references Christ's judgment at Matthew 22.37–40, namely that the whole of the law is found in the commandment to love God with the entirety of one's heart, soul, and mind, and to love one's neighbor as one loves oneself: "on these two commandments dependeth the whole law and the prophets." He thus states that the perfection of the Christian life consists primarily and essentially in one's adherence to these commands (and by consequence to the whole of the body of law at whose head these two commandments stand) as these manifest most perfectly the nature of charity. Nonetheless, there is a secondary and instrumental sense in which the evangelical counsels give rise to the state of perfection in the Christian life. These counsels are also directed to charity, but differently so than the

---

[409] ST. II-II. 184. 2.

[410] The reader will recall the discussion of these in the *prima secundae* within the *Treatise on Law* and should refer back to that discussion to complete what will be stated here.

commandments insofar as the latter address the removal of those things that are illicit and thus contributory to both mortal and venial sin and directly contrary to the virtue of charity, while the former address those things that are licit but which may, nonetheless, hinder the act of charity without being contrary to it. For example, marriage is a state which itself is holy and good. However, it brings with it responsibilities that may hinder one in one's growth into the maturity of Christian perfection, for which reason, then, some within the Christian community take up the celibate life, effectively freeing them for the opportunity to donate themselves in a more complete way to the practice of charity and aspire to that maturity of perfection available to them in this life.[411] Does this mean, then, that the state of greatest perfection is reserved for those called to the religious life, to that life wherein not only the commandments are observed, but also the evangelical counsels? Again, Thomas's response is nuanced. He states that true liberty in the spiritual realm manifests in those actions that are both internal and external, that is, in one's immanent and transitive activity. The former is a judgment that belongs to God alone and is something to which all Christians are called, regardless of the offices that they hold in life, and is something to which they must attend with all their efforts and strength if they are to attain to charity and union with God. The latter, however, culminates in the state of life that one decidedly and freely takes up, especially in relation to the variety of states that characterize the Church itself. Speaking to the latter, Thomas reminds the reader of the obligation that is implicit in a state so described, specifically that the obligation implicit in true liberty frees one for service, and that this service be taken up "with a certain solemnity" that marks the seriousness and the nobility of the state upon which one has entered. Consequently, with regard to these states that characterize the life of the Church, "one is said to be in the state of perfection, not through having the act of perfect love" (which properly pertains to one's immanent spiritual perfection), "but through binding oneself in perpetuity and with a certain solemnity to those things that pertain to perfection."[412] Thomas identifies

---

[411] ST. II-II. 184. 3.
[412] ST. II-II. 184. 4.

this with the religious and episcopal offices, to those states within the Church wherein the evangelical counsels in particular become an essential part of such states insofar as they are wholly dedicated to the work of God.[413] Nonetheless, by the fact that one takes upon oneself one of these offices does not by that very fact make one perfect in charity. Many are those who, not having bound themselves to ecclesial offices within the Church and thus to these states of perfection, nonetheless attain to the perfection of mature charity that comes from advancement in keeping not only the commandments but the counsels as well, and these in the midst of the activities that one pursues in everyday life. Nonetheless, the fact remains that the ecclesial offices within the Church are by their very nature oriented to the most effective practice of charity and thus provide the opportunity, on man's part, to manifest most effectively the immanent and mature perfection of charity in one's Christian life.[414]

Conclusion to the Secunda Secundae

In the few details that have been presented here concerning the material found in the *secunda secundae*, one readily understands why this section of the *Summa* was most popular, being separated from the whole and copied far more extensively than the other parts, as the surviving number of copies leads scholars to conclude (as well as the history of the *Summa*'s use after Thomas's death).[415] Not only does the reader find the practical details concerning the virtuous life of man as he strives, by his own agency in union with God's grace, to manifest his happiness, a picture of the specific character of true virtue, of the Christian life itself in this world as it is oriented in faith, hope, and charity to union with God in the next, anticipating whatever it can of this in the present life, but this as it has been well-ordered and presented, drawing together the wealth of the patristic tradition with that of the ancient pagan writers newly introduced into the

---

[413] ST. II-II. 184. 5.

[414] ST. II-II. 184. 5–6 and 4. See also the illuminating comments made by Jordan Aumann in his translation of this part of the *Summa* in the Blackfriars' edition, Volume 47 (1973), pp. xv–xvii, and his chapter on "Christian Perfection" (pp. 121–155) in (1962).

[415] See Boyle (1982), pp. 23ff.

West at that time. While these details offer a solid vision and the practical ways by which it might be manifested in the life of the Christian, it is something that finds its footing, so to speak, in the parts that have preceded it, specifically in the moral theory presented in the *prima secundae*, and in the nature and agency of God himself in the *prima pars*. The *tertia pars*, however, is also presumed by the *secunda pars* insofar as man's agency is found to be insufficient to the acquisition of his true end and happiness, that at every step that man takes in the *reditus* that he effects through his voluntary activity, there are the graces of God aiding him in this regard (as detailed in the *prima secundae*), as well as the providence and governance that He exerts over the whole of the universe (as detailed in the *prima pars*). This aid comes to its completion and perfection in the person of Christ, who, as the primary agent of the *tertia pars,* makes up for what is lacking in man's desire for and activity toward his happiness, effecting the specific means whereby man might be healed of his fallen condition, and thus have a real opportunity to be united to God in the next life. It is to this that Thomas now turns.

TERTIA PARS

This part of the *Summa* was to have been realized in three sections. However, only the first of these three saw completion due to the events of 6 December 1273 that caused Thomas to cease composition of his *Summa*, as was detailed in the first chapter of this reader's guide. Questions 1 through 59 are dedicated to Jesus Christ, the Word Incarnate, whose life, death, and resurrection effects man's salvation, and provides the means whereby he might really attain union with God and thus his happiness. Questions 1 through 26 are devoted to the Incarnation itself, while 27 through 59 are concerned with the particulars of Christ's life, the things that He did or suffered while united to the nature of man culminating in His resurrection, ascension into heaven, taking up His seat at the right hand of the Father, and His judiciary power. The second section is incomplete. It was to have been dedicated to a consideration of the sacraments, those most excellent means of grace that were established by Christ during His earthly ministry, and which constitute the very manner in which the theological virtues can be perfected in man, and that the Gifts, Beatitudes and Fruits come solidly to bear upon the manifestation of the Christian life itself, wherein Christ lives in man, and man in Christ. The first five questions of this treatise (60 through 65) consider matters that pertain to all the sacraments (nature, necessity, grace, character, causes, and number, respectively). The remainder of this treatise was to have examined each sacrament individually. Thomas completed three of these, namely Baptism (66–71), Confirmation (72), and the Eucharist (73–83), leaving his treatise on Penance incomplete at Question 90, having treated only of its nature, its effects, and its division into its general parts.[416] If this second section had been completed, there would have been treatments of Extreme Unction (the anointing of the sick), Orders, and Matrimony.[417] The third section was to have considered "the end of immortal life to which we attain by the resurrection,"[418] which would have been a fitting way to conclude the *Summa* in light of the actual attainment of man's final end, but this as everything that had preceded in the *Summa* would have been drawn up into Christ's salvific act, that wherein man's *reditus* is complete. Although we do have some indication as to how Thomas would have discussed these eschatological considerations, namely in light of parallel passages in his *Commentary on the Sentences of Peter Lombard* (and Questions 79 through 97 of Book IV of his *Summa Contra Gentiles*) which provide enough material for his disciples to address what was left unfinished and compose what has been called the *Supplement* (in 99 questions: 1 through 68 covering the remaining sacraments, and 69 through 99 devoted to the last things), caution must be exercised in its use, particularly as it is material written some 20 years prior to that of the *Summa* (and thus does not reflect the maturation of Thomas's thought on these matters).[419] In the space that remains to us in this reader's guide, let us look briefly at the treatises devoted to Jesus Christ, and to the sacraments, concentrating upon their more salient aspects so that we

[416] Leaving a consideration of its particular parts, "the recipients of this sacrament, the power of the ministers which pertains to the keys, and the solemnization of this sacrament" unaddressed (as Aquinas had intended, as stated in his prologue to penance at ST. III. 84).
[417] See the division offered by Thomas at ST. III. 66.
[418] The prologue to ST. III.
[419] Consider Torrell's assessment (2005), p. 62.

might have a sense as to the direction that Thomas was headed in the completion of the *Summa Theologiae*.

The Treatises on the Incarnation (1–26) and the Deeds and the Sufferings of Jesus Christ (27–59)

The first of these two parts are devoted to the Incarnation itself. Thomas divides his considerations into three. The first examines the "fitness" of the Incarnation (Question 1), the second, the mode of the union of the Word Incarnate (2 through 15), and lastly, the consequences of this union (16 through 26).

The question of the seemingly late placement of his considerations concerning the Word Incarnate, of He who effects man's return to God, has been addressed several times in this and the prior chapters; the centrality of Christ's Incarnation and of the salvific act in Thomas's thought and in his *Summa* are beyond doubt.[420] Thomas's Christology, as Kerr notes, does not begin as many modern theologians are accustomed, that is with historical considerations surrounding the person and deeds of Christ.[421] Rather, he begins with the mystery of the Incarnation itself, something that marks his Christology as one rooted essentially in the revelation of the person of Christ found in the Holy Scriptures, a decision that reaffirms the centrality of the Holy Scriptures in the development of the materials of which the *Summa* treats.

The first question asks whether the Incarnation was fitting or appropriate (*conveniens*). One should understand the thrust of this question. Thomas asks, in light of the fact of the Incarnation, where the Word took to Himself the nature of man in becoming Jesus Christ, to what degree can we understand and articulate the appropriateness of the union of the two natures in the one person of Christ? The notion of appropriateness, then, arises in light of the fact that this union, while a mystery and thus one of the many things that is revealed to man as exceeding his natural grasp, nevertheless is not "utterly incomprehensible, outrageous and unacceptable"[422] to the human mind. As it was with

---

[420] The prologue to the *tertia pars* should disaffect one of any doubt—see Torrell (2005), pp. 48–50. One might also benefit from a brief recounting of this point as presented by Kerr (2002), pp. 162–168.

[421] Kerr (2002), p. 168.

[422] Kerr (2002), p. 168.

Thomas's exposition concerning the Trinity in the *prima pars*, so too is it here that the theologian can, in prayerful contemplation of the Incarnation together with reason rightly informed by the truths it can naturally know and strengthened by the grace of God, approach "the incomprehensible love that moved God to this extreme" and to try to grasp everything that he can about this event no matter how weak his reasons may be.[423]

Article 1 states that the appropriateness of the Incarnation is found in the nature of God Himself, who, as absolute goodness, naturally communicates this very goodness, first in the act of creation and in His providence and governance of what He created (as recounted in the *prima pars*), second in the gifts of grace that he bestowed upon man as he endeavors to realize whatever he can of his *reditus* to God (as detailed in the *secunda pars*), but finally, and in the highest manner that is available to a created thing, in "joining created nature to Himself that one Person is made up of these three—the Word, a soul and flesh."[424] In this, man has not only been united to God in a new manner, he can now behold His goodness, wisdom, justice, and power manifested visibly in the very person of Christ.[425] The question of appropriateness is followed by that of motive, a determination that Thomas makes very carefully as he relies primarily and decisively upon the biblical witness. He begins by asking first whether it was necessary for the Word to become Incarnate so that the human race might be saved. John 3.16 establishes this in the affirmative, namely that "God so loved the world as to give His only-begotten Son, that whosoever believeth in Him may not perish, but may have life everlasting."[426] Thomas then qualifies the sense of necessity used in this passage, namely that the Incarnation was not the only way by which the end of man's salvation could be attained, but rather that this particular way was a better, more fitting or appropriate way by which to achieve it. Thomas shows this through an appeal to the many things that Augustine had to say on this issue, all of which are divided into two groups, those

---

[423] Torrell (2005), p. 53. Moreover, by avoiding the language of necessity here, Thomas respects God's freedom to act in this way.

[424] ST. III. 1. 1, quoting Augustine.

[425] ST. III. 1.1. sed contra quoting John Damascene.

[426] ST. III. 1. 2. sc.

that argue the appropriateness of the Incarnation as it conduces most excellently to both the human person's furtherance in good, and his withdrawal from evil. The Incarnation leads most beautifully to the establishment of and a continuous growth in faith, hope, and charity, the theological virtues so pivotal to the whole of the Christian's life in Christ, allowing him to conduct his life well in light of the example offered by Jesus which allows the human person to participate fully in the divine life as his very humanity has been taken on and redeemed by Jesus, allowing for the fullness of the deification of man spoken of in the *Treatise on Grace* in Question 112.[427] Augustine states this well: "God was made man, that man might be made God."[428] The Incarnation likewise leads most beautifully to man's flight from all that would keep him from God, specifically through the recognition of the dignity of man's very nature by the Word's assumption of man's nature in the person of Christ, something that leads man to desire no longer the devil's condition or his enticements, to take care not to damage by sin the very nature that the Word Himself found fit to take on, to rid himself of the presumption that by his own efforts he could become right with God, to cure his pride through the great humility exhibited by the Word become man, and lastly "to free man from the thraldom (*servitus*) of sin," something that could not have been effected by any one man who by his very fallen condition was incapable of satisfying the harm done to the entirety of the human race. Only God become man could effect such a thing.[429] Pope Leo the Great states this well: "Unless He was God, He would not have brought a remedy; and unless He was man, He would not have set an example."[430] This, then, leads Thomas to the heart of the motive for the Incarnation in the third article which asks whether God would have become Incarnate if man had not sinned. Recognizing the debate that this issue evokes,

---

[427] In addition to this reference to the *Treatise on Grace*, one should also reflect here upon the fact that the Incarnation is also presupposed by those questions central to the description of the Christian life in the *Treatise on Virtue*, namely those concerning the Beatitudes, the Gifts, and Fruits of the Holy Spirit.

[428] ST. III. 1. 2.

[429] ST. III. 1. 2. ad2.

[430] ST. III. 1. 2.

he reminds the reader that when it comes to those things that are freely effected through God's will, especially those things that are wholly gratuitous and not due to man, one's determinations must be guided primarily by the pronouncements made by the Holy Scriptures as it is through these that God's will is manifested to man's understanding. And so he states that

> since everywhere in the Sacred Scripture the sin of the first man is assigned as the reason of the Incarnation, it is more in accordance with this to say that the work of the Incarnation was ordained by God as a remedy for sin; so that, had sin not existed, the Incarnation would not have been.[431]

And yet, in keeping with the sense of necessity developed in the prior articles of this question, Thomas adds that the power of God Himself is not limited by the situation of man's sin, that it was well within His power to become incarnate regardless of the state into which man had fallen, a position that further heightens all that was said concerning the Incarnation's appropriateness in Articles 1 and 2.[432]

The second section of this treatise (Questions 2 through 15) considers the mode of union of the Incarnation, a very difficult section of this treatise as it considers the union of the Word and human nature from its psychological and metaphysical perspectives. As many commentators have noted, Thomas's doctrine here and in the whole of the treatise on Jesus Christ is influenced heavily by the patristic tradition from both the east and the west, as well as by the many and varied Councils that had dealt with the Word Incarnate before his day, particularly that of Chalcedon.[433] Thomas considers the many explanations offered historically to understand the union of the Word with human nature and concludes that divinity and humanity, the natures respectively of both the Word and of man, come together in the one person of Christ, not in a single nature of the divine and the human, nor in some mixture of the two, but as two natures existing and united

---

[431] ST. III. 1. 3.

[432] One should take careful note of Kerr's discussion of this point at (2002), pp. 170–172. Consider also ST. III. 3. 8.

[433] For example, see Torrell (2005), p. 53, and Davies (1992), p. 300ff.

in the one person of Christ Himself.[434] Thus, there is one person, that of Christ, who can be spoken of accurately as we would of a man and of God. Thus, Christ had a body, could experience pain and some of the emotions, enjoyed a knowledge consequent upon his experience on earth, and other things belonging to the human nature assumed but in a way that was appropriate to His person and mission, namely as He was not subject to sin, and as He was to provide a model of perfect human living for all Christians.[435] But Christ can also be said to have enjoyed the knowledge that is proper to the Word Himself, and other such things appropriate to the divine nature.[436] Both the divine and the human can be said of Christ, then, only as the Word assumed a nature other than its own, namely a human one, and that what resulted was not two beings but simply one, the person of Christ.[437]

Although Christ is fully human and fully divine, Thomas states that there were many things that distinguished Him from other human beings, specifically in the graces that He enjoyed (Question 7), the fact that He is head of the Church (8), the extent and quality of His knowledge (9 through 12), and the powers and weaknesses assumed and displayed in His soul, will, and body (13 through 15). In His divinity, Christ enjoys all that is proper to this. Since human nature is assumed by the Word, something that brings with it the fact that Christ enjoyed not just a divine but also a human mind and will, as well as a human soul,[438] Thomas argues that the humanity of Christ is something that, being distinct from His divinity, requires the graces, virtues, and gifts of the Holy Spirit of which people stand in need, as described in the *prima secundae*. Given the intimacy of the union in Christ between the human and the divine, Christ's humanity is said to enjoy the fullness of grace, that is, grace possessed wholly and perfectly.[439] And, as both Davies and Kerr

---

[434] ST. III. 2. 1–2.

[435] See ST. III. 5. 1–2 (body), 14 and 15. 5–6 (pain), 15. 6–9 (emotion), and 9. 1 and 4, and 12 (acquired knowledge).

[436] ST. III. 9–10 (knowledge)

[437] ST. III. 3. Consider Davies' discussion (1992), pp. 302–305, Nichols (2002), pp. 112–114, Wawrykow (2005 b), pp. 222–251, and Gondreau (2005), pp. 252–276.

[438] See ST. III. 5. 3–4.

[439] See ST. III. 7. 9–12.

point out, this most perfect grace bestowed upon the humanity of Christ disposes His human soul, mind, will and body to the divine most perfectly, a disposition that does not eradicate what is proper to His humanity, as if it were only the Son who was operative in the person of Christ, but rather unites His humanity with His divinity wherein Christ's actions "proceed both from a divine will and from a human will, albeit one totally in line with the divine will, and albeit one assumed by a divine person."[440] We see here, then, the process, perfected in this case, of the raising of the human by grace so that it might partake of the divine and this without the violation of the nature of all that is human, something effected freely by God's gift and lovingly sought out by man and freely accepted, as detailed in the *Treatise concerning Grace* in the *prima secundae*. Thus, Christ, having been so united in his humanity with the Word, receives not only the fullness of habitual grace, but all the gifts of the Holy Spirit and the gratuitous gifts in a most eminent way, the former as Christ's humanity is most apt to respond to the inspiration of the Holy Spirit, and the latter insofar as Christ is the "first and chief teacher of the faith," something to which the gratuitous gifts are ordered primarily.[441] Moreover, Christ possesses all the virtues perfectly, except for the theological virtues of faith and hope given that He, from the first moment of His Incarnation, both beheld and possessed God's essence fully, making the knowledge acquired by faith and the fruition that hope promises redundant.[442] In light of the fullness of grace that is Christ, and this together with the biblical witness and the discussion in the first question of the *tertia pars* concerning the appropriateness of the Incarnation, Christ is He from Whom all graces flow, that is to say, He is possessed not only of the personal graces spoken of above, but also of the "capital graces," namely those as head of the Church, of all men, and of the angels. From the fullness that He possesses, and that He is the mediator between God and man, the grace that He is and effects in the mysteries of His life, death, and resurrection, overflow into the redemption

---

[440] Davies (1992), p. 309, referencing ST. III. 7. 1. See also Kerr (2002), pp. 172–174, and Nichols (2002), pp. 116–117.

[441] ST. III. 7. 1 and 5–7.

[442] ST. III. 7. 2–4. See Davies (1992), pp. 308–312 for greater detail.

of mankind, the healing and elevation of his nature, the establishment of the Church, and the efficacy of all the sacraments, particularly that of the Eucharist.[443]

Christ's soul is also impacted in the intimacy of its presence to and unity with the Word, and this both with respect to its knowledge and power. Clearly Christ, as divine, would have possessed the knowledge appropriate to the Word. However, given the nature and integrity of Christ's humanity, Thomas argues that there would have to be attributed to his human mind a knowledge that it itself could acquire naturally, that is to say, empirically through its own experience of the world.[444] Otherwise, as Torrell notes, "his humanity would have known nothing at all and would have been assumed by the Word in vain."[445] In addition to this empirical knowledge, the perfection of Christ's humanity requires that we attribute to it a knowledge of all that can be reasoned to by the human mind, a knowledge that was infused in Him from, again, the first moment of His Incarnation.[446] Lastly, Christ, in His human nature, had to have beheld the beatific vision if He were not to have been less perfect than those humans who already beheld this vision. Nonetheless, given the nature and integrity of human rationality, this comprehension was not one that was perfect, but was sufficient nonetheless to the fruition that was enjoyed and which gave rise to the absence of the theological virtue of hope in His life, as described above.[447]

When Thomas turns to a consideration of the power of Christ's soul, he begins to note the limitations, weaknesses, or defects that were evident in the person of Christ, and this because of the distinction of natures within His person, a distinction that maintained the integrity of each nature and what was proper to each. Thus, the soul of Christ could not have been omnipotent; this belonged properly to the divine nature of Christ, to the Word.[448] Anything miraculous must be attributable, then, to the Word, and could be said of Christ's soul only as it was

---

[443] See ST. III. 8. See also Davies (1992), pp. 312–314.
[444] ST. III. 9. 4 and Question 12.
[445] Torrell (2005), p. 54 commenting upon ST. III. 9.
[446] ST. III. 9. 3 and Question 11.
[447] ST. III. 9. 2. and Question 10.
[448] ST. III. 13. 1.

used instrumentally by the Word united with it in the person of Christ.[449] The same is also said with respect to the effect that Christ could have had upon his own body.[450] These limitations are more pronounced when we consider Christ's body itself. It was fitting, Thomas argues, that His body be subject to the infirmities and defects to which the human body is heir, first, as Christ came to make satisfaction for the sin of the human race, something accomplished by taking on the penalties of man's sin, something that included death, hunger, thirst, pain, and the like; second, as this made the Incarnation something more readily believed; and lastly as this gave people an example of how to bear such things patiently and nobly in their own lives.[451] There is, however, a limit to the bodily defects that the Word assumed, namely those infirmities that were a consequence of man's sin and were thus "incompatible with the perfection of knowledge and grace" that is Christ's.[452] Consequently, Christ did not assume the defect of sin itself, particularly as this would have destroyed the very reasons why He took on man's bodily infirmities in the first place.[453] While Christ suffered from no ignorance,[454] he did experience the emotions, being possessed of a sensitive appetite. However, His experience of them differed from man's, specifically as His passions were not centered upon illicit things, His sensitive appetition being wholly rectified by and obedient to His reason (as it was for pre-fallen man), and thus presenting no obstacles to reason's operations.[455] His experience, then, of sorrow, fear, wonder, and anger (Articles 6 through 9) were of passions that are perfect, or those that occur in the sensitive appetite and go no further in their effect.

In the final section to this first part, Thomas examines the consequences of the union of the Word Incarnate (16 through 26), of which we can only make the briefest mention, something that should not prejudice the reader against the importance of this material. He considers those that belong, first, to Christ

---

[449] ST. III. 13. 2.
[450] ST. III. 13. 3.
[451] ST. III. 14. 1. See also III. 15. 5.
[452] ST. III. 14. 4.
[453] ST. III. 15. 1.
[454] ST. III. 15. 3.
[455] ST. III. 15. 4.

Himself (16–19), second to Him in relation to His Father, (20–4), and lastly to Him in relation to man (25–6). In the first of these, Thomas is quite careful to determine the statements that theologians can make about Christ, and this in light of the material that was developed in the prior questions so that one might speak as accurately as is possible concerning His person.[456] Questions concerning the unity of Christ's being (17), the relations that exist between his divine and human wills, and how the human will conforms to the divine will (18), the manner in which the natures that comprise the person of Christ are united in His activity, and the merit that results for mankind (19) finish this part.[457] Next he considers the consequences that arise from Christ's relation to His Father, and from the Father's relation to Him. In the former, Thomas explains how Christ, in His humanity, was subject to His Father both through divine appointment and His own willed obedience (20). He examines His prayer to the Father as something that is required not only by the fact that His human will stands in need of divine assistance since it is not capable of effecting whatsoever it wills (something that is not the case with His divine will), but also as it serves as an example for all Christians who undertake the will of the Father in their lives (21). Lastly, he considers His priesthood whereby Christ became the perfect mediator between God and man, not only ontologically but also sacrificially, bestowing divine graces through his person upon His people, and offering up to God a most perfect satisfaction for the sins of the human race (22).[458] With respect to the Father's relation to Christ, Thomas discusses God's adoption of man through Christ as men become members of Christ's body and thus share in His inheritance (23),[459] and Christ's predestination by the Father (24). Lastly, he examines those things that belong to Christ in relation to man, specifically His adoration (25),

---

[456] For an excellent treatment of Question 16, consider Appendix I in Colman O'Neill's translation of this part of the *Summa*, Volume 50 (1965) of the Blackfriars' edition, pp. 215–220.

[457] Again, consider Appendices 2 through 4 of O'Neill for discussions concerning this material.

[458] See Appendix 5 of O'Neill for a fuller treatment of the priesthood of Christ.

[459] See Appendix 6 in O'Neill for an excellent treatment of this question.

and his mediation between God and man as man, and through His redemptive act (26).

Among the many things that are covered in these 26 questions, one cannot help but be impressed with the care that Thomas exercises in preserving the integrity, ontologically and operationally, of both the divine and human natures of Christ so that they might be related integrally to one another and perform fully in Christ's salvific act, achieving all that is appropriate to and intended by the Incarnation itself. In effecting this, Thomas is able to describe well the love with which the Word acted in freely and graciously assuming human nature, something that not only perfects the humanity of Christ, but also overflows from this very fullness (and the deeds and sufferings that he undertook consequent to his Incarnation) into the nature of man himself, his very salvation, and the establishment of His Church with Him as her head from whom all graces, most especially in the sacraments, can be received by her members. The grace of God, then, can be said to reach us through "the mediation of Christ and so bears his imprint."[460] Consequently, Christ is not only the model of perfect Christian living and thus most worthy of imitation, He is also, and most vitally, the way by which man's "deification" is achieved, as discussed earlier in the *Treatise on Grace* in the *prima secundae*. In short, through Christ, man receives not only healing grace, but also the opportunity for that grace which elevates him so that he might participate most fully in Christ's life. The humanity of Christ, then, plays a vital role in man's deification, specifically as His humanity, in the fullness of its nature, integrity, freedom, and graced perfection, is united to and guided by the Word, and wholly obedient to the Father, something that is manifested especially in the actions that he undertook while in the flesh, the very subject of the remaining questions of this treatise.[461]

The second part of Thomas's considerations concerning the person of Christ, spanning Questions 27 through 59, take up the particulars of Christ's life, the things that He did or suffered while united to human nature. Thomas examines this in four stages, first, the coming of Christ into the world (27–39),

---

[460] Nichols (2002), p. 117.
[461] See Torrell (2005), p. 56.

second, the course of His life while in the world (40–5), third, His departure from this world (46–52), and finally, his exaltation after this life (53–59).

The first of these four begins with a consideration of Mary, the Mother of God (27–30). It should be noted that these four questions neither constitute a Mariology that stands on its own nor represent a "definitive and exhaustive treatment of our Lady."[462] Rather, these questions are developed and understood in relation to Christ, particularly in light of the architecture of the entire work and especially the purposes and teachings of the *tertia pars*.[463] Be that as it may, these four questions betray the beauty with which Thomas could write as he turned his attention to Mary's "holiness, her innocence, her human love for Joseph, and her humility before the great news,"[464] which writing at times approaches the poetic.[465] Questions 31 through 34 are devoted to Christ's conception in light of its matter, active principle, and mode and order respectively. These questions were of importance to theologians of Thomas's time, but they occupy few people today, particularly in light of the fact that much of what is developed here is "at the mercy of the biology of (Thomas's) time as regards the state and development of the foetus before birth."[466] Nevertheless, they do affirm the concrete fact of Christ's Incarnation within Mary's womb wherein He received His flesh and human soul, and His human and ancestral lineage are thus assured. In light of the blessings bestowed on Mary, the taint of original sin ends with her and she gives birth to One who is wholly free from this. The active principle

---

[462] See Kerr (2002), p. 174, and Thomas Heath's Introduction to his translation of these questions in Volume 51 (1969) of the Blackfriars' edition, p. xiii.

[463] Kerr notes the fact (2002, p. 174) that Thomas did not hold the doctrine of the immaculate conception (in ST. III. 27. 2). One might wish to consider Appendix 3 in Heath's translation of this part of the *Summa* for a good discussion of this point, as well as Appendix 1 that offers a historical survey of Thomas's teachings on the Holy Mother, particularly in light of the context and teachings of Thomas's day.

[464] Volume 51 (1969) of the Blackfriars' edition, p. xiii.

[465] See especially Heath's comments, Volume 51 (1969) of the Blackfriars' edition p. xiv.

[466] Roland Potter, translator of Volume 52 (1971) of the Blackfriars' edition of the *Summa*, p. xv.

of Christ's conception is the Holy Trinity, but, following Luke 1.35, Thomas attributes this particularly to the Holy Spirit.[467] Questions 35 through 37 consider Christ's nativity, how his birth was made known to the world, and lastly his circumcision and other religious matters observed with respect to the Christ child.[468] Thomas completes this section concern the coming of Jesus into the world ends with a consideration of the baptisms of John and Christ, Questions 38 and 39, respectively.

The second section deals with the course of His life while in the world (Questions 40–45), treating of the manner of His life, His temptation in the desert, the manner of and questions related to His teaching, the miracles He worked considered both generally and specifically, and lastly His transfiguration. Kerr notes the elementary nature of these descriptions, particularly in light of "modern historical-critical reconstructions of the life of the man who figures in the Gospels," and that this section of the *Summa* is of very limited interest to theologians today.[469]

In the third section (Questions 46 through 52), Thomas deals with Christ's departure from this world, in his passion, death, burial, and descent into hell. Four of these questions concern the passion, specifically, in itself (46), those who caused it (47), and then its effects or fruits, specifically the manner in which these were brought about (48), and then a consideration of the very effects themselves (49), the remaining concerns receiving one question each. In regards to the passion, just as the Incarnation was not a necessity imposed upon God by man's situation but was something freely undertaken by the Word, so too is the same said with respect to His passion.[470] Its appropriateness is something to which the Scriptures, both Old and New, testify: the passion displays the depths of God's love to all people,

---

[467] ST. III. 32. 1, followed in Articles 2 through 4 by appropriate qualifications of this attribution.

[468] One may wish to consider Potter's appendices on these questions in Volume 52 (1971) of the Blackfriars' translation.

[469] Kerr (2002), p. 174. Note also the judgment of the redundancy of these questions with Torrell on p. 175 and note 9. Consider also pp. xvii–xviii of Parsons's and Pinheiro's translation of this part of the *Summa* in Volume 53 (1971) of the Blackfriars' edition.

[470] ST. III. 46. 1. and 2.

something that, when properly considered, evokes their love for Him in return, wherein "lies the perfection of human salvation"; it puts before each person "an example of obedience, humility, constancy, justice and the other virtues displayed in the passion which are requisite for man's salvation"; it makes satisfaction for the sin of the human race and procures justifying grace for all and the gift of everlasting life; in light of the immensity of this act, it places a strong obligation on the human person to refrain from sin; finally, it "redounds to man's greater dignity, that as man was overcome and deceived by the devil, so also it should be a man that should overthrow the devil; and as man deserved death, so a man by dying should vanquish death."[471] In like manner, does Thomas argue for the appropriateness of Christ's suffering death upon the cross.[472] Specifically, Christ did not endure every suffering possible to man. However, he did so, generally speaking, as he endured suffering of all kinds, to every part of his body, and from all classes and manner of men.[473] The pain he endured was horrible and rose to the level of the worst any man could endure for three reasons, by reason of, first, the perfection of Christ's humanity and thus the heightened refinement and sensitivity of His person to all things; the fact that Christ did not allow any mitigation of His pain but "permitted each one of His powers to exercise its proper function" during His passion; and lastly by the fact that He accepted this pain and sorrow voluntarily so that man might be delivered from sin. Thus, "He embraced the amount of pain proportionate to the magnitude of the fruit which resulted therefrom."[474] In like manner, the faculties of Christ's soul suffered extreme anguish at His passion.[475] And yet, being divine, He continued to enjoy the beatific vision while He suffered upon the cross, a consequence of the hypostatic union.[476]

Question 47 emphasizes the fact that although others were the direct cause in Christ's death, nonetheless His death would

[471] ST. III. 46. 3.
[472] ST. III. 46. 4.
[473] ST. III. 46. 5.
[474] ST. III. 46. 6.
[475] ST. III. 46. 7.
[476] ST. III. 46. 8. See Kerr (2002), pp. 176–177 for a brief discussion of this point.

not have occurred had He not voluntarily laid down His life, and this out of obedience to His Father. This obedience was most appropriate for at least three reasons; first as "it was in keeping with human justification, that 'as by the disobedience of one man, many were made sinners: so also by the obedience of one, many shall be made just' (Romans 5.19);" second, as it reconciled man with God through being a most acceptable sacrifice; and third, as it secured victory over death itself.[477] In light of these, the Father delivered His Son up to death, inspiring Him with love to suffer on man's behalf, "not shielding Him from the Passion, but abandoning Him to His persecutors," in light of which Thomas explains Christ's cry from the cross "My God, My God, why have you abandoned me."[478] The remaining three articles of this question center upon His persecutors and their guilt in the matter.[479]

The last two questions (48 and 49) deal with the effects that Christ's passion had for mankind, namely that through His passion Christ brought salvation to all; that through the merits of his passion, this grace now extends to all His members; that through the atonement it effects, it more than sufficiently makes up for the sins of the human race; that through its sacrifice voluntarily, lovingly, and perfectly offered to the Father on man's behalf, man is reconciled to God; and that through its redemption, man is released from his bondage to sin, from the devil's power, and from having to pay a price that he himself could never pay. Through all of these, man's sin is forgiven, his punishment remitted, his reconciliation to God effected, and the gates of heaven opened to him once again, thus providing for the beatitude that has been one of the overarching themes of the *Summa* itself.

The last three questions concerning Christ's departure from this world are devoted to His death, burial, and descent into hell

---

[477] ST. III. 47. 1. Consider also what is fulfilled by Christ's obedience as listed in ad1.

[478] ST. III. 47. 3. See also ad1 and ad2. Kerr notes (2002), p. 176 that this cry "is that of a holy man who, in his suffering, remains certain of the love of his Father," something confirmed in light of the psalm to which Christ refers in his cry. See also Appendix 1 of Richard Murphy's translation of this part of the *Summa* in the Blackfriars' edition, Volume 54 (1965), pp. 181–188.

[479] For a discussion of this, see Ibid., Appendix 3, pp. 194–201.

(50–2). Concerning the appropriateness of His death, Thomas adds three more reasons to the list that has already been generated in previous questions, namely that His death showed to all the very reality of His nature as man, and that he gave all Christians an example in His death not only of how to die to sin spiritually, but also a reason to no longer fear death itself. For in His ascension, He has overcome death itself and has paid the price of man's redemption.[480] In a like manner, Christ's burial was appropriate for three reasons, namely that this assuredly established that He was in fact dead, that in His rising from His grave, hope is given to all that the same will happen to them on the Last Day, and that in one's baptism and continual death to one's sin, the Christian is in a sense buried with Christ insofar as he, having died to his own sins, is hidden or taken away from this fallen world and is prepared actively for his rising, so to speak, into the next, again, a reference to and a definite concretization of the whole of the *secunda pars*, but this made possible only by and in the person of Christ.[481] Lastly, His descent into hell was appropriate again for three reasons, namely that those who had died in sin and had descended into hell before Christ's salvific act might be afforded the same opportunities and benefits that the living and all generations to come now enjoy in light of His death, resurrection, and ascension into glory, and the power of these as they continue in the sacraments; that having overthrown the power of the devil, Christ came to deliver those who previously had been held captive; and that, having manifested His power on earth through His life and death, so too should He display this "in hell by visiting it and enlightening it."[482]

The fourth and final section details Christ's exaltation after this life (53–9). In these questions, he discusses Christ's resurrection in general terms, in relation to the status of His resurrected body, the manner in which He manifested His resurrection to others, and as it is the cause of man's own resurrection and justification (Questions 53 through 56 respectively). The last three

---

[480] ST. III. 50. 1. The remaining articles of this question deal with the status of Christ's body after His death. See Kerr (2002), p. 177

[481] ST. III. 51. 1. See also ibid., Appendix 4, pp. 202–207.

[482] ST. III. 52. 1 and ad2. See Kerr's discussion of this (2002), pp. 177–178, and Appendix 5 of Murphy, pp. 208–215.

questions treat of His ascension, the taking up of His seat at the right hand of the Father, and the judiciary power that is given to Him by the Father over the living and the dead. With respect to His resurrection, Thomas states that it was necessary for five reason; first, for praise of the Divine justice that saw it especially appropriate to raise Christ up from the dead in light of the very humility and obedience that He exhibited in laying His life down for the salvation of mankind; second, that every Christian be confirmed in their belief concerning Christ's divinity; third, to affirm every Christian's hope in their own resurrection as Christ, their head, has indeed risen; fourth, to order the lives and activities of every Christian so that they might walk "in newness of life;" and fifth, to complete the work of salvation.[483] In this, Christ's resurrection, of Him who is the first born of the dead, becomes the "efficient and exemplar" cause of man's own resurrection, and this, through God's justice as it works instrumentally through Christ's resurrection, effecting our own resurrection through His. In working all these things through Christ's humanity, the human person thus receives all the graces effected in this way, most especially that of the resurrection. As for its exemplarity, Thomas notes that Christ's resurrection is not only the first to occur, but it is also most worthy and perfect, thus standing as the exemplar to which all who are conformed to the Son, copy, so to speak, in their own resurrection. This latter applies only to the just, while the former applies to both the good and the bad, that is, to all who are subject to Christ's judgment at the end of time.[484]

Christ's ascension into heaven is something appropriate not only to His risen condition, as it is now immortal and incorruptible, but also as this increases the faith, hope, and charity of all Christians; their faith in things unseen (about which faith is, something that would have been impeded by Christ's bodily presence), their hope to join with Christ who in His assumed humanity has gone ahead to prepare a place for them, and their charity as it is now busied with and focused upon those things that will lead to heaven itself.[485] More to the point, however, is

---

[483] ST. III. 53. 1.
[484] ST. III. 56. 1. and ad3. See also Davies (1992), pp. 340–342.
[485] ST. III. 57. 1. and ad3.

the fact that Christ's very ascension into heaven is the cause of man's salvation, first, as this fosters not only a growth in man's faith, hope, and charity, but also his reverence of Him, now that He is seen in His glory as God in heaven, and secondly, that in so ascending, Christ has not only prepared the way for all Christians to follow Him and showers down gifts upon His people as He sits at the right hand of God, but also just as

> high-priest under the Old Testament entered the holy place to stand before God for the people, so also Christ entered heaven "to make intercession for us," as is said in Hebrews 7.25. Because the very showing of Himself in the human nature which He took with Him to heaven is a pleading for us; so that for the very reason that God so exalted human nature in Christ, He may take pity on them for whom the Son of God took human nature.[486]

Thus, the work of Christ as mediator between man and God is not finished with the completion of His earthly ministry, but continues before God in His resurrected state as Head of the Church and in His priestly capacity to intercede for His people, to draw everyone to the Father in the completion of the *reditus* with which the *secunda pars* is concerned, but now perfected and concretized in the person of the risen Christ.[487] In His glory, Christ sits at the right hand of God, that is to say, "abides eternally unchangeable in the Father's bliss" and reigns with Him as He has received judiciary power from Him.[488] This power, properly attributed to the Son, because He is "Wisdom begotten, and Truth proceeding from the Father, and His perfect Image,"[489] extends to all things, especially human and angelic, and will be exercised particularly at the Last Judgment at the end of time.[490]

From this brief account of the events of Christ's life, death, resurrection, and ascension into glory, one can see that Thomas's

---

[486] ST. III. 57. 6.
[487] See Davies (1992), pp. 342–344.
[488] ST. III. 58. 1.
[489] ST. III. 59. 1.
[490] ST. III. 59. 4. and 6. His treatment of the Last Judgment was reserved for a later section of the *tertia pars,* and was left unfinished at the time of his death.

intent was not to compose a biography. Instead, he dwelt upon what he calls those "mysteries" of the Incarnate Word that were directly relevant to the purposes of his Christology here in the *tertia pars*, namely, to detail those actions and sufferings that Christ undertook for the sake of effecting all that had to be realized so that man could indeed make his return to God. The very structure of the *Summa* pushes to this point where the inability of man to effect his return to God manifest in the appropriateness of the assumption of man's nature by the Word Himself, who, as Incarnate, completes in His person, with his deeds and sufferings, what is lacking to man, showing him the way he must follow, the truth he must know, and the life he must live if he is to realize his desire to be happy. In this light, Torrell is quite right to note that the four sections into which the mysteries of Christ's life are divided mirror the very schema

> of the *Summa* as a whole . . . The path followed by Jesus is in fact that of all creation and is, therefore, the path that we must take to be with him in paradise. Thus Thomas establishes the exemplary value of the mysteries of the life of Jesus, making this treatise one of the places where we can best grasp the connection between his theology and the spiritual life.[491]

We see in Thomas's Christology the final concretization of God's work, which began, in the *prima pars*, with His creative work and the establishment, conservation, and governance of the universe, but then had to be focused, in the *secunda pars*, in a more specific way (through the infused virtues, the gifts, and fruits of the Holy Spirit, the Law itself in all its forms, in short, through particular manifestations of grace) as man tries to realize the image to which he was made, and the happiness that is intended for him, something that is possible only as the *tertia pars* details God's response, in the person of Jesus Christ, to the sin and corruption that infects the condition of man and keeps him from realizing all for which he has been made.[492] In Christ is found the consummation of the entire work of theology, as Thomas

---

[491] Torrell (2005), p. 58.

[492] See Chapter One of this work where Rudi te Velde's contribution to understanding the macrostructure of the *Summa* was discussed.

declares in the prologue to the *tertia pars*. In His Incarnation and in all the mysteries recounted in the *Summa* concerning His life, are the graces whereby the healing and elevation of human nature is effected, graces that continue to exercise their effects well after the events of Christ's life and this until the consummation of time.[493] To understand how this is so, we must turn to Thomas's discussions concerning the sacraments.

The Treatise on the Sacraments (60–90)

This treatise is incomplete, as noted in the first chapter of this reader's guide. It is divided into two sections: the first dealing with the sacraments in general (Questions 60–65) and then with an examination of each of them in the second. Thomas completes his analysis of three of the seven sacraments (Baptism: 66–71, Confirmation: 72, and Holy Eucharist: 73–83). He embarks upon the sacrament of Penance and completes only his general examination of it (84–85) and its effects (86–89). He leaves off in Question 90 having enumerated its parts in a general way.[494]

Aidan Nichols states the situation very well when he says that "The mission of the Son . . . finds its expression in the mysteries of the life of Christ, which mysteries extend to our lives too, for when those lives are considered lives of Christian grace, these mysteries can be said to determine and structure them."[495] The idea here is the same one that was noted above with respect to Christ's resurrection, namely that this action, and by extension all the other actions described in the mysteries of Christ's life, those that occupy the second part of Thomas's Christology, are causes of grace not just in an efficient manner but also in an exemplarily way, which is to say, again appealing to Nichols, that "Grace in us takes the form of a real participation in the engraced being of Christ, a sharing in that being

---

[493] Consider Nichols' discussion of this point in (2002), pp. 118–120.

[494] Leaving a specific examination of these parts unaddressed (contrition, confession, and satisfaction), as well as considerations related to confession's recipients, the powers of the minister of this sacrament, and the solemnization of the rite itself, matters addressed in the *Supplement* which, as noted previously, draws upon Thomas's *Commentary on the Sentences of Peter Lombard,* a work composed some 20 years prior to the *Summa.*

[495] Nichols (2002), p. 119.

through an indrawing into the form of his mysteries."[496] In this the sacraments constitute the best of the means given by God to aid man in the attainment of his beatitude, means that are discussed throughout the whole of the *Summa*, beginning with providence, predestination, and governance of all that He created, continuing with those gifts that man needs so desperately to act for the sake of a supernatural end, those of the infused virtues, the gifts, and fruits of the Holy Spirit, the Beatitudes themselves, the law and grace, and culminating in the Word's union with man's nature in the Incarnation, in the deeds and sufferings that He endured for man's salvation, and now finally all of this as the Christian is drawn into the very life of Christ Himself through the sacraments.[497]

In his general consideration of the sacraments, Thomas treats of their nature, necessity, effects, cause, and number (60–5 respectively). He begins by affirming Augustine's description of a sacrament as a sign of something sacred that is given to man under a visible, that is, sensible form. This visible and thus readily known thing points not only at some holy thing that is unknown to him, but also to that which will make him holy. The fact that the sacrament begins with the sensible is something that accommodates the nature of man's knowing, where spiritual and intelligible things are accessed only through the material and sensual things of his experience.[498] This accommodation on God's part with respect to the human person is found in many places in the *Summa*, particularly in the manner in which He reveals Himself in the Holy Scriptures, in His creation of the multiplicity and diversity of the things of creation, and in the Incarnation itself. In their varying ways and in increasing intensity do these accommodations draw the human person ever closer to the Source whence he came. The sacraments complete this. They signify the very cause of man's sanctification, namely the passion of Christ, the form of man's sanctification, namely grace and the virtues, and lastly they signify the ultimate end of his sanctification, beatitude for all eternity. Thus, a sacrament is "a reminder of the past . . . an

---

[496] Nichols (2002), p. 120.
[497] See Torrell (2005), p. 59.
[498] ST. III. 60. 1, 2, and 4.

indication of that which is effected in us by Christ's passion . . . and a foretelling of future glory."[499]

The necessity of the sacraments for man's salvation follows upon this basic fact of human nature, that he is led to the spiritual and intellectual goods of his beatitude only through the material and sensible things of his experience. Thus, in God's providence and wisdom did He provide "man with means of salvation in the shape of corporeal and sensible signs that are called sacraments." Moreover, man's sin, as we saw in the *prima secundae*, subjects him and his passions inordinately to corporeal things. All the more, then, should the medicine, so to speak, that heals this wound in his soul be given under a form that can be recognized and used appropriately by one so diseased. Finally, the corporeal condition of a sacrament respects the fact that the majority of men find it hard to be drawn away from the material world, and thus engages them in this way, and moreover in such a fashion that they are drawn away from superstitious practices that promise falsely their sanctification. Thus,

> in the institution of the sacraments man, consistently with his nature, is instructed through sensible things; is humbled, through confessing that he is subject to corporeal things, seeing that he receives assistance through them: and he is even preserved from bodily hurt, by the healthy exercise of the sacraments.[500]

This accommodation on God's part in the giving of grace in this fashion is heightened by the fact that it need not be this way, but is deemed, nevertheless, as appropriate as has been the case with many of the things discussed in the *tertia pars*. It is interesting to note, as well, that the sacraments would not have been necessary in the prelapsarian state. For in such a state, there was nothing to be healed or elevated in man's nature, making the sacraments superfluous.[501] However, after man's sin, but before the salvific act, Thomas states that there had to exist sacraments,

---

[499] ST. III. 60. 3. The consequence of this is that a sacrament is determined by Divine institution, and not by man's—see ST. III. 60. 5.

[500] ST. III. 61. 1.

[501] ST. III. 61. 2.

specifically as there had to be "some visible signs whereby man might testify to his faith in the future coming of a Savior."[502] These were not restricted to those found in the Old Law, but include the sacraments of "the law of nature, rites and gestures in which the human instinct for beatitude came to expression even under paganism."[503] All of these, however, loose any efficacy that they had as their final cause, namely Christ's passion itself, that for which they were "instituted in order to foreshadow,"[504] has now come to pass, with the result that now, after Christ's salvific act, "no man can be made holy save through Christ."[505]

Clearly, the principal effect of the sacraments is grace. However, they do not act merely or solely as signs of grace conferred by the will of God on the occasion of the sacrament being received. They also cause grace. To explain this, Thomas distinguishes between efficient causes that are principal and those that are instrumental. Principally, no other than God can cause grace, "since grace is nothing else that a participated likeness of the Divine Nature." Instrumentally, however, something can act as an efficient cause not by reason of anything that it itself possesses by way of its form or essence, but rather by the fact that it is used for a particular purpose by the agent that wields it as a tool or instrument. Thus, although the tools used by a craftsman in the construction of a house do not cause the house principally, this being attributed to the craftsman involved as he works out of the art he possesses, nonetheless the tools are so designed and ordained to the task of construction that one can say instrumentally the tool causes the house, as the extension of the craftsman's hands and art. "And it is thus that the sacraments of the New Law cause grace: for they are instituted by God to be employed for the purpose of conferring grace."[506] One should be clear about the real efficacy of the sacrament: just as the axe by its sharpness cuts the wood when wielded by the craftsman, so too does the sacrament act instrumentally upon the soul of its recipient as God so acts. What the sacraments confer upon the

---

[502] ST. III. 61. 3.
[503] Nichols (2002), p. 123. See ST. III. 61. 3. ad2.
[504] ST. III. 61. 3. ad1.
[505] ST. III. 61. 3.
[506] ST. III. 62. 1.

soul of man is something over and above the perfections that are brought to the soul's various powers and consequent activities by the infused virtues and the gifts of the Holy Spirit. The perfections that the sacraments bring constitute God's special grace whereby He aids the Christian to achieve the very purpose of the sacrament in question. For example, "Baptism is ordained unto a certain spiritual regeneration, by which man dies to vice and becomes a member of Christ," something to which the virtues and gifts may be very well inclined, but cannot of themselves cause instrumentally.[507] One must be careful, however, not to think that the grace caused by the sacrament is somehow in it like water is in a vessel, but rather as the instrument whereby the work specific to the end of the sacrament is effected.[508] Thus, the power that is in the sacrament which brings about its effect is there imperfectly and transiently, that is to say, as wielded by the principal agent whose power is perfect, and who, in the wielding of this instrument, causes the imperfect power of the instrument to pass from it into he to whom it is applied.[509] Thomas argues that we can be more specific concerning the agent who wields this power and how it is received. He makes a distinction between two kinds of instrumental causes, namely those that are detached or separate from the agent, as in the axe mentioned previously, and those that are attached or united to the agent, in this example the craftman's hand who, together with the axe, effects the building of the house. In light of this image, Thomas states the following:

> the principal efficient cause of grace is God Himself, in comparison with Whom Christ's humanity is as a united instrument, whereas the sacrament is as a separate instrument. Consequently, the saving power must needs be derived by the sacraments from Christ's Godhead through His humanity.[510]

In light of the fact that the graces specific to the sacraments are ordered principally to the removal of any defects incurred by

[507] ST. III. 62. 2.
[508] ST. III. 62. 3. ad1.
[509] ST. III. 62. 3–4.
[510] ST. III. 62. 5.

man consequent upon his sins and to the perfection of the soul in its worship of God according to the rites of the Christian faith, and that both of these were effected through Christ's passion,

> it is manifest that the sacraments of the Church derive their power specially from Christ's passion, the virtue of which is in a manner united to us by our receiving the sacraments. It was in sign of this that from the side of Christ hanging on the Cross there flowed water and blood, the former of which belongs to Baptism, the latter to the Eucharist, which are the principal sacraments.[511]

In addition to the effect of grace, Thomas states that some of the sacraments leave their mark upon those who receive them. This mark or character is imprinted spiritually upon the soul of the Christian, deputing or appointing him to a definite purpose, namely to a spiritual service pertaining to "the worship of God according to the rite of the Christian religion,"[512] a worship that consists either in the reception of divine graces or in bestowing them upon others.[513] "The whole rite of the Christian religion," Thomas states,

> is derived from Christ's priesthood. Consequently, it is clear that the sacramental character is specially the character of Christ to Whose character the faithful are likened by reason of the sacramental characters, which are nothing else than certain participations of Christ's priesthood, flowing from Christ Himself.[514]

The faithful, so marked by and sharing in the eternal priesthood of Christ, possess this character forever. Thus, once one is baptized, for example, even apostasy will not eradicate this character from one's soul.[515] Finally, while all the sacraments

[511] ST. III. 62. 5.
[512] ST. III. 63. 2.
[513] ST. III. 63. 2–3.
[514] ST. III. 63. 3.
[515] ST. III. 63. 5. corpus and ad2.

are remedies for sin, only Baptism, Confirmation, and Holy Orders are ordered to the divine worship according to the rites of the Christian religion, and thus leave their mark upon their recipient, with the former two conferring on their recipients the capacity to receive the other sacraments, while the latter deputes one to confer these sacraments upon others. The Eucharist does not imprint a character, but is rather "the end and consummation of all the sacraments . . . it contains within itself Christ, in Whom there is not the character, but the very plenitude of the Priesthood."[516]

Thomas concludes his general treatment of the sacraments by explaining why it is appropriate for there to be seven sacraments. He does this by drawing the parallels between the life that is made possible by reason of Christ's passion and priesthood (upon which the efficacy of the sacraments are based) and that of man's corporeal condition in the world, a parallel or conformity that results in part from his hylomorphic view of human nature, as discussed in his *Treatise on Man* in the *prima pars*. The purpose of the sacraments has already been stated, namely to perfect man in his worship of God and to heal the wounds that have been caused by sin. Now, in relation to his corporeal state, man can acquire perfection with respect both to his body and as he is a member of a community. With respect to his body, perfection is acquired directly or indirectly, that is, for example, as some physiologically based system (like his digestion) attains its optimum condition conducive to its good functioning, or that its good function is achieved through the removal of something that hinders this (for example, some disease or disorder of the intestines). The former perfection, he states, arises in three ways:

> First, by generation whereby a man begins to be and to live: and corresponding to this in the spiritual life there is Baptism, which is a spiritual regeneration . . . Secondly, by growth whereby a man is brought to perfect size and strength: and corresponding to this in the spiritual life there is Confirmation, in which the Holy Spirit is given to strengthen us . . . Thirdly, by nourishment, whereby life and strength are

[516] ST. III. 63. 6.

preserved to man: and corresponding to this in the spiritual life there is the Eucharist.[517]

This, he states, would be sufficient if man were not liable to the defects that can afflict both body and soul, and most specifically sin with respect to the latter. A cure, then, is required for these infirmities, and this in a twofold way:

> One is the healing that restores health: and corresponding to this in the spiritual life there is Penance . . . The other is the restoration of former vigor by means of suitable diet and exercise: and corresponding to this in the spiritual life there is Extreme Unction, which removes the remainder of sin, and prepares man for final glory.[518]

Lastly, with respect to man's perfection as a member of community, this is accomplished in two ways:

> First, by receiving power to rule the community and to exercise public acts: and corresponding to this in the spiritual life there is the sacrament of Order . . . Secondly, in regard to natural propagation. This is accomplished by Matrimony both in the corporal and in the spiritual life: since it is not only a sacrament but also a function of nature.[519]

Absolutely considered, the Eucharist is the greatest of the sacraments, first, as it contains Christ Himself substantially, who is contained in the other sacraments instrumentally only; second, as all the other sacraments are ordered to the Eucharist as to their end; and third, as the other sacraments are completed in the reception of the Eucharist. Nonetheless, the necessity of Baptism is recognized as that which first introduces one into the Body of Christ, the Church, and makes possible, in this new life, one's enjoyment of all the other sacraments.[520]

---

[517] ST. III. 65. 1.
[518] Ibid.
[519] Ibid. Consider Torrell's comments on this choice of Thomas's at (2005), p. 61.
[520] ST. III. 65. 3.

It is clear from his treatment of the sacraments in general that there is a beautiful continuity between the graces effected by the mysteries of Christ's life, passion, death, and resurrection, and their ongoing causality, both efficient and instrumental, within the world; as Kerr states, Thomas's "Christology does not conclude with the enthronement of the risen Christ as judge of all the earth."[521] The Christian finds himself, through faith and the sacraments of faith, united to these mysteries and the causality that they exert, and in this do they receive the fruits of Christ's salvific act and a participation in and responsibility for a new way of living, and this directed perfectly to all that is required in the worship of God, and the removal of all damage to one's nature that sin has effected. In this, one is marked, particularly by one's baptism, as a new creation in Christ, ordered ultimately to the union that can be effected between God and man through the mediation of all the sacraments, but particularly that of the Eucharist in which the Christian is united with Christ Himself substantially, something that ultimately always returns one to the salvific act itself and the cross of Christ from which all graces and the Church itself flow.[522]

Many have lamented the fact that after having considered only three of the seven sacraments, that Thomas ceases in his composition of the *Summa*. Although there is a great deal concerning his views on the sacraments present in both their general and specific treatments, especially in his treatises concerning baptism and the Eucharist, enough to gain a very decent insight into the maturity of his thought in this area, we are left wanting when it comes to the final part of the *Summa* that would have dealt with eschatological issues, drawing the *Summa* to its completion in the very place where it had begun, namely in God Himself. While the *Supplement* does offer some indication of the outlines of this material (as well as the final volume of his *Summa Contra Gentiles*), missing is that beautiful continuity of thought that has permeated the entirety of the

---

[521] Kerr (2002), p. 179.
[522] See Nichols (2002), p. 124, and Kerr (2005), pp. 179–180. I have not touched upon the important question of Thomas's ecclesiology. I refer the reader to pp. 120ff in Nichols, and pp. 58–61 of Torrell (2005) for an initial discussion of this material.

material of the *Summa*, as well as the impetus that it acquired as he patiently, thoroughly, and lovingly made his way to the eschaton and the fulfillment of the purposes for which the work was written. Nonetheless, there is more than enough here in both the material of which the *Summa* treats, and the degree to which its themes and overall architecture have been realized, to captivate the minds and hearts of thinkers, both religious and nonreligious, since its composition, making this work of pivotal influence in at the very least theological and philosophical circles, something to which we now briefly turn in the last chapter of this reader's guide.

CHAPTER 3

RECEPTION AND INFLUENCE[1]

It may come as a surprise, having been exposed to the beauty and profundity that constitutes the *Summa Theologiae,* that Thomas's work was subject to ecclesial suspicion shortly after his death. The trouble that had existed between the "radical Aristotelians" within the arts faculty and "neo-Augustinian conservatives"[2] within theology, mentioned briefly in the first chapter of this reader's guide, had continued to fester even after the work of many, including Thomas, to address what amounted arguably to the status of the independence of the naturally arrived at truths of philosophy in relation to those revealed in Holy Scripture and studied and defended by theology, especially in those situations where the former contradicted the latter.[3] Such importance ascribed to pagan writers and to their commentators, especially Averroes, was argued to be an innovation dangerous to core tenets of the faith, and consequently had to be dealt with firmly and decisively.[4] Thirteen of these philosophical propositions had been condemned as early as 1270 by the bishop of Paris, Stephen Tempier, which seemed to have little effect in quelling the unrest between the opposed sides. For, in 1277, the pope at that time, John XXI, having heard of the continued and growing unrest in these scholastic and religious circles, instructed Tempier to investigate the matter and to determine those positions "prejudicial to the faith,"[5]

---

[1] I rely heavily upon the work of Torrell (1993; 1996) (2005) and Weisheipl (1974; 1983) in this chapter, as well as O'Meara (1997), Kerr (2002), and Nichols (2002). The reader should consult these works for a more robust and fully noted approach to the reception and development of Thomas's work to the present day.

[2] Torrell (1993; 1996), p. 298.

[3] See Kerr (2002), pp. 12–13.

[4] See Weisheipl (1974; 1983), p. 333.

[5] Ibid., p. 334.

who was promoting them and where, and then to send this information to him. This resulted in a list of 219 propositions culled together by a commission of 16 theologians and then, without having sent this material to the pope, was promulgated on March 7, 1277, the third anniversary of Thomas's death, leading to the excommunication of those who held these views.[6] The importance of this condemnation, for the purposes of this reader's guide, lies in its inclusion within its 219 propositions of some held by Thomas himself.[7] Although this condemnation, according to Torrell, did not have Thomas directly in its sight,[8] the implication of Thomas in it was clear.[9]

A more direct attack on certain positions held by Thomas was launched by one of his own orders, Robert Kilwardby, the Archbishop of Canterbury who, on March 18, 1277, published his own list of 30 condemned propositions of which 3 were directly held by Thomas, propositions, Kilwardby argued, that posed a grave problem to the status of the divinity of Christ's body while it lay in the tomb and which, if left unchecked, would result in a heretical position on Thomas's part.[10] Kilwardby's successor John Pecham reconfirmed this condemnation in 1279.[11] William de la Mare, who held the Franciscan chair of theology in Paris at that time, published what was called a *Correctorium,* a document that culled 118 propositions from Thomas's works, including the *Summa Theologiae,* for the purposes of warning readers of their dangers, providing them with critiques and refutations, and thus "clarifying" their reading of the *Summa Theologiae.*[12] This gave rise to a spirited defense from some within the Dominican order who referred

---

[6] Ibid., p. 335, and Torrell (1993; 1996), p. 299.

[7] Among the direct targets were Siger of Brabant and Boethius of Dacia, as Weisheipl (1974; 1983) states on p. 335. See pp. 336–337 for the Thomistic theses included in the condemnation.

[8] See Torrell (1993; 1996), p. 300.

[9] See Ibid., pp. 301–303 for the details.

[10] See Weisheipl (1974; 1983), p. 337.

[11] Weisheipl (1974; 1983), p. 338.

[12] Torrell (1993; 1996), p. 305. He states (in 2005, p. 88) that a great many of these propositions to be corrected had come from the *Summa,* "Some seventy-six in all: forty-eight from the First Part, 38 from the Second Part (the Third Part, not yet in circulation in Paris, was temporarily left uncensored)."

to Williams work as the *Corruptorium* in their rebuttals to it.[13] In a more general way, the response of the Dominican order to these and other attacks upon the work and person of Thomas can be seen clearly and unequivocally in the directives promulgated by varied chapters the Order held between 1278 and Thomas's canonization is 1323.[14] Many of these controversies are resolved by the time the declaration of Thomas's sainthood is made, and as Weisheipl states "almost all Dominicans had made the teaching of Thomas their own and considered it a privilege, as well as an obligation, to study and defend it."[15]

Torrell remarks upon the course of events here, particularly with respect to William's *Correctorium,* stating that Thomas's *Summa Theologiae* "had achieved sufficient importance even among his adversaries that, is spite of not being able to stop its spread, they judged it necessary to reduce its effect."[16] The reputation of Thomas outside his order had begun to grow, albeit at a much slower pace than within Dominican circles. In addition to the defense of his work as discussed above, much of the early work on Thomas's teachings was devoted to summaries of his *Summa,*[17] tables and concordances of his works, and to works that highlight the progress that Thomas's thought had made through the course of his career.[18] There were also translations of his *Summa* into German, Greek, and Armenian.[19] One should note, however, the great diversity of theological thought of the time, particularly with the rise of new theologians, specifically John Duns Scotus and William of Ockham, and the lack of engagement with these theologians on the part of those who studied Thomas.[20]

---

[13] Weisheipl (1974; 1983), p. 340 and Torrell (1993; 1996), pp. 306–308.

[14] See Torrell (1993; 1996), pp. 308–310 and Weisheipl (1974; 1983), pp. 341–343.

[15] Weisheipl (1974; 1983), p. 343. This is not to say that Thomas's was the only theologian studied by the Dominicans, nor that his thought received universal acceptance. See Torrell (1993; 1996), pp. 310–316, and Nichols (2002), p. 130.

[16] Torrell (2005), p. 88.

[17] O'Meara (1997), p. 157.

[18] Torrell (2005), pp. 91–92

[19] Ibid., and O'Meara (1997), p. 158.

[20] As noted by O'Meara (1997), pp. 159–160.

This first period (from his death in 1274 to 1450)[21] was followed by one that involved the *Summa Theologiae* quite heavily. This second period (from 1450 to 1800) saw a wide diffusion of the *Summa* both before, and certainly after the invention of the printing press.[22] Although the *Sentences of Peter Lombard* continued to be the preferred text for teaching theology, as discussed in the first chapter of this reader's guide, nonetheless there was a movement, beginning in the early fourteenth century, to utilize Thomas's *Summa Theologiae* instead. It was in the fifteenth century that professors began to comment upon the *Summa* both in lecture and in written form, and by the sixteenth century the practice was well established.[23] It was during this time that some of the great commentaries upon Thomas's *Summa* were composed. There was the Italian Thomas de Vio (also known as Cajetan), who wrote a very well-known commentary upon the whole of the *Summa* between the years 1507 and 1520.[24] This commentary was published with the first collected works of Thomas, and was included in the critical edition of Thomas's works published by the Leonine Commission.[25] There were the theologians who hailed from Salamanca, Spain, who both lectured upon the *Summa* and wrote commentaries upon it. Among these were Francisco de Vitoria († 1545), "the founder of international law,"[26] Dominic Soto († 1560), Melchior Cano († 1604), and Dominic Bañez († 1604), who was "councilor to and defender of Saint Teresa of Avila, to whom the Carmelite reform owed much."[27] Both Torrell and O'Meara note the importance of these men in the defense of the Native Americans, but especially Vitoria whose efforts to extend human rights to these people not only earned him the displeasure of Emperor Charles V, but also

---

[21] I follow the dates determined by Torrell in (2005).

[22] For the specifics and details, see Torrell (2005), pp. 93–94.

[23] See Torrell (2005), pp. 94–96 for these details. See also Nichols (2002), p. 133.

[24] O'Meara (1997), p. 161.

[25] See Torrell (2005), pp. 96–98 for Cajetan, and then pp. 117–120 for information concerning the Leonine edition and the history/work of its contributors. O'Meara calls Cajetan's commentary upon the *Summa* to be "outstanding" (1997, p. 161).

[26] O'Meara (1997), p. 161.

[27] Torrell (2005), p. 99.

paved the way for the better treatment of these indigenous people.[28] Lastly, there was John Poinsot, more commonly known as John of St. Thomas († 1644), who utilized Thomas's thought to engage the thinkers of the day and, to a lesser extent than the men from Salamanca, disseminated Thomas's ideas widely, reaching even into the last century in his influence upon the well-known Thomist Jacques Maritain.[29]

Thomas's influence had grown far beyond that of his own order during this second period. Torrell and O'Meara note the Jesuits in particular. According to the wishes of this order's founder, Ignatius Loyola († 1556), Thomas's thought, and especially his *Summa Theologiae,* played an important role in the education of its members. Many of its important early figures such as Francisco Toledo († 1596), Francis Suarez († 1617), and Gabriel Vasquez († 1604) studied at Salamanca under Vitoria and Cano.[30] Both Suarez and Vasequez wrote "important commentaries on the *Summa,*"[31] as well as expanding their use of Thomas to meet the problems of the day, something that brought the Jesuits into conflict with the Dominicans in some of their respective theological views.[32] O'Meara also notes the influence that Thomas's thought had had upon the mystics and spiritual writers of the sixteenth and seventeenth centuries, such as Teresa of Avila, John of the Cross, Philip Neri, Ignatius Loyola, and Pierre de Bérulle, the latter of which who influenced both Vincent de Paul and Francis de Sales. The impact of the writings of these people and all whom they influenced served to disseminate Thomistic ideas particularly in the areas of spirituality and ministry.[33]

A third period of influence, extending from the mid-1800s to the 1960s, marked a revival of Thomas's influence if not upon theology, then at least upon the greater Catholic Church itself. In reaction to the modernist trends at work within the larger culture, trends such as relativism, materialism, and subjectivism that had arisen consequent to the disappointments of the

[28] Ibid., pp. 99–100. See also O'Meara (1997), p. 161.
[29] Torrell (2005), pp. 101–103. See also O'Meara (1997), p. 165.
[30] Torrell (2005), p. 103 and O'Meara (1997), p. 163.
[31] Torrell (2005), p. 103.
[32] O'Meara (1997), pp. 163–164.
[33] Ibid., pp. 161–162.

Enlightenment and were judged dangerous to the Christian faith, many within the Church, particularly the popes of this time, had begun to search for ways by which to counter these trends and thereby protect the Faith, particularly as these trends had already found their way into the theology of the day.[34] They found this defense in the school of Thomistic thought that was seen to present a philosophical perspective that, together with its clear reliance upon Aristotle, was realistic in character, able to know the essences of things, and to speak objectively about the very things that were being relativized by the successes that the sciences, among other modern disciplines, were enjoying at that time. As Nichols states, this was the "century of Darwin, and so of the first full-scale attempt to treat human origins in systematically scientific terms," not to mention the plethora of other fields that were trying to do similar things, endangering not only the ethical doctrines of the day, but also the very cogency of the revelation found in Holy Scriptures.[35] The thought of Thomas gave a voice to those in the Church who wished not only to address these dangers, but also to engage the larger culture and to try to counter these very trends. The neo-scholasticism[36] that arose from these concerns was strongly encouraged by Pope Leo XIII, who, in 1879, published the encyclical *Aeterni Patris,* which, among other things, called for the "restoration of Christian philosophy according to Saint Thomas."[37] In the years that followed, he was instrumental in the creation of academies and schools dedicated to the study and teaching of all things Thomistic, the founding of a chair of Thomism at Louvain, making Thomas the patron saint of Catholic schools and universities, and encouraging both the Jesuits and the Franciscans to embrace the thought of Thomas in addition to their dedication to Suarez and Scotus respectively, all of which were then renewed by succeeding popes.[38] Torrell offers a very good account of the "first fruits" of these

[34] For a far more detailed approach to these matters, consider O'Meara (1997), p. 167ff, and Nichols (2002), pp. 136–139.

[35] Nichols (2002), p. 137.

[36] See O'Meara (1997), p. 169 for a definition of this term.

[37] Torrell (2005), p. 108 quoting the encyclical.

[38] See Nichols (2002), pp. 136–137.

endeavors and the limitations and failures that accompanied them.[39] Among the enduring successes are the many and diverse journals that are dedicated to all things Thomistic, the universities and institutes that were founded around the world with a special dedication to the thought of Thomas, the renewal of interest in the thought of the Middle Ages that gave rise to some excellent scholarship in the theology, philosophy, and history of the time, and lastly a goodly amount of translations of Thomas's works into many modern languages, the accuracy of which was made possible by the excellent work of the Leonine Commission charged with publication of critical editions of all of Thomas's works, something rendered absolutely necessary by the numerous variants that have found their way over time into the several uncritical Latin editions of his works that exist.[40]

The dominant character of this renewal was philosophical and not theological, a consequence of the history hinted at above. The results were mixed, but led eventually in the 1960s and especially after the Second Vatican Council, to the collapse of this renewal.[41] Nonetheless, the successes just mentioned above combined with the steady attention throughout this revival has, since the late 1970s, given rise to a renewed and intense interest in Thomas's theology as evidenced by the many and diverse publications, journals, and institutes that have arisen during this time; many of the works used in this reader's guide are the fruits of this renewal.[42] Thomas's influence in philosophical circles remains strong, but this aspect of his thought is now balanced by a greater attention devoted to his theology, and by the work of many historians who have

---

[39] See Torrell (2005), pp. 108–111.

[40] For the full details of these, see Torrell (2005), pp. 108–120. See also O'Meara (1997), pp. 168–200.

[41] O'Meara (1997), p. 198. Many postmortems are available. Referencing the works cited in this reader's guide, consider O'Meara (1997), pp. 170–173, and Nichols (2002), pp. 138–142. Kerr's book, *After Aquinas,* serves as an excellent recounting of the more particular details and struggles of this period, as well as how these are approached in the most recent work on Thomas's theology, stemming from the latest renewal of interest in his work.

[42] See Torrell (2005), pp. 127–130.

greatly aided our approach to Thomas's teachings both in their original contexts and as they have been developed by different schools of thought since.[43]

Many people, both religious and secular, have noted the enduring influence that the *Summa Theologiae* and the works of Aquinas in general have had upon the whole of Christian theology since their composition over 700 years ago. We have a body of work that is not simply relegated to the history of ideas, but manages to this day to evoke passion both pro and con, and this most certainly in theological and philosophical circles. It is rare among the authors of philosophical and theological works to have ascribed to them a particular school of thought, and rarer still to have this school penetrate to all areas of a discipline, which indeed is the case with the theological tradition of the Catholic Church where Thomas, and particularly his *Summa Theologiae,* is not only quoted at all levels and in all manner of documents that issue from the Church itself, but also forms an intrinsic part, albeit more indirectly now than was the case in the past, of the formation of its religious, the latter with which I dare say Thomas would have been pleased as was his expressed intent in the composition of the *Summa* in the first place, as recounted in the first chapter of this work. Thomas's influence, while strong within Catholic circles, is certainly not restricted to these, but has also impacted in varying ways the Eastern Churches, the Protestant faiths, and even the other two monotheisms of the Western Intellectual tradition. His works have gone well beyond these circles, and have been actively pursued by all types of scholars, particularly in the fields of ethics, law, and history/medieval studies. His works have even inspired poets and novelists, such as Dante, Sigrid Undset, J. R. R. Tolkien, C. S. Lewis, G. K. Chesterton, James Joyce, Umberto Ecco, and Flannery O'Connor (who is said to have read from Thomas's *Summa* every night before sleeping), just to mention a very few. Interest among some theologians and philosophers

---

[43] Consider, for example, Jordan (2006), and the bibliographies found in Torrell (2005), (1993; 1996), and (1996; 2003). Consider also Torrell (2005), pp. 120–127. One should heed well the concluding advice that Torrell offers in (2005), p. 133 on how Thomas's thought should be approached.

is dedicated not just to an understanding precisely of what Thomas taught, but also to its application to fields other than he had intended or even had known about. This extension of his thought in light of its spirit has met with spotty results, but indicates, nonetheless, the draw that his works have upon those who read and study them.[44] The richness and profundity of his thought is also evidenced by the plurality of Thomisms that exist to this day, Thomisms that draw at times from seemingly opposed traditions, both theological and philosophical.[45] These are but a few testimonies to the enduring influence of this work. It is my hope that this guide will encourage you to explore the *Summa Theologiae* further and in so doing avail yourself more fully of the wisdom that it contains.

[44] Consider Chapter 5: "Thomas Aquinas Today" pp. 201–243 of O'Meara (1997), as well as his conclusion.

[45] See, for example, O'Meara (1997), pp. 154–156, and, pp. 173–200, and Hudson and Moran (1992), as well as Kerr (2002), which as a whole bears witness to this point.

BIBLIOGRAPHY

There exists a number of excellent bibliographies to which the reader can refer in his desire to further his understanding of the *Summa Theologiae* and of the person and work of Thomas. Among the best of those that treat his works as a whole, offering brief descriptions of each and the translations that are available in English, is the "Brief Catalogue of the Works of Saint Thomas Aquinas" by Giles Emery, O.P., as found in Torrell (1993; 1996), pp. 330–361. This work updates "A Brief Catalogue of Authentic Works" as found in Weisheipl (1974; 1983), pp. 355–405, and "A Catalogue of St. Thomas's Works" by I.T. Eschmann, O.P., as found in Gilson (1956; 1994), pp. 381–430. The following works were used in the composition of this reader's guide, and themselves can be used profitably as well as for their own respective bibliographies.

Aquinas, Thomas (1964–1973). *Summa Theologiae,* Thomas Gilby O.P. and T.C. O'Brien, eds., 60 volumes (Cambridge: Blackfriars, 1964–1973).

— (1947) *The Summa Theologica of St. Thomas Aquinas,* Literally Translated by the Fathers of the English Dominican Province, 3 volumes (New York: Benziger Brothers, 1947).

Aumann, Jordan (1962) *The Theology of Christian Perfection* (Dubuque: Priory Press).

Boyle, Leonard E. O.P. (1982) *The Setting of the* Summa theologiae *of Saint Thomas.* Etienne Gilson Series, vol. 5 (Toronto: Pontifical Institute of Medieval Studies).

Burrell, David B. C.S.C. (2005) "Analogy, Creation, and Theological Language" in Nieuwenhove and Wawrykow, editors (2005), pp. 77–98.

Carruthers, Mary (1990) *The Book of Memory: A Study of Memory in Medieval Culture* (Cambridge: Cambridge University Press).

Chenu, Marie-Dominique O.P. (1950; 1964) *Toward Understanding St. Thomas* (Chicago: Regnery).

Copleston, F.C. (1955) *Aquinas* (Middlesex: Penguin).

Davies, Brian O.P. (1992) *The Thought of Thomas Aquinas* (Oxford: Clarendon Press).

Emery, Gilles O.P. (2005) "Trinity and Creation" in Nieuwenhove and Wawrykow, editors (2005), pp. 58–76.

Gilson, Etienne (1956; 1994) *The Christian Philosophy of St. Thomas Aquinas* (Notre Dame, IN: University of Notre Dame Press).
— (1957) *Painting and Reality* (Ohio: World Publishing Company).
— (1965) *The Arts of the Beautiful* (New York: Scribners).
Gondreau, Paul (2005) "The Humanity of Christ, the Incarnate Word" in Nieuwenhove and Wawrykow, editors (2005), pp. 252–276.
Hart, David Bently (2005) *The Doors of the Sea: Where Was God in the Tsunami?* (Cambridge: Eerdmans).
Hudson, Deal W. and Moran, Dennis, editors (1992) *The Future of Thomism* (Notre Dame, IN: University of Notre Dame Press).
Jordan, Mark D. (1988) "Medicine and Natural Philosophy in Aquinas" in *Thomas von Aquin,* ed. Albert Zimmermann, *Miscellanea Mediaevalia* 19 (Berlin and New York: Walter de Gruyter, 1988), pp. 233–246.
— (1992) *The Alleged Aristotelianism of Thomas Aquinas.* Etienne Gilson Series, vol. 15 (Toronto: Pontifical Institute of Medieval Studies).
— (2003) "The *Summa*'s Reform of Moral Teaching—and Its Failures" in Kerr (2003), pp. 41–54.
— (2006) *Rewritten Theology: Aquinas after His Readers* (Oxford: Blackwell Publishing).
Kerr, Fergus O.P. (2002) *After Aquinas. Versions of Thomism* (Oxford: Blackwell Publishing).
—, editor (2003) *Contemplating Aquinas: On the Varieties of Interpretation* (Notre Dame: University of Notre Dame Press).
Loughlin, Stephen (2008) "Thomas Aquinas and the Importance of Fasting to the Christian Life," in *Pro Ecclesia* 17, pp. 343–361.
Marenbon, John (1987) *Later Medieval Philosophy: 1150–1350* (London: Routledge).
Merriell, D. Juvenal C.O. (2005) "Trinitarian Anthropology" in Nieuwenhove and Wawrykow, editors (2005), pp. 123–142.
Nieuwenhove, Rik Van, and Wawrykow, Joseph, editors (2005) *The Theology of Thomas Aquinas* (Notre Dame: University of Notre Dame Press).
Nichols, Aidan O.P. (2002) *Discovering Aquinas. An Introduction to His Life, Work, and Influence* (Cambridge: Eerdmans Publishing).
O'Meara, Thomas F. O.P. (1997) *Thomas Aquinas: Theologian* (Notre Dame, IN: University of Notre Dame Press).
Pasnau, Robert (2002) *Thomas Aquinas on Human Nature* (Cambridge: Cambridge University Press).
Pieper, Josef (1954; 1966) *The Four Cardinal Virtues* (Notre Dame, IN: University of Notre Dame Press).
— (1966; 1989) *Living the Truth* (San Francisco: Ignatius Press).
— (1986; 1997) *Faith, Hope and Love* (San Francisco: Ignatius Press).
— (1988; 1990) *Only the Lover Sings: Art and Contemplation* (San Francisco: Ignatius Press).
Pinckaers, Servais O.P. (1991; 2003) *Morality: The Catholic View* (South Bend, IN: St. Augustine's Press).

— (1993; 1995) *The Sources of Christian Ethics,* translated from the 3rd edition by Sr. Mary Thomas Noble, O.P. (Washington, DC: Catholic University of America Press).

— (2005) *The Pinckaers Reader: Renewing Thomistic Moral Theology* (Washington, DC: Catholic University of America Press).

Rikhof, Herwi (2005) "Trinity" in Nieuwenhove and Wawrykow, editors (2005), pp. 36–57.

Sokolowski, Robert (1982; 1995) *The God of Faith and Reason: Foundations of Christian Theology* (Washington, DC: Catholic University of America Press).

Stump, Eleonore (2003) *Aquinas* (London: Routledge).

Torrell, Jean-Pierre O.P. (1993; 1996) *St. Thomas Aquinas. The Person and His Work,* vol. 1, trans. Robert Royal (Washington, DC: Catholic University of America Press).

— (1996; 2003) *St. Thomas Aquinas. Spiritual Master,* vol. 2, trans. Robert Royal (Washington, DC: Catholic University of America Press).

— (2005) *Aquinas's Summa. Background, Structure and Reception,* trans. Benedict M. Guevin, O.S.B. (Washington, DC: Catholic University of America Press).

Tugwell, Simon O.P. (1988) *Albert and Thomas: Selected Writings,* The Classics of Western Spirituality (Mahwah, NJ: Paulist Press).

Velde, Rudi A. te (2003) "Understanding the *Scientia* of Faith: Reason and Faith in Aquinas's *"Summa Theologiae"* in Kerr (2003), pp. 55–74.

— (2005) "Evil, Sin, and Death: Thomas Aquinas on Original Sin" in Nieuwenhove and Wawrykow, editors (2005), pp. 143–166.

— (2006) *Aquinas on God: The "Divine Science" of the* Summa Theologiae (Aldershot: Ashgate Publishing).

Wawrykow, Joseph (2005) "Grace" in Nieuwenhove and Wawrykow, editors (2005), pp. 192–221.

— (2005 b) "Hypostatic Union" in Nieuwenhove and Wawrykow, editors (2005), pp. 222–251.

Weisheipl, James A. O.P. (1974; 1983) *Friar Thomas D'Aquino: His Life, Thought, and Works* (Washington, DC: Catholic University of America Press).

Yates, Francis A. (1966; 1992) *The Art of Memory* (London: Pimlico).

INDEX